DISTRICT PLANNING
A Handbook

This book has broughtout on the 60th birthday of Dr. K.V. Sundaram as a tribute to his contributions to the theory and practice of District Planning

DISTRICT PLANNING
A Handbook

R.P. MISRA
Editor

CONCEPT PUBLISHING COMPANY, NEW DELHI-110059

ISBN 81-7022-313-X

First Published 1990

Published by
Ashok Kumar Mittal
Concept Publishing Company
A/15-16, Commercial Block, Mohan Garden
NEW DELHI-110059 (India)

Lasertypest by
Microtech advance Printing Systems Pvt. Ltd.
H-13, Bali Nagar
NEW DELHI-110015

Printed in India by
D.B. Offset Works
New Delhi-110028

DR. K.V. SUNDARAM

CONTENTS

PART II: DISTRICT PLAN OF CHITRADURGA
— **R.P. Misra** and **P.S. Tewari**

PREFACE

This Book centres on the theory and practice of district planning. It contains materials which constitute the foundation of the district planing process in India.

The district plan of Chitradurga district of Karnataka State, prepared by the Editor in 1976, is summarised in Part II of the book. It offers an example of the use of the principles enunciated in different chapters of Part I.

The book is divided into two parts. Part I contains eleven chapters which deal with the concepts, basic issues and methodology of district planning. In the opening paper "On the Task of District Planning", Misra highlights certain neglected dimensions of district planning and emphasises that district planning must be viewed as an instrument intervening between grassroots micro-spaces and national macro-spaces. According to him, the biggest task in district planning is to empower the people and to plan for small projects with small resources. In this context, he refers to the Gandhian perspective of the Indian village with its ever-widening circles surrounding the individual and the community and must be based on the local realities as observed and felt by the local people.

Arun Sinha's paper gives a cogent account of the experiences of district planning in the country, the *Panchayati Raj* and the planning process; and sets forth the "stages" in preparation of district plans. He also underlines the importance of training for making district planning effective.

This is followed by a classic paper by veteran statesman M. Visvesvaraya, in which he has elaborated his ideas on District Organisation and Village and Town Organisations and outlined a methodology for planning and development of rural areas including the essential surveys to be conducted and the policies, institutions, equipments and administrative practices to be set up to augment the production of commodities and services. Despite the fact that the paper is an old one the principles enunciated here have much validity even today. It also proves that the concern for district planning is not as new as many of us are led to believe.

Ajit Kumar Singh critically examines the existing mechanism for disaggregating plan outlays from the State to the district level in Uttar Pradesh and sets out certain general principles as well as alternative models for such allocations. In a critical review paper, Palanidurai analyses the trends in de-centralised planning in Tamil Nadu and Karnataka and examines as to why de-centralised planning could not take off in Tamil Nadu while it succeeded in Karnataka. The Editor has also included two papers by Sundaram, one in which he has vigorously advocated the necessity to revitalise *Panchayati Raj* and encourages localism in district planning and impart appropriate training to officials and non-officials at district level and below. In another article, he has discussed the difficult tasks of area specific sectoral mix and integration in district plans. The principles of spatial integration as explained in Misra's paper on spatial planning. There are also two papers which are extracts from well-known documents, one from an FAO publication "Toward Improved Multi-level Planning for Agricultural and Rural Development in Asia and the Pacific" and the other from Planning Commission paper deals with the methodology for the preparation of district plans, including the guidelines for sectoral planning in a district frame.

Nine chapters of the book (Chapter 12 to 20) constitute Part II of the book. They have been devoted to a case illustration in district planning – the planning for Chitradurga district, a drought-prone district in Karnataka. (This is a Summary of the plan prepared in 1976.) These chapters are intended to illustrate the methodology for district planning and set out the various steps – goal setting, strategy formulation, project identification and formulation for land and water resources development, agriculture, horticulture, animal husbandry and allied sectors, infrastructural and social services development and rural employment. In the last chapter on "Development Administration", a model of development administration at district level has been outlined based on functional principles.

The Editor, while selecting the articles for this volume, has not only sought comprehensiveness in coverage in terms of substance and content, but also a certain balance between theory and practice. An attempt has also been made to highlight the basic issues involved in district planning, as this book is being published at time when so much interest is being evinced on planning at the sub-State level. He is particularly happy that the publication of this volume co-incides with the 60th birth anniversary of Dr. K.V. Sundaram, who has contributed so immensely to the theory and practice of district planning. It is hoped that the volume will be welcomed by all those interested and involved in de-centralised planning and will serve as a basic reference book for students, acdemics, statutory authorities, planning organisations and specialist.

R.P. MISRA

LIST OF CONTRIBUTORS

R.P. Misra, Professor of Regional Planning, Department of Geography, Delhi School of Economics, University of Delhi, Delhi.

Arun Sinha, Adviser, Planning Commission, Government of India, New Delhi.

M. Visvesvaraya, Former Dewan of the princely State of Mysore.

G.V. Viswanath, Director, Industrial Finance Corporation, Government of Karnataka, Bangalore.

K.V. Sundaram Project Co-Manager and Chief Technical Adviser, In-service Training Project – Agricultural Project Analysis and Rural Development in Nepal, FAO, Kathmandu.

Ajit Kumar Singh, Professor of Economic, Giri Institute of Development Studies, Lucknow, U.P.

P.S. Tewari, Prof. of Geography, University of Madras, Madras, T.N.

K.V. Palanidurai, Deputy Adviser, Planning Commission.

PART - I

PRINCIPLES AND PRACTICES

1

INTRODUCTION

R.P. MISRA

PLANNING is now a widely accepted way to handle complex problems of resource allocation and decision-making. It involves the use of "collective intelligence and foresight to chart direction, order, harmony and progress in public activity relating to human environment and general welfare.* It has become particularly necessary in the context of limited resources and growing demand for better and richer standard of life by the fast growing population in Third World countries.

Planning in India started as a centralized macro-effort. It followed the Soviet practice. The States of the Union were least concerned. They did not attempt planning, nor even projects' formulation. The Central government took responsibility of thinking and working for them. And since the party in power was the same at the Centre and the States, there was voluntary willingness on the part of the States in this regard. The States implemented relevant projects/schemes but left it to the Centre to determine what was good for them. This led to a situation where States abdicated their roles in planning and when they did realize this, after a decade or so, they fell back on the methods and approaches of the Central government.

The State plans largely consisted of the ongoing Central schemes with a view to get the largest amount of grants. Since they did not get

* Charles E. Merriam, Pacific North-west Regional Planning — A Review, *Bulletin No.6*, Division of Power Resources, Olympia, USA.

into the habit of mobilizing State resources, they did not think of programmes and projects of their own. They manipulated data to generate resource gaps. The State which had larger gaps got larger funds. As such, both the Central and State plans were inflated and were always beyond the capacities in terms of resource mobilization and efficient implementation of projects and schemes.

State planning even at present is essentially a secretarial exercise. It is only putting together of sectoral proposals, utilizing terminologies which are now well-known to government officials through refresher courses, on the job training, foreign visits, etc.

District planning is the Indian version of regional planning for an administrative unit. Its rationale lies in the presence of an administrative apparatus necessary for plan implementation. This advantage, however, imposes several disabilities for realistic planning. As a result, district planning is yet to take off the ground, although it is being experimented/practised for quite some time. This paper attempts to delineate the task of district planning in years ahead.

The Problematique

Perspectives

Today planning in India is being done not only at the National and State levels but also at district and local levels. The idea is that such a process would generate developmental impulses at all territorial levels. It would help solve problems wherever they are; would mobilize resources wherever they can; and would involve people individually and in groups in developmental processes in each area and locality. This came to be known as multi-level planning system, i.e., planning being done at a number of territorial levels.

The multi-level decentralized planning system in vogue in India, however, suffers from almost the same deficiencies as does the national planning system. It is technocratic in approach and lacks popular involvement. Its conceptual and theoretical foundations are weak and it is impregnated with a value system which is different from that of the people who are the main concern of development. In a multi-level planning set-up, the macro or micro issue is not simply an issue of scale, nor only an issue of resource allocation. One may venture to say that it is not only the issue of decentralization of power and authority. It is an issue of a new way of looking at development process – an issue of a new development style. It must be viewed as a two-way process – top-down and bottom-up simultaneously; it must be seen as the concern of the people; it must inform all aspects of life – economic, social and cultural. If people's primary institution for collective action is the community, community participation, i.e., role for ordinary people in matters affecting their lives, must become the cornerstone of planning.

Thus, the problematique of multi-level planning in general and district or local planning in particular lies in the satellite imagery view – i.e., looking at the people and their problems from above, thereby seeing the forest but not the trees. Recent thrust on decentralization and participatory planning, etc., has only brought the developers – theoreticians as well as practitioners – down to the aeroplane or helicopter. They have not yet come to the ground. Recruiting the local leaders often with dubious credential is not people's participation. It often amounts to curling participation of the common men and women.

In the top-down planning process, the micro-spaces, i.e., villages, communities, small towns, ethnic groups, etc., are perceived as transitory and on the way out. They are considered as drags on the modernization process. They have to be tolerated for the time being. This way of looking at micro-spaces by the group, which can be said to be responsible for initially creating the problem, is a problem in itself. It is a problem of both epistemological as well as practical import.

When we look at the reality from the air (from the top), we get only a photographic image or data-based image. Secondly, the viewer gets the image as he likes. The human world on the ground is thingified. Living communities are reduced to groups and places which can contribute to 'nation-building'. The history, culture, feelings, emotions, perceptions, etc., are treated as noise in data system deserving contempt.

The micro-spaces we come across are of two types. The first is the product of the dynamics of history and geography. It is a space inhabited by people bound together by a set of formal and informal relations. There are rules and standards of conduct, some of them respected but many others transgressed in practice. Yet, they are community forming rules. Villages, neighbourhoods, small towns, cities, wards, ethnic communities and similar grassroots formations constitute these micro-spaces. Some of them are large in scale but the factors which bind them are essentially the same which bind small-scale communities. One must, however, keep in view the limitations imposed by distance for inter-personal communication.

The second type of micro-spaces are the ones created by the micro-processes. These are administrative regions, divisions, districts, *talukas*, or revenue villages. They may also be small but they have not resulted from micro-processes moving horizontally but as channels for the macro-authorities to wield power down to the grassroots level. These micro-spaces are atomized parts of the macro-spaces.

District is thus an atomized part of the national level macro-space and hence district planning, as it is conceived presently, cannot be a very effective tool to generate development from below. It remains a technocratic and bureaucratic exercise. When we plead for restoration of power to the people at the grassroots level, we have no misgivings about the distortions in community integration and change processes therein. It would, therefore, be highly misleading to treat them as instruments of change in all circumstances. These communities do have people who resist change and who promote degeneration of life. It is myth to think that micro-spaces consist of people who live in peace and harmony. Oppression, violence, division and hate are frequent within or between them. What sets them apart from macro-spaces is that life within them is still defined by human beings belonging to them in all their richness and weaknesses, their complexity, their uniqueness and their unpredictability. As against this, the life at the macro-level is governed by external forces and institutions and not by endogenous human beings.

District planning must be viewed as an instrument intervening between grassroots micro-spaces and national or international macro-spaces. That district planning is still struggling to find a place in the planning system and is overwhelmed by macro-planning culture, is, therefore, understandable. District planning with a human face is too tall an order for institutions which have been created to disrupt the community which is the central theme of micro-level planning.

Empowering the People

It is contended that local communities are powerless, they are weak, they cannot survive on their own without being integrated into bigger, more powerful entities. One may say that this itself should be adequate reason to empower them. But that apart, let us not forget that the macro-spaces have powers which emanated from micro-spaces to begin with. Have we not noticed some of the mightiest empires having crumbled when people regained and used their inherent power. Think of the Shah of Iran; think of recent happenings in Poland, Hungary, Czechoslovakia, East Germany or even in the USSR. Think of the Greens in Western Europe; protest movements in the USA; student uprising in China, etc. Do these happenings not show that the real power lies with the people but this power is often usurped by a ruling class denying the people even the opportunity to perceive that the real power belonged to them.

People at the top feel powerful only because they are able to take advantage of a number of apparatuses and devices which can weaken the power-base of people at the grassroots level. They control the commanding heights, occupy strategic positions and use various means of power to quickly transform their otherwise meagre potentials into instant power over the others. This power holds good only so long as the micro-spaces are ignorant of themselves being the power-base or are so weakened by the macro-space that they cannot assert. Resistant to macro-powers is and often unorganized. A guerilla war is always on. The macro-spaces fail to subdue the micro-spaces but the uncoordinated and unorganized, as the micro-spaces are, they seldom get back the power that belongs to them.

The question that comes to our mind is: if people are and have power, where is the question of empowerment? To answer this question, we have to look into space specificities of the source and nature of power. Power should not be equated with political power which can be transferred and re-transferred. Each human formation has its own way of creating and exercising power. Each formation has long history of resistance and self-defence behind it. Each has a unique experience still visible as tradition, convention, modes of behaviour, folklores, etc. They are best adapted to each particular group's culture and opportunities.

They cannot be discarded as outdated nor they can be replaced by universal recipes.

Gunnar Myrdal once said that there was only one economist who knew India. That was Mahatma Gandhi. Here was a man who knew the power invested in rural communities. He made his people realize and used this power to wrest power from the mightiest empire of the world. He inspired millions of people to follow his footsteps, for each of them knew his strength emanating from the power regained. Gandhi could pick up idioms which made the people of India realize their inner strength and the shallow power-base of the colonial administration.

Lenin, Mao, Ho Chi Minth, Castro, etc., had similar messages.

How tragic it is that, in country after country, people have been weakened in the name of development. They have been led to the garden path of formal power structure to deprive them of their informal power. The power of Gandhi, Mao, Ho Chi Minh, etc., was the collective power of the people. It was not a macro-power in micro-vacuum.

Small or Large

Research on micro-macro relationship has greatly suffered from a confusion between what is real and what is apparent. For our planners, anything small is outdated. It is too small to generate development. Because development must be macro, big. It is seldom realized that what appears small is the very heart of the big, in the same way as the heart of the macro-space lies in the strength of the micro-space. The biggest task is to transcend the artificial dichotomy between the small and the big and not to have big projects, with big resources to spend, where small projects, with small resources, can do the job.

The planner of today, however, goes for large projects because the reality he addresses is of his own making; not the one that is experienced and evolved by the people. The design of the projects are influenced by motivations different from those of the majority of the people. Quick and spectacular results are considered essential for rapid change. It is seldom realized that lasting change cannot occur in a macro-space if they do not stem from changes within its constituent micro-space. The result is that while the macro-spaces (nation regions) grow in terms of production and incomes, the people in micro-spaces decay; poverty grows, unemployment increases and marginalization of the weak expands. District planning has to counter these macro-planning exercises to ensure development where the people matter.

Gandhian Perspective

Gandhi considered Indian village as the basic societal unit with maximum autonomy and maximum inter-dependence. It was localized but not isolated. It had no frontiers as modern educated men have. It had a wider ever-expanding horizon without defined limits. That is how the notion of *Vadudhaiv Kutumbakam* came into being.

Gandhi considered this widening horizon as oceanic circle with each individual and community as the micro-space. As these circles meet and cut across each other the inter-dependency increases without hurting the autonomy. Moreover, life becomes an integrated whole. There are no sectors like education, health, economic, social, etc. Each human activity is localized yet it is part of a micro-world representing thousands of years of communal life and collective memory or wisdom reaching far beyond any particular activity. In the ever-widening set of concentric circles, the one closer to the core, defined more concretely the unique world of individual concerns, aspirations and hopes, merges in the concerns, aspirations and hopes of the larger society.

The need to regenerate these micro-spaces as centres of the ever-widening circles surrounding it is basic to all human formations. Yet in the contemporary world where a host of violent divisions and alienating elements are permeating all life spaces, it has become a challenging task. Pollution of human spaces by micro-forces needs to be critically studied and understood before any attempt is made to fight its causes and consequences.

District Planning

Development from Below

Keeping the above analysis in view, we have to think of district planning as a co-ordinating process of local or micro-spaces. It has to derive inspiration and support from local communities of the district and it has to work to strengthen them and, thus, to strengthen the national unity.

The major thrust of district plan, therefore, must be to create conditions for generating micro-level development initiatives. It should attempt to unite the people for common causes, build their confidence, build integrated self-managing micro-societies and promote self-reliance. Success of a district plan should be seen in the degree of local initiative rather than in action from above. Micro-spaces or local communities as stated earlier have wider links which wane or weaken as distance increases. The contention that the information society of our future would remove the distance factor completely is unrealistic. It is the inter-personal links sustained through history, geography, culture, conventions and folklore which give rise to a community of people. There is indeed a larger society which is seen by people through occasional visits, books, newspapers, electronic media, etc. It is not homogeneous, it is subjected to mental constraints and is always seen in abstract terms. Members of the larger society are welcome in the community because it is the communities which make a society. Diversity is respected and appreciated. There is tolerance of cultures other than one's own.

What is the district in this context? It is a natural area, say, a valley, a desert, a forest, etc., which gives a sense of environmental unity; it is not a problem area which gives a sense of common suffering or purposes; it is not a homogeneous culture zone either. It has been artificially created by the British and the inheritors of the British to rule a nation State. It is only an administrative area.

A district, thus, suffers from very initial drawbacks, for, we now know that the planning is not administration. It has a human face which is plastered by theories, models, projects, managerial tools and techniques, abstractions, generalizations giving rise to social Darwinism — human being preying on other human beings. The poverty that we witness in India is a blot on our body politic. District planning has to be a major instrument to remove it. But it can do so only if the plaster that casts its face is removed first.

To say that the district boundaries be changed is to ask for something that is not practical. Nor is there any urgent need to do so, for people do not live by boundaries. They do not respect even international boundaries. Boundaries have meaning only to rulers and planners. And if district planning gets oriented to people, then the district boundary cannot be a major hurdle.

The traditions, cultures, sub-cultures, styles of life and living are very much influenced by geography and history. Keeping these two factors in view, one can always identify micro-areas within the district space which need special and specific attention. But such an exercise should not lead to truncated thinking. Spatial analysis must be backed by spatial synthesis.

District Planning Machinery

It is not very pertinent to dwell here on the existing planning machinery at the district and still lower levels. At present each district has a planning officer whose job is to prepare district plan. The chief planning officer in effect is the Collector of the district. The Chairman of the *Zila Parishad* (District Council) is the *de jure* head of the planning and development agency, but he functions under such serious constraints and has so little time to devote for development (being a political person), that the Collector remains the boss.

The sectoral officers are asked to prepare plans for respective sectors, they prepare projects giving justification for each. All these sectoral plans are put together and total cost estimates worked out. Each department is asked to prune its sectoral plan in the light of the scarcity of resources. Only those sectors for which more funds are earmarked under some special schemes, sponsored by the Central or State governments, get larger share. All sectoral plans are mechanically cut to size and finally put together to constitute the district plan.

For the last 25 years this exercise has been going on in one form or the other and crores of rupees have been spent on projects washed away and re-done in successive plans. One fails to see even one primary school with infrastructure deserving the emphasis this great country of ours laid on education. School buildings fall down within a year of construction; Harijan colonies without inhabitants abound in plenty. Roads constructed in 1950 and 1960 have been washed away and become public hazards because of poor or no repairs; many new roads built during the last ten years do not exist at all.

None appears to be concerned about all this. Those who are the beneficiaries of development – the politicians, the bureaucrats and the contractors – have become promoters of development. The people are unconcerned. They have never been consulted. They get some marginal benefits but such benefits have been there even in the British days. They are now so deeply caught in the net that they have lost most of the freedom of action. There is despondency, a feeling of hatred and even revolt, but also helplessness. Each village has agents of the middlemen; they are informers, beneficiaries, contractors, musclemen, etc. These agents have horizontal as well as vertical links.

The financial aspects of local level planning have received lot of attention in recent years. Some States have done well and committed resources for district level planning by earmarking certain projects and the costs thereof to district authorities. In many States, the progress in decentralization is slow and tardy. The States which have done well are also the States which started thinking of decentralization as early as 1960s. Mention may be made of Karnataka, Maharashtra and Gujarat.

Availability of funds is not the only issue. The real issue is the approach, the perspective, the methodology and the people's involvement. As stated earlier, the real purpose of district planning is to generate development from below – from micro-centres, from villages, from city wards and from small towns – focussing on the poor, neglected and oppressed. Roads are needed, buildings are needed, factories are needed. But all these can be used and they are being used to further oppress the people to take them to the road to serfdom or violence. What is, therefore, needed most is the action to help people help themselves.

In 40 years of planning, could India not develop even one district of the country to an extent that mass poverty was eliminated? Could it not develop ten villages which could be called model villages? In Israel one could see all theoretical and conceptual models, development applied in the field. Why did India not apply even the model which Mahatma Gandhi presented? Nothing could be done because the very conception of planning is elitist, bureaucratic and technocratic. Its human face is missing.

Toward Realistic District Planning

District planning should no longer be a local replica of national planning. In fact it should try to fill those gaps which national planning leaves unfilled. While national planning has to be based on abstraction of field level realities, the district planning has to be fully aware of these realities. While the macro-level national planning sees the forests, district planning must see the trees. In the case of the latter, each tree is important for the quality of the forest is ultimately determined by individual trees. It is unfortunate that district planning, instead of carring for the trees, deals with forests which at the micro-scale cannot be visualized fully.

The task of district planning has thus to be complementary and supplementary to macro-level national planning. It is the task of enabling the people and communities to take responsibilities of development on their own shoulders. In other words, the main task of district planning is development from within.

Planning is not a desk work. It is more so at the micro-level. Planner's job is to seek information all the year round. The data so obtained must enter the planning process. He has to be continuously involved in various kinds of surveys for feedback on:

1. Geographic situation
2. Socio-economic situation
3. Institutional strengths and weaknesses
4. Leadership/change agents

5. Needs and possibilities.

In the absence of such feedbacks, the planner at the apex, no matter how competent he is, can achieve precious little. The sad part of the story is that this feedback in our planning system is not only lacking but also considered unnecessary. It has now been replaced by a pernicious system of allocation for and expenditure on projects which can be accounted without any accountable targets. The money goes in the pockets of the developers and not to the people.

For district planning to succeed we have to return to Gandhian thinking and economics. We must base our models and projects on the local realities as observed and felt by the people. We have to go back to employment oriented projects of lasting nature. We must promote production by the masses rather than mass production by a selected few.

All this needs a community bias in our thinking to overcome the urban bias toward gigantism of the last 40 years. Local institutions need to be strengthened with a view to promote change and development from within. Voluntary agencies, which have feel for rural society and are known for community development, can play a catalytic role in the new dispensations for district planning.

2

DECENTRALIZED DISTRICT PLANNING
The Indian Experience

ARUN SINHA

Introduction

THE INDIAN experience of decentralized planning presents a mosaic of varying patterns and different hues. It has had a chequered progress though interest in the concept of the decentralization of the planning process, once aroused, never flagged. Recently it seems to have acquired renewed vigour thanks to the relentless espousal of its cause by the Prime Minister himself. This has generated for the concept of decentralized planning wide-spread support. This thrust and the rekindling of public interest could not have come at a more opportune time. We are poised on the threshold of a new Five Year Plan. What is more, over a long period, since the early 1970s in fact, considerable planning capability in terms of manpower, training and, a reasonably adequate methodology has been developed. It should not therefore, be at all difficult now to exploit fully the new resolve to make district level planning the starting point of the States' plans, during the new Five Year Plan period, commencing next year.

The concept of planned development made its debut in the 1950s, at the national level, when the Planning Commission was set up by the Government of India. The Planning activity remained centred around the Union and the States. However, from the Second Five Year Plan onward, decentralized planning also began to receive attention. Progress was slow. Attention continued to be rivetted largely on the national and State level plans, and the planning process. The reason partly was that soon after independence there was total pre-occupation with growth oriented development. It was only when the attention shifted to the re-distribution of the gains of growth to bring about improvements in the living condition of the backward and the poor, that the concept of decentralized planning really began to be taken seriously. The requirement for balanced regional development further necessitated that the planning process should be decentralized, and made more responsive to the wishes of the people at the grass-root level.

The pace of decentralization in the field of planning remained uncertain for other reasons as well. Let us take the constitutional position first. Decentralization of the planning process was envisaged in the same Directive Principles of Policy, set forth in the constitution, which also became the source of planning in India. The functions assigned to the Planning Commission were a follow-up of the Directive Principles which amongst other things laid down that "The State shall strive to promote the welfare of the people by securing and protecting, as effectively as it may, a social order in which justice, social, economic and political, shall inform all the institutions of the national life". The Directive Principles further obliged the State to direct its policy towards securing for all citizens, men and women equally, the right to an adequate means of livelihood. The State was also directed to ensure that the ownership and control over material resources was so exercised that instead of resulting in the concentration of wealth and control of production to the common detirment, the economic system benefitted all. These Directive Principles necessitated that development should be planned in the way it was envisaged. But the same Directive Principles also clearly laid down that the State would take steps to constitute village panchayats and vest them with such power as would be necessary for them to function as self-governing units. Notwithstanding this clear direction, the cause of decentralization has not been as well served as was expected. Why? Is it only because of our pre-occupation with growth in the initial years rather than with the redistribution of economic gains? That is only part of the answer. A more fundamental answer is to be found in the federated structure envisaged by the Constitution makers.

The political and administrative structure, which is served through planning, has as its pivots the centre and the States. They have a well defined role. There is also a third area which is the concurrent jurisdiction of both the Centre and States. "Economic and Social Planning" is in the 'Concurrent' list. The structure below the level of State is left to be tackled through a process of decentralization. Each State has to decide for itself how far it is prepared to go. The political and administrative structure indicates a preference for centrist tendencies. The Constitution, as it has been worked, clearly shows a bias in favour of what might be called 'the top down' approach involving, where necessary, devolution of authority and functions from a higher unit of administration to the lower units. In this scenario, it is easy to appreciate why decentralization of the planning process has been slow.

There are two other reasons which must also be taken note of. Both have relevance for any one wanting to appreciate the difficulties in the path of decentralization of the planning process. The idea in bringing out these is not to discourage or create despair, but to set out clearly the environmental constraints that must be overcome if the planning process is to be decentralized.

The first of these constraints is linked with the political administrative structure. It has already been pointed out that the structure favours the 'top down' approach. Our systems also favour centralization of authority. And this applies as much to the administrative machinery as to the political wing of the Government. On the political side the Parliament and the Legislatures are the real sources of power. Consequently Members of Parliament and of Legislatures, as representatives of a constituency of people, exercise considerable influence not only in the national and State arena but even more so in their local area. Similarly, on the administrative side too the flow of authority is from top to bottom. The confluence of interest of both political personage and of administrative personnel therefore tends to favour the higher echelons of administration. In this, the political and administrative power centres tend to make common cause in their reluctance to let go their sphere of influence.

The second environmental constraint is the requirement of the planning process per se. Planning is an intricate exercise requiring skills and techniques which are not readily available in a developing economy, starting almost from scratch. Infact at the initial stage of the planning exercise the concentration on job expertise was naturally at the central level. It is only gradually that it spread to the States and levels below. Lack of requisite numbers of trained planning personnel at the district level, therefore, poses a serious constraint to the spread of decentralization in the area of planning.

This difficulty is further compounded by the fact that while there are many definite advantages of decentralized planning, it must contend with, and transcend partisan approaches to development when advocated by locally influential people. This makes the micro-level planning exercise at times more difficult than the macro-level exercise. In the politico-administrative set up like ours, it requires very very careful handling to persuade people to accept the true advantages of planned development. The temptation to go in always for apparently simple solutions, however, ill-advised from the planning point of view, is always lurking in the background. It requires a considerable degree of communication skills, patience and hard work to overcome such disadvantages. Hence, all the more need for adequately trained planning personnel at the local level. Without this even if the planning process was decentralized, it would be difficult to exploit its full potential.

This theme is the setting against which the progress of decentralized planning should be viewed. On the one hand, there has been an unmistakable intention to promote a decentralized, even participative system of administration and planning. On the other, there is an equally decisive, mandate again from the constitution, favouring concentration of administrative, financial and decision-making authority at the level of Centre and the State. This tendency affects the planning process as well. Between the intention to decentralize and the inclination to centralize, reconciliation is sought to be achieved by a conscious process of devolution of authority and functions to local levels such as the District, Block or Village. Progress is somewhat tardy because of inherent pulls and pressures. It is hoped though that the advantages of decentralized planning, already well recognised, will overcome any latent doubts. There is even talk of a constitutional amendment to ensure that the local level democracy envisaged in the Directive Principles of Constitution gets its rightful due. With or without such an amendment, however, it seems clear that the process of decentralized planning has come of age.

Decentralization – A Necessity

It has always been recognised that in a country of India's size, there is really no option but to decentralize the administrative and planning system. There are 25 States apart from a few Union Territories directly administered by the Centre. Each of these States is further divided into districts. There are as many as 451 districts, Talukas/Blocks (5082) and then Mandals (group of villages) and villages. There are vital areas of development such as public health, education, land reforms, agriculture, irrigation local government etc., which can best be attended to at the local level. The community development experiment, launched in the early 1950s, clearly established that a decentralized system of administration, accessible to people and responsive to their needs could very much accelerate the process of development. Infact, to consolidate the gains from this experience a Committee was constituted under Shri Balwant Rai Mehta. This Committee recommended the idea of 'planning from below'. It also recommended setting up of 3-tier body of representatives of people. It was the beginning of Panchayati Raj System. The mechanism for decentralization of authority and functions at the local levels was thus created.

The Panchayati Raj system was implemented by different States with varying degrees of success. Maharashtra and Gujarat were forerunners and have continued the experiment. In other States, Panchayati Raj system does not seem to have made much impact. In Maharashtra and Gujarat a number of activities relating to agriculture, irrigation, education, health, etc. were transferred, alongwith the staff, to the Panchayati bodies primarily to district and block levels. In respect of these transferred activities, the State also transferred funding provision and the authority to over-see the implementation and monitoring of their progress and generally to decide how the transferred activities should benefit the people. In a limited sense, therefore, the planning function also came in the hands of these elected bodies. The natural culmination of this initial step would have been to have transferred the planning function for the whole of the district in the hands of district panchayats. Instead a separate District Planning Board was created to organise the preparation of plans for the district. In other States also such District Planning Boards, Planning Committees have been constituted to lookafter the work of planning at the district level. In two States i.e. Andhra Pradesh and Karnataka recently, on the introduction of democratic decentralized institutions – Zilla Praja Parishad, Zilla Parishad – Planning funtions were also transferred to these bodies.

Decentralized Planning and the Planning Process

District Planning is an integral part of the planning exercise which at present begins at the national level. At the top is the National Development Council (NDC), comprising representatives of the Central

Government, and the Chief Ministers of the State Governments and the Council is presided over by the Prime Minister himself who is also the Chairman of the Planning Commission. Below the NDC, it is the specific responsibility of the Planning Commission to organise the planning process and to coordinate and promote activities at all levels. Besides long-term perspective plans, the main activities centre around Five Year Plans and annual plans. In case of Five Year Plans, the work starts with almost two years of the previous plans still left. By this time, a mid-term review of the previous plan would also be available and Steering/Working Groups set-up, to identify important issues, policies and programmes, which must figure in the next five years. The States are also requested to take similar action. Since it is proposed that the next Five Year Plan of the States should be based on district plans, Districts too have been advised to draw up a draft Five Year Plan. These would have to be integrated in the State's Five Year Plans. The Steering Groups and Working Groups are engaged to identify major planning issues. A paper is put up to the NDC indicating the approach and the strategy to be followed up in formulating the next Five Year Plan. Before it is taken up for discussion in the NDC, it is made available to the States so that their comments may also be incorporated and a meaningful discussion may take place in the NDC. Presumably where it touches upon activities included or likely to be included in the district level planning system, States would also consult the districts before formulating their views. After the Approach Paper is discussed and finalised in the NDC, it becomes the basis for formulating the Five Year Plan at the national, State and even district level. It needs to be pointed out that a substantial part of the planning activity also covers public and private sectors. The Approach Paper, therefore, tries to assimilate the view points of public and private sector also.

The Approach Paper sets out broad national objectives and the strategy for achieving it. Keeping this in view, the State and the district level planning bodies are required to work out what they would like to do in the course of the next five years, and how the resources for the same would be mobilised. The district planning bodies in turn may have to consult village and block level planning bodies to prepare the draft Five Year Plan for the districts. The plans of these districts are then integrated into the State plans. The integration is largely in respect of sectoral requirements as also inter-district schemes and programmes. There is also a question of resource allocation. The State level draft plans are then discussed at the central level where again the question of resources assumes considerable importance. State plans comprise their own resources, and the resources made available to them on the basis of an approved formula — known as 'Gadgil formula' – by the Centre. In addition, the Centre also takes up special Area Programmes like Hill Areas Development Programme, Tribal Areas Sub-Plan, etc. mainly with a view to redress regional imbalances. There are besides a large number of central schemes aimed at promoting desirable types of activity. The centrally sponsored schemes are funded both by the Centre and the States on the basis of an agreed principle. They, therefore, tend to affect the allocation pattern of resources in the State's Plan while at the same time providing additional support to the States' own efforts.

Like State Plans, Plans of Central Ministries are also prepared. They are finalised only at the Central level. Finally the Central plans and the State Plans are brought together and the total picture emerges of the National Plan. After it has received the approval of NDC and the final adjustment in respect of central assistance, market borrowings, assistance from external resources, etc. is also made in this meeting. States do try to ensure that outlays earlier agreed to by them in respect of district plans are not reduced as far as possible. Even so, it is possible some adjustment may become necessary particularly in the sectoral allocations. This final position is then communicated to the district level officers who can then begin to implement the plan schemes.

This is broadly how the district plans fit into the general planning procedure. There are considerable variations in the manner in which this procedure is followed at the district level. In some cases very detailed district plans are prepared while in other cases, planning is left mostly to sectoral departments. It is expected that this year almost all districts would be preparing district plans. Between 30 to 40 per cent of the State Plans would generally be allocated to the district sector schemes. Of this about 80 per cent is provided for ongoing and continued schemes. The balance is generally available for taking up new schemes at the district level. For some years past, now provision is also being made in the State Plans for untied amount. This has been done to encourage the planning exercise at the district level. There are of course certain guidelines like this fund should not be utilised/used on non-poductive schemes or schemes of long gestation etc. but basically funds can be utilized by the district planning authorities in their districts. This has greatly aroused interest in the planning activity at the district level. In some States, a part of untied funds is being used as incentive money requiring matching contribution to be raised by the district people themselves.

The Parliament, it becomes a reference point for preparation of annual plans during the next Five Year Plans. The Annual Plans are also prepared more or less in the same fashion. In the case of Annual Plans also, the planning exercise really starts with a letter of Planning Commission to the States requesting them to formulate draft plans. While doing so, important areas are highlighted. There are detailed formats also prescribed in which the information is requested to be supplied both in respect of financial and physical development. Simultaneously the States are also required to indicate details of resource estimates. The States in turn communicate to the districts the likely availability of resources and the basis on which the districts should prepare their plans. In a number of States there exists detailed sectorwise, districtwise break-up of flow of funds. Information is also available in respect of flow of credit from various financial institutions and Banks. Taking account of this and other information as may be necessary, the Districts prepare their own plans. After they have been approved by the District Planning Boards they are forwarded to the State Planning Department/ Board for integration with the State Plans. When the States have finalised their own plans they bring it for discussion with the Planning Commission officials. The discussions take place both in respect of resource estimation as well as plan outlays. In respect of Plan outlays, sectoral allocations and sub-sectoral allocations are gone into in great detail in Working Groups comprising not only representatives of the State but also of Planning Commission and representatives of Administrative Ministries at the level of Government of India. The Working Groups evaluate the current performance and level of development, identify the needs and recommend what should be provided for within the parameters of available resources. The sectoral requirements are then integrated in a discussion between the State Plan Advisers in the Planning Commission and officers of the State Government. The State Plan Advisers then give their recommendation regarding plan size to be fixed and the various sectoral and sub-sectoral outlays within it. This report is discussed finally in a meeting taken by the Deputy Chairman where the Chief Minister of the concerned State is also present. The final plan size for the next year is fixed in this meeting. In the light of this decision if there are any sectoral adjustments required they are carried out by the State Plan Advisers in consultation with the State Government officers.

Decentralized Planning Set-up

The Planning process outlined above needs to be supplemented with some more details to give a true picture of how planning activities are organised at the district level. There are broadly two kinds of administrative structures discharging planning functions in the district. One is represented by District Planning Boards which are nominated and usually have a Minister of State presiding over it. The other is an elected body called Zilla Praja Parishad or Zilla Parishad. Only Andhra Pradesh and Karnataka have entrusted planning functions to an elected body. Under either of these systems, there are a large number of departmental heads – Central and autonomous agencies which owe a loose allegiance to the planning body. They are basically field organisations working under a departmental hierarchy. Their interaction with each other at the day-to-day level is frequent but in matters of policy they generally tend to reflect the view-points of their departments. Even a Statistical Organisation which keeps statistics from various departments, tends to rely on the statistics brought out at the State level rather than compiling it straightway at the district level itself. The point being made is that the approach is largely sectoral and department-oriented even at the district level. It requires a great deal of work to develop the kind of integration needed to bring about a homogenated area development approach.

A consequence of the predominantly sectoral or departmental outlook is that officers tend to look upon planning as a marginal activity. The planning function is relegated to a secondary status within a departmental organisation. Planning becomes a primary responsibility of only the core planning staff working under the direct control of the district Collector or the Zilla Panchayat as the case may be. Since the Planning Board of Panchayat is an influential organization of the district, and the planning staff also has the support of the Collector and an equally senior officer who is the Chief Executive of the Zilla Parishads, it is able to obtain a fairly satisfactory response from representatives of various departments. However, as pointed out earlier, this response would increase very considerably if the heads of offices of different departments could be persuaded to accept planning as a significant part of their activity. It is hoped that it would be possible to bring about the needed change through training programmes. Attention to this aspect is being given.

By now, considerable literature has accumulated on the methodology to be adopted for district level planning. As far back as 1969, Planning Commission had issued very detailed guidelines to the States and through them to the Districts indicating how the plans should be prepared. Later, in 1982, Planning Commission set-up a Working Group to review the progress of District Planning and to suggest further action required to be taken. This Group gave its Report in 1984. In respect of the guidelines issued in 1969, the Group came to a conclusion that they were much too detailed and needed simplification. Accordingly, new guidelines were incorporated. The Report of the Working Group on District Planning has become the basic literature guiding the district planners. Here and there, States have brought about improvements and adjustments and the Planning Commission also has issued supplementary instructions from time to time but, by and large, methodology enunciated in the report has remained the backbone of District Level Planning.

Stages in District Level Planning

In a very general way the following would be the stages in the preparation of district plans:

(I) Pre-requisite – State Level Action :

(i) Indication to a district of the likely availability of resources or atleast the likely increase in percentage terms over the previous year's allocations,
(ii) National and State level objectives to be kept in mind,
(iii) Programmes like Minimum Needs Programme or Employment Programmes where a certain level would have to be maintained.

(II) District Level :

(i) Meeting of district level officers to discuss State-instructions and work out a-road programme of action. Similar meetings are indicated to be held at Block/Mandal Levels,
(ii) Preparation of sectoral profiles based on data showing development and gaps. Data is analysed, achievements and progress reviewed and the strengths and weaknesses of existing approaches are identified,
(iii) Preparatory proposals are worked out keeping in mind sectoral

priorities and there may also be consultation with at least a few prominent members of the public,

(iv) Programmes having a bearing on other sectors are discussed in meetings where departmental views are reconciled,

(v) After the Sectoral views are firmed up, plan proposals indicating schemes, priorities, locations, benefits, expenditure requirements, phasing, etc. are made over to the core planning personnel,

(vi) Planning people scrutinise the proposals in the light of National, State policies as well as the feasibility of schemes,

(vii) The District Planning Body discusses with sectoral departments plan proposals and decides what sectoral relativities should be recommended, and

(viii) A Draft District Plan is prepared and submitted for the consideration of the State.

It needs to be mentioned that there are considerable variations even as between district to district within a State. The variations arise because even though general instructions exist, there is no manual yet which dictates the exact sequence of events. Differences also arise depending upon the degree of importance given to planning by different participants in the planning process. Thus following the same format one can see variations in quality of planning output of different districts.

Decentralized Planning – Need for Trained Staff

One of the reasons why district planning could not make much headway and gain credibility is the lack of adequately trained staff. Since 70's steps have been taken to not only augment the strength of plan ning personnel in districts but also to diversify the skills and expertis amongst them. Where such staff is fully in position and has remaine so for sometime there is a definite improvement in the quality of plan They are fully familiar with techniques of spatial planning, need fo projectisation and other skills which help to determine function: hierarchy and location priorities, etc. The planning staff also acts as guide to officers of various departments and helps them to prepa details of schemes and programmes in a planned manner.

One of the main arguments in favour of decentralized planning its accessibility to people and its capacity to evoke responsive cooper tion from them. This is an area which has not been attended to very much except in a limited way. Consultation with Members of Parliament, Legislature and even elected representatives to Panchayati Raj Bodies may be there but it is at best marginal. That perhaps is the reason why when the interaction does take place, it is quite often one-sided. It, therefore, tends to be construed as interference or consultation without really caring for it. It is, therefore, being recommended to the local level planners that the process of consultation should be made regular and its scope should be widened.

Finally, a word about the latest developments. Three types of steps are being taken to improve the level of decentralized planning. In the first place, data collection, storage and its constant upgradation is being attended to. As computerised district information network is being established to ensure linkage of data throughout the State and even the country. While working out the data requirement for planning purposes attempts would be made to identify core data requirement while leaving an option open to tap subsidiary data to be retrieved from the files of monitoring data. How the data would be captured, what would be the frequency of a particular data collection are the kind of issues being presently sorted out. Reconciliation and dovetailing of data available from multiple sources is also one of the important parameters of this exercise to fill the data gap.

The second attempt is in the direction of improving training facilities and relating them to the specific category of planning personnel. Broadly there are two categories of officers : officers whose primary responsibility it is to plan and those for whom planning is but a part function. Amongst these two broad categories also there are functionaries at different levels requiring different kind of orientation and training. These aspects are being attended to. At the same time how to fit in large members of functionaries in the training programmes is also receiving attention. Finally, there is also the question of course content and an appropriate mix of instructional systems.

Lastly, consultants have been engaged to work out detailed plans on a pilot basis. The idea is to see how far the methodology developed till now can in practice deliver good plans. One cannot ignore theory and yet one has also to be realistic and aware of what is happening in practice. It is hoped that when these various plans are fully ready they would not only indicate how a plan should be prepared but also which of our present notions should be given up. Amongst these experiments the foremost is the one undertaken by National Institute of Rural

Development. They are helping the district officers to learn to prepare plans. Full results are yet to be made available but the stress has been on putting into practice whatever has been learnt in the classroom. The most important lessons would, however, be available from their record of how it goes in practice.

The Indian experience with the decentralization of the planning process shows that much has been achieved but much more remains to be done. The need now is to recognise that the main objective of decentralization was to bring the planning process within reach of the people. It is time that we went whole hog towards this goal. This may also prove to be the ultimate strength of the decentralized planning process.

3

DISTRICT DEVELOPMENT SCHEME*

Economic Progress by Forced Marches

M. VISVESVARAYA

Introduction

AN INDUSTRIAL Revolution was gradually brought about in England and Europe about the middle of the past century by the invention of power machinery and the development of the factory system of manufacture. A decade, later, revolution has come about during the past 30 years, due to such new forces and inventions as development of electric power, advances in industrial chemistry, replacement of the domestic system of manufacturing by the factory system and the startling growth in transport and communications.

While these discoveries and advances have greatly benefited the western nations there has been no organized effort to introduce them into India. As a result of the competition of imported machine-made goods with local products, the people of India have lost their age-old occupations and a substantial portion of their employment and income, and with the growth of population vast numbers of them have been forced to live below the poverty line.

* It is classic literature on District Planning prepared by M. Visvesvaraya as early as 1939 and published by the Bangalore Press, Bangalore. It has been reproduced here as it is.

This is mainly due, on one side, to lack of encouragement from State policies and, on the other, to unhealthy traditions, illiteracy, want of adaptability and the apathy of the people themselves. There are large numbers of citizens who favour rapid industrialization, the wider use of machinery and tools, mass production methods and the adoption of newer business practices which no nation, which desires to be progressive, can do without. But there is also a vast multitude of illiterates and not an inconsiderable number of public leaders who long for rural life and the peace and quiet of the older times.

The actualities of the situation demand great changes. These changes should be brought into being by Government ignoring political differences and working in the closest association with leading businessmen, financiers and economists in the country. On every current problem, *pros* and *cons* should be weighed, formulae and policies based on world experience evolved and a constructive plan prepared, which the country can unhesitatingly accept and follow. And when the plan is ready, a workable organization should be brought into existence to give effect to the measures recommended.

The country has to be equipped with sound economic policies, institutions and machinery and the average citizen instructed in business discipline and effective working habits.

In an undeveloped country, like India there is need for improvement and development in many directions. There is insistent demand, for instance, for improvement under communications, housing, water supply, sanitation and other social wants. But all these needs should yield priority to economic advancement, because, if production from agriculture and industries is increased, there will be rise in income all round and the growth of income will enable the people to raise their standards of living. Animalities are fundamental. Physical wants should be supplied first. Our chief concern as a first step should, therefore, be to give the masses opportunities of earning a reasonable income to provide themselves with the normal wants of existence.

The immediate object of the proposals outlined here is to urge that at least one district in every Indian Province be taken up for intensive development by planning. To treat one district in this way will not put any appreciable strain on the resources of a local Government. The district chosen may need financial support for the scheme for the first four or five years only, after which the experiment ought to be able to pay for its own way. There should be no difficulty in equipping one chosen district for this short period with picked officials, experts, enthusiastic public workers and adequate financial and other machinery to step up the ratio of its productive power.

Planning is needed to introduce a new business order into the districts in which discipline, integrity, devotion to duty, value of time and corporate effort should all be recognized and made to play their legitimate part. If work is found for every able-bodied person and productive activities are systematically stimulated, industry, alertness and discipline may become the rule, and a situation may arise in due course in which goods and services would be available in increasing quantities to render living conditions for every one more secure.

When the public obtains clear proofs of the benefits of the measures undertaken in one district, other areas will begin to take lessons from it, and it would not be long before the great majority of the people of a Province or State begin to appreciate the methods adopted and become warm supporters of planned development.

Main Lines of Development

The basic wants of a family may be taken as six in number – Food, Clothing, Housing, Education, Recreation and Amusement, and Work.

The people will have to obtain these wants by engaging themselves in the various occupations and professions open to them. As vast masses of the rural population lead a hand-to-mouth existence any scheme intended to redress their condition should aim primarily at making provision for the necessities of life. The poorer classes constitute more than 75 per cent of the population and if the standard of living of these classes is raised, those of the middle and upper classes will rise automatically.

The information collected in statistical tables for each residential area or region by means of surveys will reveal approximately the productive capacity and income of the area. It will show whether the income is sufficient or not, and, if insufficient, to what extent it is so, to supply the inhabitants with the minimum wants of a healthy and decent existence.

The tables and information gathered will reveal the total population of the district, its average annual income and in what proportion each of these is distributed between the various occupations. They will also give a clue to the changes and adjustments to be made from time to time in order to maintain a proper balance of occupations and secure a progressive rise in the standard of living.

All income and standards of living will be dependent in the last resort on the output of work of the people. Their economic condition is determined normally by their productive activities and capacity. In almost every country there are great inequalities in the income of individual citizens due to privileged position, inherited property and nature of occupations followed. But, generally speaking, the prosperity of any people or community will depend on the character of the occupations which they have chosen for themselves and the vigour, skill and ability with which they apply themselves to their various callings.

The survey and statistical statements collected will reveal how the average individual income in a village, town or city stands as compared with that needed for normal subsistence. Enquiries made in districts situated far apart show that at the present time the income of an average family is in the neighbourhood of Rs. 25 per month. Among three-fourths of the rural population, the average does not seem to exceed Rs. 12. To enable an average family to provide itself with the bare necessities of life, a minimum monthly income of Rs. 40 seems necessary even from Indian standards. Our first endeavour should, therefore, be to suitably provide the population with gainful occupations and services to secure this minimum income for every family in the district.

Obviously, the only way to secure a rise in income is by giving the necessary training and inducing the people to work harder, to work longer hours where necessary, to develop skill and capacity and produce commodities of quality and value. If intelligence and skills are developed hours of labour can be shortened.

The statistical statements resulting from the surveys will suggest to trained minds and experts the directions in which industries and employment should be increased or multiplied in order to raise the income.

With the aid of statistics, the district economic council and the development office superintendent with their expert staff will be able to advise the local village councils in what directions their productive activities should be extended and strengthened to give them a substantial increase of income.

It has been stated that one of the six wants of a family for healthy existence is work. It is natural in an undeveloped country, like India, that this wholesome precept should be lost sight of and large masses of the rural population should have come to regard work as an unpleasant necessity.

The appalling amount of unemployment and particularly short employment is due to this wrong conception of life, the ignorance of the population, lack of guidance by public leaders of Government and the utter absence of economic planning and organization.

The aim of the district development scheme is to lead the people to work under discipline, to take up the most profitable occupations within their reach, to double their average income and mitigate their existing poverty and distress. In their very attempt to double their present average income, the people of a district will acquire the initiative, vigour and co-operative effort necessary to provide themselves with their further wants.

Steps should be taken to give whatever temporary relief is possible to the poorest classes by organizing for their benefit new units of work and new occupations as an emergency measure.

The main lines of development will include the following policies and measures:–

1. The public should be induced and trained to make up their mind to work harder, more methodically and in closer co-operation with their neighbours to increase production. All successful nations owe their prosperity and long life to their active policies and habits.
2. A survey should be made of economic conditions to find out the present defects which afflict the people and the directions in which reforms and remedies are necessary and to create and select occupations for them.
3. Occupations which give the highest remuneration or profit should be chosen.
4. The district should be equipped with appropriate institutions, directing staff and policies to promote development.
5. Elementary education should be spread rapidly, particularly among the adult population. Without education and an informed public, it would be futile to attempt building up efficiency or prosperity. All this should be done by planning.

District Organization

The population of an average district in British India is about one million souls. The total yearly income of such a district, at Rs. 50 per head of population, may be taken to be about Rs. five crores. The aim is to double this income within a period of seven to ten years. It is proposed to do this on the footing of a plan and a programme, carefully thought out, and with the aid as well of an agency specially chosen for the purpose.

The supervision and control of district development work will be invested in a development officer and staff working in close association with a district economic council. The economic council will be made up of seven to twelve members, nearly half of whom will be elected by the people of the district. The executive work of the council will be attended to by the district development officer, who will have two deputies and a staff of some twelve assistants. The development officer and staff will be expected, while working in close co-operation with the council, to carry out the orders of the State or provincial government concerned. The district economic council and the officers of the development department will be jointly in charge of the operations for increasing the goods and services in, or the income of the people of the district.

The district development officer will be responsible for giving effect to the plan and programme approved by the district economic council and sanctioned by the provincial government.

The development officer will work in co-operation with the Collector and the heads of various Government departments and local bodies in the district. He will take instructions in important matters from the department of the provincial government to which he is directly responsible.

The economic council will take into account the resources, both material and manpower, available in the district to the fullest extent possible while preparing the plans and schedules of work to be executed in each official year. The council will also prepare a Five-Year Plan embodying forecasts of developments in various departments of district economic life for the ensuing five years, including the year for which a working plan and budget are prepared.

A plan, schedule of works and a budget are the three essential parts of a district development scheme. All these will be constantly undergoing revision and development at the hands of the economic council and the district development staff. They will be prepared in accordance with the provisions of the scheme and the instructions of the controlling authority in the provincial or State government concerned.

The services of qualified public-spirited citizens who volunteer for this scheme may be utilized in any capacity they may be wanted by the district development officer. They may serve as individual officials or in committees constituted for local objects under the scheme. While so employed, they will be subordinate to the development officer and will carry out the duties and observe all the rules and discipline expected of them. The services of such men may be utilized for one year at a time, with the approval of the economic council.

Village and Town Organizations

For the purpose of encouraging self-government among the rural masses it will be convenient if a group of villages, perhaps 10 or 12 in number, are treated as a village union or unit and operated together. The combined population of the group may ordinarily vary between 5,000 and 10,000. The office of the village council should be established in a centrally situated village within the group. The village council should consist of seven to twelve members elected for a year at a time from among the most competent residents in the area by an assembly of headmen of families residing in it.

Two or three village officials including an accountant will constitute the village office and they will work under the direction of the village council and its elected Chairman. The Chairman will, during his term of office, be responsible to the District Collector and to the district development officer for the performance of all the duties assigned to the village council under the scheme. Where necessity arises and funds permit, other special establishments will be employed for specific constructive duties as required.

The village office will maintain statistics of production and income of the population in each of the constituent villages and prepare a report embodying the necessary statistical tables at the end of the year. The report will give the income in each village and the average income per family and per head of population in the whole union.

Under the advice of and in accordance with the instructions issued by the district development department, the village council will prepare lists of raw materials and other resources available to give employment to local labour and of industries and trades which require encouragement in the coming year. The village council will also indicate, under the advice of the development officials, the amount of capital and material needed and how it is proposed to obtain them. The estimates and plans when prepared will be submitted to the district development officers for approval and after sanction is obtained the proposals will be given effect to.

The village community will be encouraged to concentrate attention on gainful occupations and the new activities in the village, such as extension of irrigation, use of fertilizers, establishment of new industries, expansion of old industries and promotion of trade and traffic calculated to bring increased income and revenue to the village population.

At the same time, under the advice and direction of the officials of the development department, a forecast of production and income for the ensuing period of five years may be prepared. Endeavours would also be made in some villages to achieve an increase of income amounting to as much as 50 per cent by the end of the fifth year of the programme. Such increase may not be possible in every village. But there may be some villages in which by rapid nurturing of new industries the income could be more than doubled.

It must be understood that in the case of the agricultural population income is certain to be reduced now and again by bad years, that is, by seasonal variations due to shortage of rainfall or in a lesser degree to excessive rain or heavy floods or inundations. Safety, therefore, lies in increasing employment in industries and other occupations.

The results of each year will be recorded in suitable statistical tables, registers and reports, copies of which will be kept in the village union office, and also in the district office of the development department.

In every district there will be a dozen or more towns and occasionally one or two cities, and in each such town and city, an urban development council should be established to encourage the growth of industries, trade and other occupations and to collect and record statistics of production, service and income.

Detailed methods of development can be worked out for each city and town, according to the nature of its occupations and commercial activities and aptitudes.

Separate forms of reports and statistical tables to be maintained by the village and urban councils, respectively, will be prescribed by the development department with the approval of the provincial government.

The constitution of the village union here suggested is largely based on the one adopted in Japan under similar conditions, when self-government was first conferred on rural areas in that country. Some half a dozen or more villages were grouped together to form a self-governing unit. In that way 72,000 villages in Japan were grouped into 12,000 self-governing units.

This scheme of rural self-government is working well in Japan and may be advantageously adopted here. We are at present concerned in creating an organization mainly for the purposes of economic betterment. When it begins to work successfully, other functions of the district administration may be transferred to the village council. In Japan, the village councils tax themselves and spend liberally on education. They also collect the taxes due to the district and provincial governments and remit the collections to the Governor of the Prefecture or district. With the exception of the police duties, the village council and headmen administer all the affairs of the village union. It is important that the constitution of the village government should be changed at the source in order to give a desirable training in constitutional government for our rural population.

Occupational and Production Survey

Almost the first work of the development department should be to investigate how the people of the district are employed, how many of them in agriculture, what number on industries, trade, transport and other services and what their aggregate income is in each of those classes of occupations. A survey will give a clue to the true resources and earning capacity of the people and to the distribution of the total population and income in the respective occupations.

A survey of industries should be given precedence because they typify occupations which have been neglected in the recent past and which, for that very reason, are likely to give handsome returns for some time to come, if undertaken at once and pursued on lines suggested by recent world experience.

One of the first labours of the survey would, therefore, be to collect data for industries in each village union and in each urban unit area under the following heads :

(i) Number of establishments or separate units of work;
(ii) Capital invested;
(iii) Labour employed;
(iv) Products and their value; and
(v) Per capita value of industrial output in each unit area.

An account should be compiled of the condition of existing industries in the district and a list prepared of other new industries that can be profitably started. This will be among the earliest results of the development programme.

The next most important work to be undertaken would be a comprehensive survey of occupations in the district. They may be considered under four classes as under :

1. Industries and crafts;
2. Agriculture and allied occupations;
3. Trade and transport; and
4. Services, professional, public, domestic, etc.

This survey should lead to the collection of information under each of these groups of occupations regarding products (where there are any) and their values, total population including dependents maintained and the amount of income in each group. In this way the income, or the approximate income, of the entire population of a village union, town or city will be ascertained, and statistical tables will be compiled giving the total income, per capita income and other data for the entire district. Simultaneously, a register should be prepared of able-bodied persons who are unemployed and of approximate numbers of persons who suffer from short employment. This information is also necessary to give a complete idea of the economic situation in the district.

The Table 3.1 will reveal generally in what way the population of an average district is distributed at present, and in what directions changes and re-adjustments are necessary to bring them into line with people of progressive countries, whose occupations are more wisely balanced.

The distribution of population in the second column of Table 3.1 is based on the Census figures of 1931. Those in the third column are taken from a statement giving occupations in 14 countries based on information in the *Statistical Year Book of the League of Nations*, 1933.

A glance at the above table will show how heavily agriculture is overweighted and how great is the necessity to afford relief to the soil by transferring the surplus population now dependent on agriculture to industries and other gainful occupations.

An occupational survey of the kind suggested is likely to reveal the following more obvious defects in the economy of the State :

TABLE 3.1 : Population distribution — occupation-wise

Class of Occupation	Percentage of total population: As employed at present	Percentage of total population: Approximately as it should be employed in future
1	2	3
1. Agriculture and Allied Occupations	67	31
2. Industries and Crafts	10	33
3. Trade and Transport	6	18
4. Services: Government Domestic, Professional, etc.	17	18
Total	100	100

(i) That the people are insufficiently employed and, although prepared to work, their opportunities of obtaining suitable employment and earning a decent living are limited;

(ii) That the income of the people in most districts, save in irrigated tracts or industrial neighbourhoods, is below what is necessary for a normal healthy existence;

(iii) That for want of mass education and training the people have not acquired the capacity and practices of self-help, initiative, courage to start new enterprises and skill to secure new sources of income; and

(iv) That for lack of proper business conditions, credit and co-operation are at a discount and new business undertakings are of necessity slow to take root.

Aids to Development

Sound policies, institutions, equipment and administrative practices can all help in the production of commodities and services. These may be considered under two heads, namely, (1) Principal Aids, and (2)

Subsidiary Aids.

The principal aids to development, aids which are practically indispensable for the purpose, may be stated to be banking facilities, statistics, tariff protection, mass education and travel conveniences.

The subsidiary aids usually provided are commercial museums, exhibitions and fairs, research, marketing and transport facilities, workshops and training institutions, and commercial and trade schools.

Each of these aids will now be briefly explained.

Principal Aids

Banking Facilities: Government should use its credit to keep large sums of money in circulation in the district for purposes of production by raising the capital required wholly or partly in the district itself. Government is in a position, with the aid of existing banks, to reduce the rates of interest on loans prevailing in the rural tracts. Special precautions should be taken that the security of the loans advanced is not jeopardized.

How important and urgent this reform is will be understood from the fact that the peasantry is steeped in debt and there are regions in which the interest rates charged for loans are as high as 18 to 25 per cent, per annum.

Statistics: The maintenance of reliable statistics is one of the essential features of the district development scheme. In reports on Indian economic life, it is usual to be content with general assertions. If disciplined progress is to be maintained, developments in every sphere of progress should be measured, wherever it could be done, by the yardstick of statistics.

Tariff Protection: One of the greatest needs, if not the greatest need for the encouragement of industries, is protection against undesirable imports and dumping by foreign countries. Raw materials produced in India are exported to foreign countries and are brought back again here in a manufactured state. This deprives local labour of its scant supply of remunerative employment and is in many ways an injurious and anomalous practice.

Tariff protection is not a matter which Provincial or State governments can deal with. In order to secure adequate protection to local producers and manufacturers, the Government departments concerned (as well as committees of leading public men and businessmen in the district and in the province) should keep questions connected with protection under continuous study and make representations as required, from time to time, both to Provincial and Federal Governments and Legislatures.

Mass Education: Mass education should be vigorously pushed forward along with development activities. Real economic progress cannot be secured, and, when secured, will not long survive unless backed by a well-informed enlightened public opinion.

Here, again, there will be obstacles. Experience shows that farmers and working classes are likely to welcome the extension of elementary education while the richer land-owning classes are prone to oppose their tenants receiving education through fear that they might get out of control. This is a very selfish reason for obstructing progress. The general advancement of the country cannot be allowed to be retarded by allowing such notions to prevail.

Travel Conveniences: Local travel agencies managed on business lines, if brought into existence, will materially assist further intercommunication and commercial intercourse, and help to promote unity between all parts of India.

A good number of well-managed hotels should be established in towns and cities, with the aid of Government subsidies where necessary. They should be subject to the disciplinary control of the development department.

Lodging houses should be started in centrally situated villages subsidized by village councils. Such help would probably be required for five or six years only, until people get used to hotel life and business habits and a demand is created.

If model hotels are established in cities and towns and model lodging and boarding houses in villages, the business life of a district will be appreciably quickened.

The Americans and the Japanese are practical people. The writer has met university graduates in hotel management in America. Clean, cheap lodging houses are a marked feature of Japanese village life.

Subsidiary Aids

Commercial Museums, Exhibitions and Fairs: There should be a commercial museum with adequate staff – one at least at the headquarters station in each district – to exhibit sample products, chiefly to serve as patterns for local manufacture. Labour-saving tools and machinery should be also exhibited. The museum should serve as an agency from which should emanate all proposals for holding periodical exhibitions and fairs in the principal towns and business places in the district.

Research: In western countries considerable importance is attached to research and enormous sums are spent on it. Scientific research will be needed and should be encouraged both in industries and agriculture.

In agriculture, provision should be made for a wide range of experiments in scientific methods of production, fertilizers, eradication of pests, marketing problems, crop insurance, utilization of farm wastes, irrigation and the like.

A laboratory is necessary in many a modern industry for regulating manufacturing processes. Raw materials require to be tested and finished products made to conform to standard specifications.

Marketing Organization: At the present time, due to the ignorance of the cultivator, the middle man takes advantage of his helpless position and buys the produce of his labour too cheap and sells it at rates advantageous to himself in the nearest town or city. Some organization is needed to provide the illiterate cultivator with adequate marketing facilities. One way would be to establish business offices and godowns for co-operative marketing, to which the cultivator may take his produce for sale.

Transport Facilities: Both for products of new industries and for transport of raw or semi-raw materials intended for manufacture, railways should be induced to charge low freight rates. This question should be studied in comparison with practices in foreign countries. Cases in which rates are disadvantageous to industry should be brought to the notice of the Central Government and redress obtained.

A Central Workshop and Training Institutions: An experimental and demonstration station may be usefully established at the headquarters town of the district in which instruction is given, say, in some half a dozen industries likely to prove profitable to the people of the district.

Side by side with the experimental and demonstration station, a central workshop should be maintained to give practical training in manufacture. For all practical purposes, in these days, a well-equipped central workshop will be a more useful institution to the people of a district than an arts college.

Trade Schools: Either classes should be attached to existing schools or separate trade schools should be maintained to give instruction in various occupations, such as weaving, tailoring, smithing, carpentry, etc. Along with such training, an elementary knowledge of economics should be imparted.

One or two independent commercial schools and also commercial classes in existing middle and high schools should be established in the district to give training in economics, commerce and business practices.

Every young person, as he leaves the school, should regard himself as so much mechanical power for the production of wealth and be able to take his place in a farm, factory, office or shop as soon as he completes his education. He should start life adequately equipped to brave the struggles for existence. Moral education is also necessary. School boys and girls should have an elementary knowledge of the forces which shape their lives and an adequate training in business habits, discipline and value of time in order to grow up to be efficient citizens.

"Decades ago", says a British Consular Report, "in most households in Japan a screw-driver or a spanner were unfamiliar instruments: but today small boys make wireless sets and are interested in any kind of mechanism."

Quite three-fourths of the juvenile population who pass through our educational institutions in the districts should have practical training of some sort, so that in after life every single individual among them may be a producer or worker who would be adding to the wealth of the district.

Policies and Implications

Some practical measures which suggest themselves in this connection may be stated here to serve as a reminder to those actually engaged in rural uplift work.

Attention has been drawn to the fact that the present average per capita income in India is about one-tenth or less than one-tenth of what it is in Western Europe. Radical changes will be necessary in the economic structure and policies in the districts, if the present income is to be substantially raised.

Certain new policies and practices are recommended in the district development scheme proposed to change the economic structure in a district. This is in accordance with the principles followed in economic planning and involves public control of the economic structure. Such a control exists today on a wider scale in Great Britain. Under the proposed scheme, this control will be exercised by the district development department and the district economic council working jointly.

The supreme control of the local government over all district development works will remain unaffected.

Selected men, whether officials or non-officials, should be trained and employed on the scheme. Only enthusiastic officials and popular leaders who can render disinterested public service should be chosen for the work.

Among the officials and volunteers employed in the district under the development department, a reasonable proportion of the employees should, if possible, be persons who have been educated or have widely travelled abroad.

New occupations should be started and old ones expanded as required, particularly such as would give an abundant supply of the basic wants of the population – in food, clothing and housing.

Units of production and business undertakings should be multiplied by bringing capital, labour, organization and managerial ability together, wherever there may be scope for income and profit.

The most promising source of income at the present time is industries. Both large-scale and minor industries are wanted but this scheme is confined to a district and is, therefore, concerned with minor industries only.

Under each of the six wants of the human family referred to earlier the commodities and services, required to meet each want, should be roughly estimated and lists or tables prepared, showing how much grain, cloth, housing materials, educational and other facilities are available and how much more are needed. The figures gathered together will only be approximate but from them rough schedules of development can be prepared to support a forecast of future wants.

Statistics of production particularly under agriculture and industries should be collected first and maintained in every village union, in town unit areas as well as in the district as a whole. Preparation of occupational statistics should follow.

Statistics of changes in the occupational structure as far as can be ascertained should be published along with annual reports.

Tariffs should be watched and adjusted from time to time. Tariff protection is occasionally objected to as making articles of common use costly for the poor. It may have this effect temporarily but the sacrifice is necessary in the wider interests of the country to make it self-sufficient in regard to many of the products in ordinary use which the people can easily manufacture for themselves.

Rural indebtedness is another evil which should be attacked and remedied at the very outset, wherever possible. This has been attempted with success in a small district like Bhavnagar. The influence of money-lenders should be utilized in a healthy direction to build up a new credit system for the village.

There should be reform and re-awakening in universities to train young persons in the science of better living, so that a good proportion of them, after they pass through the university portals, may be able to enter a farm, factory or shop and carry on business with success after a brief apprenticeship, if necessary.

Some of the textbooks used at present in Middle and High Schools which give instruction in morals or business life will require rewriting to suit the altered present-day business conditions.

To make the people industry-minded and to create an atmosphere of progress, propaganda should be resorted to by writing and distributing leaflets, the delivering of public lectures, etc., to spread among the people information bearing on :

(i) Past experience and present state of industries in India;
(ii) Recent experience in the same field in progressive countries;
(iii) A knowledge of up-to-date machinery in common use; and
(iv) Modern processes of production and the latest industrial and commercial practices

The public should be kept informed up to date, by propaganda from time to time of the true position of affairs in the following respects:–

(1) Specific facilities and concessions given by Government to encourage industries;
(2) The nature of and conditions under which expert advice provided by Government can be procured;
(3) The distribution of population and income by occupations; and
(4) Maintenance of accurate current records and statistics.

At present large numbers of people suffer from unemployment and short employment. No efforts should be spared to start new units of work for their benefit, wherever there may be scope for them.

In both rural and urban unit areas, much of the success of the proposed scheme will depend upon the growth of the working capacity of individual families and citizens. This should be stimulated by well-devised propaganda, by giving prizes and by other methods of encouragement, with the aid of public-spirited leaders and local committees. Progress in this respect should be also watched by means of statistics maintained specially for the purpose.

The co-operative spirit among the people should be particularly stimulated, opportunities being provided for them to work together in association in production and profit-making occupations.

Also, the district development department, with the aid of the economic council, should be able to check mal-practices in business concerns by exercising some sort of paternal control and by bringing to bear on them the moral influence of the community.

A Concrete Programme

There is at present no plan, nor are there any national policies, to guide us in the solution of new economic problems as they arise from time to time. Such planning on a national scale will require the active cooperation of the people and the ungrudging support of the Government. Till a national plan comes into existence, individual districts whose administration is within certain limits in the hands of the people themselves are in a favourable position to attempt planned development.

The Provincial Governments can now plan and make available an increasing amount of goods and services for the use of their people. The district development scheme herein proposed gives the outlines of a desirable plan. It aims at making an intensive effort to increase production by persuading the people to work harder, and under discipline, to work more intelligently and effectively. The various proposals which comprise the plan will now be briefly recapitulated in a connected form.

Size and Resources of a District – For purposes of illustration, the following hypothetical data may be assumed for a district in British India in which the scheme may be brought into operation :–

Area of District	5,000 sq. miles
Population	1,000,000
Annual Revenue	Rs. 80 lakhs
Amount of Capital to be made available for expansion of industries and for improving agriculture and developing occupations	

generally	Rs. 80 lakhs
Yearly Grant	
for maintaining the district development scheme	Rs. 5 lakhs

The cost of maintaining the development department may be taken at Rs. 5 lakhs for the first three years. If a larger sum can be spared so much the better. Of this sum, Rs. 3 lakhs may be utilized for the district organization and staff and Rs. 2 lakhs for a central workshop and other training institutions.

The sum of Rs. 5 lakhs should, in the first instance, be met by a provincial grant. If everything goes well, the income of the people will increase and the Government revenue also, with it, from new industries and employments. The demand on provincial revenues is likely to grow less and less from the third year onwards.

Main Lines of Development

The chief object of planning, in the present case, is to ascertain the demand and supply of the normal wants of the people, to preach the gospel of work and the value of co-operative effort, to create new sources of production, to bring work within the reach of every able-bodied citizen, and by all these measures to double the income and standard of living of the people in the course of seven to ten years.

It is proposed at the beginning to limit the scheme to the reconditioning of one district only in each Province or State in the manner described.

District Organization

This will consist of:–

1. An Economic Council;
2. A District Development Department, and Budget; and
3. A Five-Year Plan.

The economic council may consist of seven to twelve members.

District economic conferences will be held at regular intervals in the year to which officials and experts and leading businessmen and active citizens from all parts of the district will be invited.

The district should be properly equipped with offices, institutions and policies and with staffs of officials and experts who would be able to guide the population to start new works and new occupations. Mere advice will not prove sufficient. The officials should guide in establishing and operating new units of work and continue to advise until occupations are more correctly re-distributed.

The district population particularly needs instruction in company formation and co-operative business practices. This is an equipment to which little or no attention has been paid hitherto. Certain Indian communities are adepts in this class of work. Their special knowledge and practices in this respect might be advantageously put into a modern form and widely disseminated.

The district development department and the economic council will jointly operate the scheme. They will maintain statistics of production on modern lines, review the situation once a quarter and issue yearly reports of progress with appropriate statistical tables.

Village and Town Organizations: These consist of village and town councils and their establishments.

The village councils and their headmen will administer a group of villages with a population varying from 5,000 to 10,000. They will be allowed to tax themselves for the purpose. *Panchayats*, wherever they exist, may help them with funds to make a beginning.

In the first three to five years, Government may subsidize the village councils but thereafter the councils should be made to depend upon their own taxes.

The urban units will be provided with funds for their work by the municipalities or other local self-government bodies concerned, and as in the case of the village councils, they will be also aided by subventions from the Government during the first five years.

Eventually when the village units are found working satisfactorily most of the functions of the district administration in the area may be safely transferred to village councils.

Survey and Statistics: A survey will be carried out of production, income, number of workers employed, etc., in industries, agriculture and other occupations in each unit area and the district as a whole.

Statistical tables will be compiled showing the distribution of population and income by occupations, to serve as a guide in planning for the future.

Aids to Development: Simultaneously certain facilities are needed to create an industrial and developmental atmosphere. The more important of these are banking facilities, statistics, tariff protection, mass education and travel conveniences.

Capital is required for new industries and for expansion and improvement of agriculture and subsidiary rural occupations. In the initial stages, the amount required may be taken at about the same figure as the total yearly revenues of the district.

This sum may in most cases be raised, with the aid of a Government guarantee of interest for a term of years, from well-to-do classes of the population in the district itself.

A beginning may be made by raising a loan equivalent to about 25 per cent of the revenues of the district for utilization as capital on minor and cottage industries. The percentage may be gradually increased as demand arises for financing new ventures.

The loan should be advanced, as far as possible, not by a Government department but by independent financial organizations, such as local trusts, branch banks or co-operative societies.

Citizenship Training: For training the people for industries and business life, a central workshop, an experimental and demonstration station, a museum, trade schools, commercial classes, farms, etc., will be brought into existence as required.

The cost of these, unless Government itself comes forward to provide them, should be met by appeal to local industrialists and merchants, leaders and philanthropists backed by handsome subsidies and subventions by Government.

Propaganda, Reviews and Reports: Suitable propaganda will be carried on by the district economic as well as local councils and by the Government department to popularize the scheme. Statistical tables and charts will be maintained to measure progress and these will be exhibited in village *chavdis* or halls.

Development Schedules and Budget: Estimates of work to be done and their cost will be collected in the form of schedules for each unit area. Schedules of development for the first year and approximate schedules for five years will be prepared for each village and each urban development unit first, and from these for the whole district. All works and improvements to be carried out in the year in the village unit area and in the urban unit area including training for industries should be brought on a schedule in this way and the budget for their execution based thereon.

The budget should be duly approved by the district economic council and the development department before the commencement of the new financial year. The funds required in each union should be raised by a local tax or supplied by a local *Panchayat*, if there be one.

The district budget will make provision for the expenses of the economic council and the development department with all its staff, contributions to institutions, associations, committees, etc., and contributions or subventions to the village and urban councils.

Annual Reports: An annual report embodying the results of the surveys and other progressive measures undertaken in the district during the year should be prepared and copies of the same recorded in the offices of the local councils as well as in the district development office at the headquarters of the district. Copies may also be furnished to other offices as required.

Code of Rules: A code of rules for the administration of the district development scheme should be prepared and maintained. The compilation would be somewhat imperfect at first but as work progresses it is bound to be gradually improved, from year to year, with the experience gained in advancing the scheme.

Aims Redefined

We live in a stubborn material environment and generally we have to work hard to get what we want. Work is necessary for the production of consumers' goods and services required to supply the various wants of a human family. Where more work is put into gainful occupations, there will be more income, and the greater the income the higher the standard of living. Prosperous nations are not always those that live in tracts where nature is propitious but those who have learnt by past experience and suffering that conditions of living can be improved only by industry, organization and technical skill. Increase of commodities, will be secured through longer hours of labour, teamwork, discipline, skill put into labour and by better organization and planning. To show the way to these various expedients is the object of the district development scheme here described.

The proposed district development scheme, if brought into operation in the spirit indicated above, is expected to provide an effective starting point for the economic reconstruction of the countryside. As explained before, the specific aim of the plan at the outset will be to stimulate the productive capacity of the district and double its income in seven to ten years time. Since there will be wanting men, money and directing ability to do this on any vast scale, it is proposed to confine the scheme at the outset to one or two district(s) only in each Province and State.

Developments in other spheres – political, social or cultural – should be attempted by creating other independent agencies and not be mixed up with this scheme. Although all such beneficial measures should be worked together and in close harmony, the immediate aim of the scheme under consideration is economic betterment. Material wants in which we are very poorly equipped at present must rank first and as they are fundamental to the very existence of the population they are important enough to be treated as a class by themselves.

Many wrong traditions have to be wiped out and numerous modern practices and policies assiduously cultivated in order to make the people trust one another and co-operate more freely for attaining national aims and ends. Numerous existing retardative practices have to undergo a revolutionary change.

It was owing to these traditions and practices that India, notwithstanding that her population is over 30 times as large, has had to yield pride of place in industry and trade in recent times to a well-knit small nation like Canada.

There is no responsible agency or organization at present to correct defects in the economic life of the people and stimulate progress. So a district development department associated with a district economic council is proposed for the purpose.

The scheme aims at securing bare subsistence wants mainly for the rural population. It is intended for the rehabilitation of a district – not a Province or the country as a whole.

There are too many people employed in some occupations and too few in others, and production is impeded. To remedy this, a balanced re-distribution of occupations is urged.

Industries were badly neglected in the past. To make up speedily for past losses, special measures are contemplated to expand them and increase the proportion of the working population on them to three or four times its present strength.

There is not enough money in circulation in rural parts, either for investment or for use as working capital for the volume of business that is needed to secure comfortable working conditions for the people. Steps should be taken to ensure the freer circulation of capital, even if it necessitates Government sharing unfavourable risks.

The average citizen should be educated and encouraged to work the proposed plan. He should be induced by lure of income and profit to raise his economic status.

4

DISTRICT PLANNING
Some Basic Issues

G.V. VISWANATH

IN THE papers already placed before this conference, and in those to follow, ample and adequate description of the methodology of the District Planning and the Panchayat Raj systems, in Karnataka and elsewhere in the country, would be found. It is not, therefore, proposed to repeat them here. On the other hand, this chapter attempts to focus attention on certain larger issues connected with rural development, in the broad sense of this word, which is the basis of district planning.

Panchayat Raj, the autonomous institutional framework for rural development that we have now adopted, is not new to India. Since several centuries, through the rise and fall of kingdoms, and periods of great political upheavals, the autonomous village administrative systems have been providing stability and conservation to the social, political and economic life of the people. Enough material has come to light in recent years, in the works of Dharmapal and others, to show that at the beginning of the colonial era, the rural areas not only enjoyed a high degree of local autonomy, but were also economically and socially viable.

The old self-governing village institutions and the economic self-sufficiency of the villages formed the basis of Mahatma Gandhi's idea of *Gram Swaraj*, where "the village is a complete republic, independent of its neighbour for its own vital wants and yet interdependent for many others in which the dependence is a necessity". This was Gandhiji's prescription to overcome the ill-effects of a centralized colonial economy, which reduced the rural population in particular to conditions of economic and social serfdom and destitution. He felt that this was the only remedy to the increasing poverty and degradation of life in the villages. The reasoning is obvious. The then rulers had vast powers to exploit the raw-materials and labour of the rural areas to stifle any economic activity which could compete with their own or lead to self-sufficiency. The answer to this situation, as Gandhiji saw it, was for the village economy to free itself from the grip of the larger colonial economy. At least initially there may be a shrinking of economic activity, but it would provide freedom to the rural areas from the predatory clutches of the system. Thus, *Gram Swaraj* was the first requirement for the regeneration of rural India, which meant the country as a whole, since an overwhelming part of its inhabitants lived in rural areas.

Even prior to independence many of these ideas had resulted in attention being paid to rural problems. There were institutions like District Boards and other Local Boards in many States. After independence, there was a commitment to develop rural areas and to bring the rural people into the main stream of national life. We had the District Development Councils and the Taluk Boards and similar institutions.

There has been, however, a growing realization that all these efforts were pitfully inadequate and did not even scratch the surface. The vast majority of our people who lived in the rural areas had not really begun to participate in economic development. Hence a new framework in the form of Panchayat Raj system has become necessary. It has already been introduced in many States, and the model followed in Karnataka seems to have gone the furthest. In the Karanataka model, for the first time an elected body, independent of Government, would plan and execute development schemes. This amounts to the very substantial transfer of political power and economic resources.

The success of the *Panchayat Raj* institutions which are coming up in the country would depend upon the political awareness of the people who form a part of the system. If there is political backwardness, we may be sure that old despotism and tyranny would creep back, with even more economic and political authority and even less accountability or restraint. So, to bring about social and political awareness among the people is very much a part of the process and necessary to ensure its success.

However, the Panchayat Raj systems provide only the framework. It is the means to an end and not the end in itself. We have also to appreciate that it is only the Government's developmental activities which are transferred to the new institutions. We have to observe that, first, governmental intervention in the form of development activities is only a small part of the total socio-economic activity. Secondly, even for this small part to take place, there has to be a transfer of resources from above, from outside. A continuous infusion of funds is what would make the whole system work. This does not amount to autonomy or self-sufficiency, as Gandhiji saw it. But whether, in course of time, it would generate local resources and lead to greater autonomy is the important consideration.

Very briefly, let us recollect that 77 per cent of our population live in rural areas. Rural poverty is really staggering: learned estimates varyingly place 60 per cent to 40 per cent as being below the poverty line. Even if we adopt the official estimate currently available of 40.4 per cent, we would see that more than 250 million people live below the poverty line and hence unable to meet the requirements of a bare livelihood. Thus, rural poverty is appalling and wide spread.

Even after so many years of independence we have not been able to cope with this problem. We inherited and continued to build upon the same economic system, which prevailed earlier, a system which is not easy to dismantle or even change. Our patterns of economic growth have become fixed along these lines. In the '50s and '60s we thought the solution lay in big industries and dams, in centralization and greater efficiency. Today we are no longer sure that this is the complete answer, but we find it not easy to get away from it, even if we wish to. Our economy still remains largely a centralized one, with resources being drawn away from the rural areas as remorselessly as it was during the colonial era.

In recent years, the migration that is taking place from rural to urban areas has reached alarming proportions. If this is not halted or slowed down somehow, it is feared that all civic life in our cities would breakdown. But why does this happen? Apart from the obvious attractions of city life, the main cause of migration is economic. It is not true that a village provided agricultural occupations alone. There were a hundred occupations in a village; apart from agriculture and allied pursuits, there were weavers, potters, carpenters, black-smiths, builders, shopkeepers, oil-mongers, musicians, dancers, entertainers, priests, astrologers, story-tellers, teachers and so many others. The village economy can no longer sustain such a variety of occupations which it did in the past. Some of them have perhaps become redundant, but other alternatives have not taken their place. So people have lost their vocations and their means of livelihood, and migrate to the cities in search of bare existence. If the flight of resources from rural areas is not halted, it would not be possible to halt migration either.

Is it possible, even remotely, that the developed sector is, unwittingly, treating the vast rural areas as its internal colony? We must really go into this question of transfer of resources from rural areas in the form of men, material and talent. We have accepted as axiomatic that many of the measures we have undertaken are of real benefit to rural economy. But a sugar factory which crushes 1,500 tonnes of cane deprives 15,000 families of employment in the *gur* industry. If the bullock-carts begin to use rubber tyres, an inexhaustible market would be opened out for exploitation by urban manufacturers. We have to assess the total impact of setting up an industry in a rural area and find out whether it actually contributes to or takes away from rural economy. No doubt, large centralized industries have an efficiency of their own. They help in increasing production in many cases. But the important question is: whom does this increase benefit? Where does this increase go? Not back to the rural areas!

So ours in an unenviable position. Because, we are aware of the absolute need to bring the rural areas into the main stream of economic progress. At the same time, we don't know how to do this. There are forces at work in our economy which have a momentum of their own, and are not amenable to change. We find that we are pursuing contradictory goals, that some of our activity at least has a result which is opposite to that intended. But as long as we recognize, and are aware that there are contradictions, and view them objectively, without attempting to see that which we would like to see, we would surely have taken a step forward. But one idea stands out today: that Mahatma Gandhi's concept of village autonomy is more valid than ever before.

The *Panchayat Raj* institution is a breakthrough, we may say, in bringing democracy and democratic planning nearer to the people in the rural areas. If we must build upon this, it is inevitable that we give substance to *Panchayat Raj* through the concept of village autonomy.

5

REVITALIZING DISTRICT PLANNING*

K.V. SUNDARAM

The first step for effective district planning is to have elected *panchayat raj* bodies in all States. Unless the *panchayat raj* bodies come into existence and go through a learning process, they can never acquire the capabilities to deliver the goods and improve their performance.

Elections serve as the best instruments for weeding non-performing institutions when the time comes. The second step is to integrate development administration into the *panchayat* system. Several States have squandered the funds provided by the Planning Commission by not employing technical personnel of the right calibre in the district planning cells. Maharashtra and Gujarat made a breakthrough in the '70s and '80s by devising suitable allocation formulae which are being adapted now by a number of other States with necessary changes according to their circumstances.

Panchayat Raj Institutions

THE RECENT Prime Ministerial mandate on district planning infuses great hopes in an area plagued with a lack of political will and bureaucratic disinclination. If the PM's statement on the subject is to be taken seriously and acted upon sincerely, the Planning Commission and the State administrations have to identify the numerous ailments which characterize district planning in different parts of the country today and launch appropriate and sustained action intended to deal successfully with these problems.

The first step for effective district planning is to have elected

---

* Reprinted from *Economic Times*, June 9-10, 1988.

panchayat raj bodies in all the States. Whatever hurdles are there militating against this step must be ruthlessly overcome. It is here that the Prime Minister has to show great political courage and determination and demonstrate his keen desire for clean politics. Unless the *panchayat raj* bodies come into existence and go through an experiential learning process, they can never acquire the capabilities to deliver the goods and improve their performance with experience.

In a democracy, elections serve as the best instruments for weeding non-performing institutions when the time comes. This is the natural process of selection in politics. The ruling party will do well to go by such ethics.

The second step is to integrate development administration into the *panchayat raj* system. This would mean clothing these institutions with adequate powers and resources to enable them to function as truly effective instruments. The district level *panchayat* must assume supremacy as the authentic approval body with powers to screen all proposals and programmes of the line departments.

The apex body will be the district *panchayat* itself. It will be in the nature of a district assembly—a supreme decision-making body reviewing, approving and authenticating the district plan prepared by the second level planning organization, which may be designated as the "district planning committee". The district *panchayat* has to be an all-embracing body – the nerve centre with the representation of chairman of *panchayat samitis*, members of the executive committee of the district *panchayat* and the district heads of sectoral departments. To enlarge its representation, some special invitees may be added to its composition particularly for the purpose of carrying on its transactions in regard to planning. These special invitees could be :

- all MPs and MLAs hailing from the district;
- chairmen of all municipal bodies in the district; and
- representatives of statutory authorities, if any, operating in the district.

Such a composition will pave the way for the representation of all shades of opinion and for the integration of all planning activities going on in the district. The presiding deity of this set-up is normally the chairman of the district *panchayat*. A question may be raised as to how national and State level politicians will attend a meeting presided over by a local politician? In fact, it is this vexed question that has led some States (e.g. Gujarat, Maharashtra, West Bengal) to create a separate organization, called the district planning and co-ordination council or district planning and development council, as in Maharashtra or the district planning board as in Gujarat, with a Minister of State as chairman.

But, the dilemma can be solved through healthy precedents. For instance in such meetings where the plan is to be approved or vital planning decisions to be taken, the senior-most politician may be given the right of precedence or the privilege of presiding over and guiding the deliberations. Experiences in Gujarat and Maharashtra have shown that when a Minister of State is appointed as the chairman of the district planning body, he often finds little time to devote to this work and meetings often get postponed.

The second tier institution in the planning set-up envisaged here is the establishment of what may be called a District Planning Committee (DPC). It will be somewhat similar to the executive committee constituted in a number of States. It will be the real planning body preparing the draft district plan, aided in this task by a multi-disciplinary planning cell whose capabilities have to be consciously built up. At present, this apparatus is quite weak, notwithstanding the financial incentives provided by the Planning Commission through its scheme of strengthening of the planning machinery at the district level.

In fact, several States have squandered the funds provided by the Planning Commission by not employing technical personnel of the right calibre in the district planning cells. In the case of States which employed some technical staff, they were not properly trained and usefully employed in the planning tasks. There is a great leeway to be made by the States in this regard.

The third institutional tier to be considered is the one at the block level. It will be a body with the president of the *panchayat samiti* as chairman and with members consisting of the *pradhans* of all *gram panchayats* and the block level officers of departments. This body has the crucial task of throwing up the felt needs of the block level community and their development priorities. At this stage of development, it is too much to expect the blocks to come up with a well-conceived block level plan.

The government of West Bengal, which has operationalized district planning to some extent, has been realistic and has desired the *gram panchayats* to prepare a needs statement and the *panchayat samitis* to prioritize the needs statement on the basis of the total financial ceiling indicated to them. An arrangement on these lines will be the most practical so far as sub-district level planning is concerned.

Another essential step to get district planning moving in the right direction in the States is by paying attention to the financial aspects of decentralization. For a long time, district planning did not take off in the country, as the districts were not told about the ceiling within which to plan. This led them to the preparation of a catalogue of schemes or needs, which does not have much relevance. No priorities were laid down and the exercise was one of blowing up the needs.

Thus, no realistic district planning materialized in spite of the appeals and coercions of the Planning Commission. The Planning Commission has emphasized, from time to time, the importance of effecting financial decentralization from the state to the districts based on sound methodologies, taking note of the relative level of development among the districts.

Maharashtra and Gujarat made a breakthrough in the '70s and the '80s by devising suitable allocation formulae which are being adapted now by a number of other States with necessary changes according to their circumstances.

Thus, the problem of inter-district allocation methodology has, to a great extent, been solved; nevertheless, there are still related problems which are posing serious difficulties.

Encouraging Localism

A point of great significance in local level planning is the freedom available to the district planning body to deploy the resources in accordance with the local priorities and needs.

This aspect, referred to as 'localism' in planning, i.e., autonomy to utilize the development funds according to the local perceptions of needs and priorities, is not conferred on the districts by the usual procedures of allocation. This is because most of the allocations indicated to the districts are already pre-empted for various departmental schemes and are provided in the budgets of the sectoral departments. The actual decision-making powers in regard to the utilization of these funds vest with the departmental heads and not with the district planning body. It is in this context that the idea of 'untied funds' has been mooted.

This is, in effect, making a separate allocation of funds to the districts by the States apart from the allocations made department-wise. This is to be accompanied by a budgetary innovation of starting a new budget head for 'District Plan Schemes'. The 'untied' funds are intended to be used for topping up outlays of other departments/agencies as may be required, or for initiating vitally important new schemes as per the perceptions of the block/district planning authorities. Wherever, such untied funds are now provided, they constitute a relatively small sum.

Nevertheless this kitty could be considerably enlarged and real 'localism' conferred on the district planning bodies. This is by directly vesting with the district *panchayats* the vast pool of funds which the Centre now spends towards its numerous poverty alleviation programmes – The Integrated Rural Development Programme (IRDP), National Rural Employment Programmes (NREP), and Rural Landless Employment Generatic Programme (RLEGP) along with a considerable sum of money coming from credit institutions. This money should be provided as a bulk grant to the district panchayat. This will provide a great deal of flexibility to the district planning bodies, as they could then prepare schemes with the full knowledge of the totality of needs and the totality of other schemes being implemented by diverse authorities.

The jurisdictional dilemma could be broken and all the available funds could be used within the framework of a district plan so as to maximize the benefits to the rural population.

If one is asked to single out the most important prerequisite for the success of decentralized district planning, one would unhesitatingly put it as development of trained manpower. Dag Hammarskjold once remarked:

> "Great economic development programmes have been planned which were held back more by a lack of men to direct them than by lack of capital. Great national problems of social welfare are failing to move forward primarily for a lack of experienced officials to undertake the manifold administrative tasks which they entail. Fundamentally, man is the key to all problems, not money. Funds are valuable only when used by trained, experienced and devoted men and women. Such people on the other hand, can work miracles even with small resources and draw wealth out of a barren land".

With the right development polices and programmes, training will ensure the success of development efforts. At the district level, in particular, there is acute shortage of skilled planners. As talents normally tend to float to the top, the lower levels always remain deprived of talented manpower. Training, therefore, assumes a rather special significance at the district level, because the district personnel must acquire skills, knowledge and attitudes needed to cope with the growing complexities of the development challenge.

Training, in our country, however, has not received its proper attention. Expenditure on training comes to an infinitesimally small fraction of the total costs on development projects. The few institutions that occasionally run courses for district planning have yet to standardize their training methodology for district planning as well as the teaching materials. Lecture-oriented training predominates with little field orientation.

For district planning, in particular, the sandwich training which combines institution-based and on-the-job training will be the most productive and useful. Experimentations on these lines are called for. As district planning is multi-sectoral planning, detailed manuals for the district level planning of each sector of activity have to be prepared.

In some other countries, innovative attempts are being made to solve the 'personnel' problem. Bangladesh, for instance, is posting senior officers to the *thana* level to improve the quality of grass-root level planning. So far as India is concerned, a really massive training effort is needed if the personnel at the district level are to be upgraded and equipped to shoulder the serious tasks of planning. Since the personnel constraints are bound to continue for a long time to come, vigorous efforts have to be made to associate the academic community, universities, research institutes and scientific bodies — in a big way to assist the district personnel in preparing plans in a scientific manner. Some of the success stories in local level planning show that significant achievements are possible through such efforts.

Kundrakudi in Tamil Nadu is a standing example. This author documented the success story of Kundrakudi for the Planning Commission in 1985 and attributed its success to a combination called 'TAD MIX' (i.e. Technocratic, Academic and Democratic Mix). Here a local democratic institution — the village planning forum — was assisted technically by a dedicated band of scientists from a national research laboratory — the Central Electro-Chemical Research Institute — and technocrats in government departments also actively co-operated. The trigger function was provided by a charismatic religious leader. To bring about this 'TAD MIX' on a country-wide scale is an extremely difficult, if not impossible job.

What this discussion points out is that district planning is a hard path. Currently, it suffers from several ailments. Institutionalization of planning, increased localism and trained manpower are some of the remedies that may be prescribed to prop up the ailing district planning process.

However, strong political will, bureaucratic abetement and public participation are the foundation medium through which these remedies have to be administered, if these are to be effective. Can all these synchronize in their right combinations, sequence and in right time to produce the desired effect? Herein lies the challenge of district planning.

6

ALLOCATION OF PLAN FUNDS TO DISTRICTS IN U.P.

AJIT KUMAR SINGH

Introduction

THE NEED for decentralized planning has been repeatedly emphasized in Five-Year Plans of India since the inception of planning. However, progress in this direction remained slow and faltering. One of the main reasons for this was that the required procedures and organizations were not set up in the right earnest nor were efforts made to operationalize the process of decentralized planning. Some progress in this direction was made after the guidelines for formulation of district plans were provided by the Planning Commission in 1969.[1] In more recent years, particularly since the Fifth Five-Year Plan, concrete steps were undertaken in a number of States, notably Maharashtra, Gujarat, Karnataka and Uttar Pradesh, to decentralize the planning process to the district level. These efforts have been examined in detail by the Working Group on District Planning set up by the Planning Commission, which also gave detailed suggestions for operationalizing the process of decentralized planning.[2]

Any scheme of decentralized planning requires a sound mechanism for sharing the resources among the different levels of the planning hierarchy as well as among the different participatory units. In the present article we propose to critically examine the existing mechanism for disaggregation of plan outlays from the State to the district level, drawing upon the experiences of the above-mentioned

States which have made more noteworthy progress towards decentralized planning.

Division of Resources Between State and District Plans

The issue needs to be discussed at two levels. First, how much of the total State plan outlay should be earmarked for the district sector plans, and secondly, how the share of each district in the total district sector outlay is to be determined?

Presently, the share of district sector outlay in total State plan outlay is 30 per cent in U.P., 35 per cent in Gujarat, 40 per cent in Maharashtra, and 45 per cent in Jammu and Kashmir. In Uttar Pradesh the figure of 30 per cent was arrived at after examining the existing level of outlay on district and State sector schemes. It was found that nearly 53 per cent of the State plan allocation was accounted for by power and major and medium irrigation projects, while another 17 per cent was spent on other schemes in the State sector, thus leaving a residual share of 30 per cent for the district sector schemes. For the eight hill districts of the State, for which a separate sub-plan is prepared, the allocation between the district sector and the State sector plans' outlay is in the ratio of 50 : 50.[3]

In actual practice, even the proposed share of 30 per cent for the district sector schemes was never realized. In fact, it has gone down from 28.74 per cent in 1982-83 to 25.50 per cent of total outlay in 1986-87. In case of the plain districts the share has gone down from 26.10 per cent to 22.70 per cent over the same period.

Thus, the criterion of adequacy has not been met in case of U.P. as far as the planning for the decentralized sector is concerned. In particular, the existing allocation to the districts has constrained the capacity of the districts to take up new scheme suited to the needs of the area. An exercise by the State planning department revealed that in 1984-85 the proposals for new schemes amounted to Rs. 10.69 crores or only 3.4 per cent of the total outlay for the district sector. In as many as 15 districts funds allocated were not sufficient even to meet the requirements of the on-going schemes, while in another 10 districts only token provisions were made for new schemes.

There is thus a clear case for raising the quantum of flow to the district level at least in the State of U.P. The share of districts in plan outlays has to be commensurate with the planning functions entrusted to them. "But", as argued by the Working Group on District Planning "any proportion arrived at by a State should not be continued on a permanent basis, but should be constantly watched in a dynamic context and revised".[4]

In this context at the State level powers and functions should be decentralized and gradually transferred to the district level as their capacities for planning are built up. At present when the scarcity of resources at all levels is acute and a large chunk of plan funds has to be devoted to large infrastructural projects, the claims of the State sector cannot be overlooked. We would, therefore, suggest that *if the share of the district sector is kept between 35 to 40 per cent of State plan outlay, it would meet the requirements of both desirability and feasibility during the next plan.*

Disaggregation of Plan Funds among Districts

Let us now turn our attention to the second issue, i.e., how the share of each district in the total district sector outlay is to be determined. Here questions of inter-regional equity are involved. The existing mechanism of distribution of plan funds among districts in the States, where the system of decentralized planning has made greater headway, is based upon a multi-indicator formula basically centred around the considerations of population, levels of development and existence of problem areas. Appendix .6.1 gives the details of the distribution formula adopted by the States of Maharashtra, Gujarat, Karnataka and Uttar Pradesh.

In the current thinking and practice consensus has emerged around some general principles which should govern the distribution of outlay among districts. First, it is commonly felt that population alone cannot be a sufficient criterion for allocation of funds and some mechanism should be built into the allocation system to ensure a more favourable treatment to the relatively backward or otherwise physically handicapped districts. Secondly, there should be some free or untied funds at the disposal of the district planning bodies which can be used by them at their own discretion to undertake programmes specifically related to the total needs. Thirdly, the system of allocation must also contain some provision to encourage mobilization of local resources. The implications of these principles need careful consideration.

The use of a multi-indicator formula abounds with many problems for which no simple solutions can be offered. A number of issues are involved here, such as, what indicators should be used ? What should be their relative weights ? What should be their specification ? Whether sectoral or composite indicators of development should be used ? etc. While *every State has to devise its own detailed formula for allocation of plan funds to districts in the light of its own specific situation and priorities*, some general observations on these issues are called for.

Population

The weightage of population has been kept at 50 per cent in U.P. and Karnataka, it is 60 per cent in Maharashtra, where additional weightage of five per cent to urban population is also given. On the other hand, Gujarat has given a weightage of only 40 per cent to population and has also excluded population of towns with more than 50,000 for computing the population. This is a sound practice, which other States should also adopt. In our view the weight of population in the formula should not exceed 50 per cent, if the problem of backward districts is to be tackled effectively.

Weaker Sections

All the four States also give weight to two categories of weaker sections, namely, Scheduled Castes and Scheduled Tribes and small and marginal farmers and agriculture labourers (except in Maharashtra). The weight given, however ranges from five per cent in Maharashtra to 17.5 per cent in Gujarat. Since these two groups are already included in total population and there is much overlap between the two groups as well, *it would be adequate in our opinion to give a weight of 5 per cent each to these two categories of weaker sections.*

Backwardness

The weightage of backwardness has been kept at 19 per cent in Maharashtra, 30 per cent in U.P., 35 per cent in Karnataka and 40 per cent in Gujarat. The items covered and weights given to different indicators of backwardness also vary from State to State. All the four States have given consideration to backwardness in agriculture, industry, communication and irrigation (except U.P.). The formula adopted in U.P. and Karnataka also takes into account backwardness in health facilities and power supply. In addition, U.P. has made provision for drinking water and Karnataka for backwardness in financial structure and for incidence of unemployment. Maharashtra and Karnataka have also given a weight of six per cent and 10 per cent respectively, to the special problem areas, but in Gujarat and U.P. there is no such provision. Surprisingly no State has taken into consideration backwardness in education for allocating plan funds.

In U.P. all aspects of backwardness have been given equal weight of five per cent in the formula for allocation of plan funds. While backwardness in agricultural and industrial output has been given equal weight of five per cent in Maharashtra, Karnataka and U.P., Gujarat has given a weight of 10 per cent to agricultural backwardness as compared to five per cent to industrial backwardness. Gujarat has also given relatively higher weightage to backwardness in communication than other States.

While some degree of arbitrariness will always be there in any system of weights, the practice of assigning equal weights to all indicators of backwardness as done in U.P., does not seem justified as it bears no relation to either the contribution of the factors to development or to the pattern of plan allocation. Thus, in U.P. the study of sectoral allocation pattern under district sector schemes revealed that in 1984-85 agriculture and allied sectors (including rural development and minor irrigation) received 51.6 per cent of total outlay as compared to the share of 16.3 per cent for roads, eight per cent for health facilities, six per cent for drinking water facilities, 2.2 per cent rural electrification and two per cent for industries, while all the items were given an equal weight of five per cent in the allocation formula.

If the approach based upon multi-sectoral indicators of backwardness for allocation of plan funds is continued, attempts should be made to devise a more rational system of weights. It would be more appropriate that the weights attached to different sectoral indicators have greater correspondence with the share of those sectors in total plan allocations, which can be taken as an index of the plan priorities.

A study of the per capita plan outlay district wise in U.P. during the periods 1982-83 and 1987-88 reveals that the present formula of allocation is not yielding satisfactory results from the point of view of regional equity. Taking the 48 districts of U.P. plains for analysis, it was found that the value of coefficient of correlation between per capita plan outlay and per capita district commodity output was only –0.1947 and that between per capita plan outlay and composite index of development was –0.6836 (Table 6.1).

TABLE 6.1: Correlation Matrix

	X_1	X_2	X_3
X_1	1.0000	–0.1947	–0.6836
X_2	–0.1947	1.0000	0.4639
X_3	–0.6836	0.4639	1.0000

Note: X_1 = Per capita District Plan Outlay 1982-88.
X_2 = Per capita District Commodity output (average 1981-84).
X_3 = Composite Index of Development, 1980-81.

If we compare the per capita district plan outlay of individual districts the unsatisfactory impact of the present formula would be further apparent (see Appendix 6.2). To give a few glaring instances: Fatehpur and Ballia have the rank of 30 and 31, respectively in the composite index of development, but their plan allocations in per capita terms come to Rs. 186 and Rs. 310. Similarly, Shahjahanpur, Pratapgarh and Sultanpur, which rank 36th, 37th and 38th, respectively in the composite index of development received plan allocation; of Rs. 190, Rs. 230 and Rs. 350, respectively, in per capita terms. Similar discrepancies can be observed on comparing the ranks of districts in per capita output and per capita plan outlay.

The operation of the present formula of allocation of plan funds among districts in U.P. has tended to favour the backward districts as a whole, but it does not yield fully satisfactory distribution of plan funds if one looks at inter-district allocation within the developed or backward group of districts. While some backward districts have benefitted very substantially, others have gained only marginally. Therefore, there is a need to look afresh into the various aspects of the formula including the variables of backwardness to be taken into account, their relative weights and their proper specification.

Alternatives

We may at this stage consider some alternative models for allocation of plan funds among districts to ensure inter-district equity. One approach can be to classify all the districts into different groups according to levels of development and fix certain norms for distributing plan funds for each category giving weightage to backward districts so that they get plan allocations on per capita basis in a predetermined ratio. Following classification and weights may be taken as illustrative of this approach:

	Level of Development	*Weights*
(i)	Very Developed	1.00
(ii)	Relatively Developed	1.10
(iii)	Less Developed	1.25
(iV)	Backward	1.50

For classifying districts according to the level of development a composite index may be prepared using multi-indicator approach. As the exercises done by the Chakravarty Committee on Backward Areas[5] show even simple device for preparing composite index like ranking method or relative index may help in identifying the hardcore backward districts.

Apart from simplicity, the chief merit of this model is that it ensures a more balanced inter-district allocation of funds in consonance with the priority accorded by the planners to the objective of development of the backward districts. Its major drawback is that it slurs over finer differences among districts within the same group. However, this problem can be minimized if one takes a larger number of groups into account.

The second approach which is worth considering is that recommended by the Fact Finding Committee on Regional Imbalance in Maharashtra.[6] In addition to the State level schemes, State pool of district level schemes and other district level schemes, the committee suggested the creation of a "State Pool for Removal of Specific Backlog" by taking out outlays meant for selected schemes from other three pools. The suggested pool was to cover 26 sub-sectors or items pertaining to socio-economic infrastructure including road development, irrigation, rural electrification, health and education services and land development schemes. In fact, "the Pool for the Removal of Specific Backlog" was to be the single largest component of the plan outlay (i.e., around 40 per cent).

The Committee recommended the following procedures for allocation of funds from the "State Pool for Removal of Specific Backlog" :

(a) Identification of approved outlays for specific relevant sectors/sub-sectors/schemes/programmes in the Annual Plan each year;

(b) Reserving 15 per cent of the outlays for completion of on-going works/projects not relevant to removal of backlog and for meeting the needs of natural growth; and

(c) Allocating the balance of 85 per cent of the funds, sector by sector, to all districts with a backlog in proportion to their backlog measured from the present State average.

It was also emphasized that these allocations must be treated as earmarked for removing specific backlog and should not be diverted to any other purpose. Consequently the committee suggested slight modification in the allocation formula to cover the normal district sector schemes by taking out the weights given to backwardness in communication and irrigation and adding them to population.

Thus the committee suggested a novel way for reducing inter-district disparities in development through a continuing process of lifting up the bottom. In our opinion the model of allocation suggested by the committee is worth adopting by other States on several grounds. It provides a clear-cut mechanism for transfer of resources to the districts meeting the requirements of inter-regional equity. It gives weight to the extent of backlog in each specific item. It also enables the State planners to ensure that the district plans adhere to national priorities. Finally, it suggests a strategy of balanced regional development by providing a minimum level of socio-economic infrastructure in each district. The only drawback in this scheme is that it tends to restrict the freedom of the planners at the district level. However, this drawback can be minimized by suitably adjusting the share of plan funds going to the "specific pool" and other district level schemes.

Need of Untied Funds

Two other considerations relevant for disaggregation of plan funds to the district level may be mentioned at this stage. The first is of making a provision of "free" or "untied funds" which can be utilized by the district planning body for taking up some local development programmes to meet local aspirations and requirements. The Working Group on District Planning has endorsed this approach as in this way, "some degree of localism in planning could be built into the district planning process." In Gujarat 15 per cent of district sector outlays are earmarked for such discretionary or free funds. Karnataka also has a lump sum provision for this purpose.

Incentive Provision

Secondly, the mechanism of division of plan outlays among the districts should have an incentive element built into it. As pointed out by the Working Group on District Planning, this would increase the sense of participation among people and motivate them to mobilize local resources.[7] In Gujarat five per cent of district sector funds are kept reserved for this purpose to provide grants on matching basis on a graded scale according to the level of backwardness. In U.P. three per cent of the outlay is allotted to the districts on the basis of their performance in the national savings programme. This is, however, creating certain distortions as more developed districts are benefiting more under this provision. In this connection one can think of some alternative indicator like performance in family planning programme or poverty eradication programme, etc.

Conclusion

The recent efforts towards decentralization of planning to the district level are a move in the right direction, though still falling short of the ideal to be achieved. The scheme has to be extended and improved in the light of the experience gained over time. There is a need to gradually increase transfer of power and resources from the State to district level as the planning capacities at the district level are improved.

As far as the question of allocation of plan funds among districts is concerned, the present formula is not producing a fully satisfactory result although it is weighted in favour of the backward districts. The questions related to the indicators of backwardness, their relative weights and specification need a fresh look in the context of each State.

While the details of the allocation formula may differ from State to State, certain broad features of the formula would be common to all. As discussed above it is generally agreed that the allocation mechanism should:

(i) maintain a proper balance between the share of the State and the Districts in plan funds,

(ii) give adequate weight to backwardness,

(iii) include an element of incentive, and

(iv) provide for earmarking of certain amount as untied or free funds to be used for schemes of local development.

In this connection we would strongly recommend the adoption of the scheme suggested by the Committee on Regional imbalances in Maharashtra under which a 'State Pool for Removal of Specific Backlog' is to be created. The funds under this pool are to be distributed sector by sector to all districts in proportion to their backlog measured from the present State average.

Funds under other district sector schemes should continue to be allocated on the basis of the present formula appropriately modified. An illustrative formula is given in Appendix 6.3 for this purpose.

The move to the new mechanism of allocation should be done in such a manner which does not disturb the present momentum in growth in individual districts or sudden curtailment of funds. Finally, a certain measure of stability in the plan allocations over a given plan period would be desirable. The pattern of inter-district allocation needs to be scrutinized at the end of each Five-Year Plan period and modified as required.

REFERENCES

1. Planning Commission (1969). *Guidelines for Formulation of District Plans.*
2. Planning Commission (1984). *Report of the Working Group on District Planning.*
3. Government of U.P., Planning Department, *Draft Annual Plan 1987-88*, 1, pp 60-61.
4. *Ibid.*, p 43.
5. See Government of India (1981). *National Committee on the Development of Backward Areas, Report on General Issues Relating to Backward Areas Development.*
6. Government of Maharashtra, Planning Department (1984). *Report of the Fact Finding Committee on Regional Imbalance in Maharashtra*, Ch.XVII.
7. Government of U.P., *op. cit.*, p 43.

APPENDIX 6.1

Comparative Statement — Formula for Disagregation of Plan Funds to District Level

(Weightages in percentage)

Sl. No.	Criteria	States			
		Maharashtra	Gujarat	Karnataka	Uttar Pradesh
1	2	4	5	6	7
1.	Population				
	(a) Total Population	60.0	40.0*	50.0	50.0
	(b) Urban Population	5.0	—	—	—
2.	Backwardness of weaker sections:				
	(a) Population of Scheduled Castes and Scheduled Tribes	5.0	15.0	2.5	5.0
	(b) Small and marginal farmers and Population of agricultural labourers	—		2.5	10.0
3.	Backwardness in respect of:				
	(a) Agriculture production/value of outpu:	5.0	10.0	5.0	5.0
	(b) Irrigation	4.0	10.0	5.0	—
	(c) Industrial output	5.0	5.0	5.0	5.0
	(d) Communications	5.0	10.0	2.5	5.0
	(e) Drinking water	—		—	5.0
	(f) Financial infrastructure as measured by the size of population served by each commercial and co-operative Bank	—	—	2.5	—
	(g) Medical and health facilities (No. of Hospital Beds)	—	—	5.0	5.0
	(h) Power Supply	—	—	5.0	5.0

(Contd.)

1	2	4	5	6	7
4.	Backwardness in respect of the targets of other selected minimum needs	—	5.0	—	—
5.	Special Problems:	—	—	—	5.0
	(a) Drought Prone Areas	3.0	—	2.5	—
	(b) Coastal Areas	1.5	—	—	—
	(c) Forest Areas	1.5	—	2.5	—
6.	Local tax efforts	—	—	5.0	—
7.	Incidence of unemployment as measured by the proportion of registrants at the employment exchange	—	—	5.0	—
8.	Unallocated amount for meeting special problems	5.0	—	—	—
9.	Incentive provision	—	5.0	—	—
	Total	100.0	100.0	100.0	100.0

* For computing the population for the purpose of the formulate in Gujarat only rural population and population of towns with less than 50,000 people were taken into account.

Source: *Report of the Working Group on District Planning*, Annexure 4.1.

APPENDIX 6.2

Districtwise level of Development, Per Capita Commodity Output and Per Capita District Plan Outlay in U.P.

District	Composite index of development 1980-81	Rank in descending order	Per capita commodity output (Rs.) 1981 — 84 (Total)	Rank in descending order	Per capita district Plan outlay (Rs.) 1982 — 88	Rank in ascending order
1	2	3	4	5	6	7
Meerut	2.4685	1	1,197	3	136	1
Ghaziabad	2.4249	2	1,649	1	144	2
Muzaffarnagar	1.8252	3	1,107	7	153	4
Bulandshahar	1.3422	4	960	13	167	12
Kanpur	1.3236	5	986	11	183	17
Lucknow	1.2395	6	742	31	146	3
Saharanpur	1.2183	7	1,158	4	156	6
Varanasi	1.0891	8	747	29	169	13
Bijnore	1.0697	9	1,015	9	164	8
Agra	0.8114	10	691	36	154	5
Allahabad	0.7974	11	897	15	166	11
Gorakhpur	0.7467	12	573	45	191	22
Aligarh	0.7439	13	900	14	158	7
Moradabad	0.7278	14	770	26	165	10
Lakhimpur-Kheri	0.7075	15	875	17	213	38
Bareilly	0.6555	16	832	20	164	9
Rampur	0.6483	17	675	39	178	16
Mirzapur	0.6365	18	1,134	5	279	43
Jhansi	0.6271	19	974	12	196	28
Farrukhabad	0.6262	20	724	32	185	19
Etawah	0.4512	21	744	30	196	27

(Contd.)

1	2	3	4	5	6	7
Rae Bareilly	0.4311	22	754	27	198	29
Faizabad	0.3982	23	612	42	183	18
Mathura	0.3960	24	1,242	2	173	14
Jaunpur	0.3926	25	544	47	205	36
Barabanki	0.3661	26	798	24	202	34
Azamgarh	0.3388	27	703	34	195	25
Deoria	0.2910	28	688	37	201	33
Ghazipur	0.2906	29	660	40	194	24
Fatehpur	0.2775	30	826	21	186	20
Ballia	0.2758	31	537	48	310	44
Badaun	0.2754	32	820	22	207	37
Pilibhit	0.2260	33	1,111	6	201	32
Mainpuri	0.1013	34	753	28	193	23
Etah	0.1542	35	803	23	176	15
Shahjahanpur	0.1275	36	836	19	190	21
Pratapgarh	–0.0281	37	719	33	230	40
Sultanpur	–0.1099	38	590	43	350	46
Basti	–0.3340	39	565	46	243	41
Unnao	–0.3680	40	702	35	199	30
Sitapur	–0.4639	41	854	18	195	26
Hardoi	–0.4036	42	679	39	204	35
Gonda	–0.5158	43	616	41	199	31
Bahraich	–0.6411	44	578	44	217	39
Jalaun	–0.8637	45	781	25	415	48
Lalitpur	–1.0332	46	882	16	333	45
Banda	–1.0786	47	993	10	267	42
Hamirpur	–1.1313	48	1,064	8	359	47

Source: (a) Composite index of development has been taken from R.T. Tewari, *Patterns of Development in India*, Ashish Publishing House.
(b) Value of per capita commodity output has been taken from State Planning Institute, U.P.
(c) Figure of per capita plan outlay have been obtained from Planning Department, U.P. Government.

APPENDIX 6.3

Illustrative Formula for Disaggregation of Plan Funds to the District Level

	Criteria	Weightage (in Percentage)
1.	Population:	
	(a) Rural Population	50
	(b) Urban Population	5
2.	Weaker Sections:	
	(a) Population of SC & ST	5
	(b) Number of Small & Marginal Farmers & Agricultural Labourers	5
3.	Backwardness in:	
	(a) Agricultural Sector	15
	(b) Industrial Sector	5
4.	Problem Areas like: Drought Prone Area, Flood Affected Area, Coastal Area, Forest Area and Size of District	10
5.	Incentive Provision	5

7

DECENTRALIZED PLANNING IN INDIA
Experiences of Karnataka and Tamil Nadu

K.V. PALANIDURAI

Introduction

SUCCESSIVE five-year Plans have laid emphasis on local level planning – such as planning at village, block and district levels – for effectively tackling the twin problems of poverty and unemployment. References to the virtues of grass-roots planning and exhortation to the States to adopt this approach in the planning process at sub-State level abound in almost all the Five-Year Plan documents. The creation of Panchayati Raj Institutions in 1959, systematic efforts initiated by the Planning Commission with the issue of detailed guidelines for formulation of District Plans in 1969, Block level planning recommended by Dantwala Committee, the introduction of Integrated Rural Development Programme (IRDP) on a country-wide basis during the Sixth Five-Year Plan are some of the major land-marks in India's efforts to decentralize the planning process. Despite the acknowledged merits of 'planning from below' and the efforts taken by the Central and State Governments during the past three and a half decades, planning in India, by and large, continues to be centralized at two levels – the Union Government and State Governments. The progress, if anything, towards decentralization in planning, implementation and decision-making to district and block levels has been sporadic and tardy.

The Seventh Five-Year Plan has emphasized the need for decentralization of planning and development administration below the

State level and advocated a gradual step by step approach towards decentralized district level planning. Reviewing the past attempts for adoption of 'grass-roots planning', the Seventh Plan has noted: "though *Zilla Parishads* and *Panchayat Samitis* have been established in several states, the actual decentralization of political and administrative authority has been generally of a limited nature. Nor have sufficient arrangements been made in the organization of technical, administrative personnel at the State level and below to facilitate decentralization. The lack of adequate machinery for decentralized planning and administration thus continues to be a critical weakness in the existing system".

The Planning Commission constituted a Working Group on District Planning in 1982 under the Chairmanship of Dr. C.H. Hanumantha Rao, the then Member of the Planning Commission, and the recommendations of this Group formed the basis for evolving the decentralized planning approach outlined in the Seventh Plan. The Working Group reviewed in greater detail the experiences of different States in the formulation of district plans and observed that "the ideas relating to decentralized local level planning have been somewhat nebulous and the progress in the various States somewhat halting". The practice of States showing the district sector outlay in their plan documents was considered merely as an exercise in disaggregation of the State Plan outlay and would not amount to decentralization of planning process. The touchstone of decentralization would be the freedom available at the district level to "plan according to local potentials". According to this Group "the present state of art of district planning in the country clearly shows that the activity has remained a non-starter all along because all the essential elements or ingredients that we referred to did not exist as a total package. Somewhere the structure existed, the personnel were not there or personnel existed but skills, powers or authority were lacking. Somewhere the district planning process got choked on the way and could not follow. Somewhere the flow began but directions were not clear and so on".

The Working Group has made a number of far-reaching recommendations for operationalizing the decentralized planning concept. In order that the States at different levels of development may move towards decentralization over a definite period of time, the Working Group had advocated a progressive or stages approach. The Stage I will be a phase of initiation which will evolve, *inter alia*, establishing planning procedures, disaggregating outlays between the State and district sectors, evolving criteria for inter-district allocation of plan funds and strengthening of planning capabilities at the district level. Stage II will be one of "limited decentralization" when planning for certain sectors of activity like Minimum Needs Programme, Agriculture and Allied Activities and all target group-oriented planning will be brought within the purview of district planning. Delegating extensive powers to the district level will be specially sought to be achieved during this phase. Stage III will be the final stage which will encompass all district sector activities. During this stage a set of wide ranging administrative, financial and decision-making powers will devolve upon the districts and a high level of popular participation will be sought to be achieved. It is envisaged that all the States in the country would reach the final stage by the year 2000 A.D.

The Seventh Plan had accepted the recommendations of the Working Group and stated that "during the Seventh Plan period the decentralization of the planning process and full public participation in development will be pursued on the lines suggested by the Working Group. These steps will seek to ensure the achievement of the twin objectives of effective implementation of the anti-poverty programmes and ensuring a balanced regional development at least in respect of the Minimum Needs. District Planning as advocated in the report of the Working Group should be vigorously pursued. Eventually, the decentralization of planning should be extended further to the Block level, particularly, for the effective implementation of anti-poverty programmes."

We are now at the mid-point of the Seventh Plan period. Having charted a course for decentralized planning and fixing the destination, are we moving towards the goal and at the required pace to reach the goal by 2000 A.D.? The success of achieving the objective largely depends on the steps taken by the 25 States in India. An attempt is made in this chapter to assess the progress towards decentralization in the planning process during the first three years of the Seventh Plan in two southern States, viz., Karnataka and Tamil Nadu. This chapter also seeks to identify the factors responsible for the success or otherwise in the implementation of the scheme of decentralization in these two States. A brief review of the progress in other States is also presented.

Progress Towards Decentralized Planning in the States – an Overall Assessment

The concept of decentralized district level planning outlined in the

Hanumantha Rao Report has been accepted in principle by all the States except Sikkim, Goa and Tripura. Sikkim is a small State with four small districts. Considering the size of the districts within a small State, it is decided to suitably strengthen the planning machinery at the State level, so that it can take up formulation of integrated development plan for each one of the four districts. Goa, which has attained Statehood recently has also taken a similar view. Tripura has proposed to decentralize planning to the Block level. Kerala has accepted the concept of district planning in a rather qualified manner and it would like to commence the exercise limiting it to formulation of Special Component Plan for the Scheduled Castes and Scheduled Tribes at the district level.

A recent review by the Planning Commission reveals that "although the need for decentralized planning has been recognized and several measures have been taken to effectively decentralize planning process, the progress has not been uniform in all the States. Consequently, the pattern and level of decentralization achieved in various States has also not been uniform. While some States, like, Karnataka, Gujarat, Maharashtra, Jammu & Kashmir and West Bengal have made appreciable progress, some others have made a beginning or are still in the process of completing some necessary preliminaries".

The progress in setting up district planning machinery has also not been satisfactory. In order to encourage the States to establish planning cell at the district level, the Planning Commission introduced a Centrally-sponsored Scheme on a cost-sharing basis during 1982-83 and continued it in the Seventh Plan. Many States have not taken full advantage of this scheme. The position regarding setting up planning machinery at the district level is briefly indicated below :

(a) States which have set up District Planning Machinery	Bihar, Karnataka, Orissa, West Bengal
(b) States which have set up the machinery but require strengthening	Andhra Pradesh, Himachal Pradesh, Gujarat, Kerala, Jammu & Kashmir, Maharashtra, Manipur, Meghalaya, Nagaland and Uttar Pradesh
(c) States which have not	Assam, Madhya Pradesh, Punjab,

yet set up the District Planning Machinery	**Rajasthan and Tripura**
(d) States for which proposals have been approved by the Planning Commission but personnel are not in position.	Tamil Nadu (only three districts on a pilot basis), Haryana

The Panchayati Raj Institutions have been assigned a crucial role in the decentralized planning envisaged by the Working Group. But, unfortunately, they have not been closely and actively involved in the district planning in most of the States. West Bengal is the only State in which Panchayati Raj Institutions have been intimately associated with district/block planning and implementation of development schemes. The finding of a recent study on "West Bengal Land-Scape" by Shri Arun Ghosh vividly describes the extent of involvement of the Panchayati Raj Institution in the planning process. Referring to a meeting of the Block-level Planning Committee in one of the districts, the study states: "The discussions continue well into the evening. If these discussions are any guide, if this is representative of the functioning of the *Panchayat* System throughout West Bengal, then the *Panchayat Raj* experiment is safe and, in fact, can no longer be stated to be an experiment. Genuine democracy exists, the awareness of the people has been aroused, their active participation in the development process is now a function of the authority and the command over resources that can devolve on them."

Karnataka has ushered in a new era of democratic decentralization in 1987 with the establishment of *Zilla Parishads* and *Mandal Panchayats* which are endowed with powers, functions and resources. Andhra Pradesh has also introduced major reforms in the *Panchayat Raj* set up in 1987 and established *Zilla Praja Parishads, Mandala Praja Parishads* and *Zilla Pranabha Abhivirudhi Mandali.* In other States, wherever Panchayati Raj Institutions exist they are generally represented in the District-level planning body, which in several States functions as an advisory or reviewing body (for example, District Development Council in Tamil Nadu). But the most unfortunate part is that Panchayati Raj Institutions are dormant in a number of States, and the elections to local bodies have not been conducted for several years. Uttar Pradesh, Rajasthan, Bihar and Madhya Pradesh come under this category.

An appraisal of the progress towards decentralization reveals a depressing picture. While the developments in a few States, like Karnataka, West Bengal, Gujarat and Maharashtra, are noteworthy, the measures so far taken by the other States have not shown any significant impact or improvement on the planning process at the sub-State level. The slow progress is largely due to lack of political will and commitment to make the scheme of decentralized planning a success. In the absence of a clear directive from the political authority at the State level, the bureaucratic response to Planning Commission's persuasions and preachings on decentralized planning has been lukewarm. If the same trend continues in the remaining two years of the Seventh Plan, the goal of achieving 'localism' in the planning process by 2000 A.D. will remain a distant dream. Karnataka's experiment in the democratic decentralization is the lone exception. In fact, Karnataka has made big leap forward, skipping the stages approach recommended by the Planning Commission and nearly achieved the target set for 2000 A.D. by 1988. The credit for achieving this measure of success goes to the political leadership in Karnataka and its willingness to share power with newly created district level institutions.

Trends in Decentralized Planning in Tamil Nadu and Karnataka

Though the concept of decentralized planning (or grass-roots planning) has been accepted since the beginning of planning era, planning and decision-making function remained centralized at two levels – the Centre and the States, during the first two decades of planning. Some attempts were made during the Third Five-Year plan, for preparation of State Plans for rural development on the basis of district and block plans. This period also witnessed the introduction of Panchayati Raj Institutions and the concept of democratic decentralization on the recommendations of a Study Team constituted by the Planning Commission popularly known as Balwant Rai Mehta Committee. Despite all this not enough progress has been made in building up appropriate administrative and information systems in evolving operational methodologies for formulating district plan. This state of affairs was attributed partly to the fact that operational decisions were taken essentially in departmental organizations at the State level, and partly of the inability of the State Planning Departments to handle the enormous volume and variety of data and issues relating to evolving an integrated plan at the district level. On the eve of the Fourth Plan (1969), the Planning Commission issued detailed guidelines to all the States for formulation of district plans. This was the first systematic effort of the Planning Commission to motivate the States to take up district planning seriously. The response from the States was a mixed one.

Tamil Nadu was perhaps one of the few States which took up district planning, following the 1969 guidelines of the Planning Commission. District Planning Cells were set up in 1972 in each of the districts and these cells were entrusted with the responsibility of formulating a perspective plan for the district covering Fifth and Sixth Five-Year Plan periods. Though Tamil Nadu had formulated district plans in a systematic way, these plans never became operational or action plans. The absence of an executive body with elected representatives at the district level to take follow up action on the district plan, and the failure on the part of the State level departments to take note of the district plans while formulating their annual plans have reduced the entire district planning exercise meaningless and irrelevant in the planning process. The District Planning Cells were wound up in 1974 after completion of their main task of bringing out the district plan documents. Tamil Nadu did not pursue the concept of district planning thereafter. The planning process continues to be on the conventional lines with a sectoral bias.

Karnataka started the experiment of district planning in 1978 with all seriousness. As a first step in the introduction of district planning, efforts were made by the State Planning Department for two to three years to develop district-wise and taluka-wise data relevant to decentralized planning. To facilitate the formulation of programmes based on local needs and taking note of the handling capacity of the planners at the district level, the development schemes were classified into two groups – District Sector Scheme and State Sector Scheme. District Planning Committees were constituted for each district. Financial allocations were indicated to the district for the purpose of formulation of plan, and allocation was arrived at on the basis of an objective criterion which gives weightage to population and backwardness. By taking sustained interest, ever since 1978-79, the State has experimented with different approaches to district planning. With the establishment of *Zilla Parishads* in 1987, Karnataka has achieved a major breakthrough in decentralized planning. The clear demarcation of areas for planning at district and State levels, devolution of powers to local institutions and provision of plan funds are some of the salient features of the planning process at the district level. It is reported that the State's Annual Plan for 1988-89 for the first time has been formulated on the basis of district plan proposals formulated by *Zilla Parishads*. The measures implemented so far, the manner in which the State has been boldly facing the teething troubles in operationalizing the decentralization concept and, above all, the political commitment displayed at the State level, clearly show that Karnataka is genuinely interested in making decentralized planning a success.

Thus, the experiment in two States, viz., Tamil Nadu and Karnataka, during the past 15 years provide us two extreme examples of sub-State level planning. Tamil Nadu, making an early start, formulated the district plan, but failed to operationalize it and gave up the exercise after initial enthusiasm waned Karnataka started the exercise much later and showed sustained interest in district planning and ultimately made it a reality.

The evolution of planning process at grass-roots level in India is best illustrated by the Tamil Nadu and Karnataka experiments. Any study on the extent to which the various States in India have succeeded in decentralizing the planning process would show that majority of the States fall under the category of Tamil Nadu. What made the Karnataka experiment a success? Why Tamil Nadu experiment failed to take off? The answers to these questions would provide us some insights and possibly some lessons to the other States which are in the process of implementing decentralized planning.

District Planning in Tamil Nadu: A Non-Starter

Tamil Nadu had set up a State Planning Commission in 1971, and claimed that it was the first State to have set up such a planning body at the State level. The Commission was entrusted with the responsibility of formulating a Perspective Plan for the socio-economic development of the State covering Fifth and Sixth Five-Year Plan periods. In order to accomplish this task, the commission organized (i) preparation of sectoral profiles, (ii) formulation of district plans and (iii) some special studies which would serve as input for formulation of Perspective Plan. Tamil Nadu's economy was divided into 15 sectors (Agriculture, Animal Husbandry and Dairy Development, Fisheries, Forestry, Rural Development, Urban Development, Fuel and Power, Transport, Mineral Resources, Large Industries, Small Industries, Education, Health, Human Resources Development and Financial Resources) and for each one of the sectors a Task Force with one of the members of the State Planning Commission as Chairman was constituted to formulate a perspective of development for the sector. The Task Force comprised non-official experts also as members, besides officials. A senior official drawn from the respective (discipline) department functioned on a full time basis as the Secretary of the Task Force. For the formulation of district plan, a District Planning Cell was created in each district. This planning cell was headed by the District Collector and consisted of a District Planning Officer (who was drawn from the cadres of Deputy Collector in the Revenue Department/Deputy Directors in the Rural Development Department), the District Statistical Officer and the district level officers concerned with development departments. The State Planning Commission provided the guidelines for formulation of district plans and organized a training programme for the District Planning Officers and District Statistical Officers to give them the necessary orientation. The "development district" which roughly constitutes half the size of the revenue district was selected as the unit of planning. Thus ten large districts were divided into two development districts and three small districts retained as single development districts. In this way Tamil Nadu prepared plans for its 23 'development districts'. The planning process at the district level involved the following steps:

(i) assessing the availability of human and material resources;
(ii) identifying the constraints to district development;
(iii) identifying the main economic activities and activity centres to be developed;
(iv) listing the subsidiary and supplemental activities to be promoted in their order of importance;
(v) determining the infrastructural facilities, inputs and services for the main economic activities;
(vi) indicating the basic requirements of backward areas and backward classes;
(vii) collecting the requirements of various areas, determining the location of projects and organizing them spatially in an integrated manner with a view to secure optimum coverage;
(viii) assessing the physical and financial resources potential; and
(ix) projecting the trend in development of the district and the State of resources and institutions.

The District Planning Officer collected basic data at the *taluka*/block level, held series of discussions with other district level officers and formulated a set of schemes/programmes taking into account the local resource endowments and the problems. There were frequent informal interactions between the team of officials in the State Planning Commission, engaged in the preparation of sectoral profiles, and the district planning officers, which enabled a two-way flow of information and helped in ensuring the priorities and objectives of the Perspective Plan. Between 1971-73 the District Planning Cells were engaged in the formulation of district plans and the cells were disbanded in 1974, after their main task was accomplished.

The efforts of two years' labour of 13 District Planning Cells have not been put to any worthwhile use as the district plans prepared by them have not been meaningfully integrated with the State's Fifth Five-Year Plan/and the Annual Plans. It is likely that quite a few schemes contained in the district plans might have figured in the State's Five-Year Plan, but no serious effort was made to implement the district plans as such. Thus the Planning process during Fifth Plan continued along the conventional lines of formulating sectoral plans at the State level and consolidating them into State's Annual Plan.

Tamil Nadu had not made any attempts to decentralize the planning process at district level during Sixth Plan. The State Planning Commission continued to exist, with periodic reconstitutions and without any well defined role. Sometimes the Commission functioned as a plan review body, sometimes engaged in carrying out special studies, sometimes involved in the formulation of Annual Plan. The position obtaining in the State during the Sixth Plan was: "According to the existing arrangements, planning for development is done at the State level. The heads of development departments formulated Annual or Five-Year Plan proposals, pertaining to their departments and these are overseen and revised by the Secretaries to Government incharge of the administrative department at the Government level after taking into account the plan priorities and directions of Government."

As far as the district planning, the position described by the State Government, was: "No separate machinery for planning exists in the districts. All planning is done at the macro-level in the State. The strategy and sectoral priorities for development are by and large determined at the State level. Though a system of communication and information flow exists at the district level, the information emanating from the lower levels is analyzed and studied only at the State level taking policy decision."

Progress during Seventh Plan: The State Government has accepted, in principle, the concept of decentralized district planning advocated by the Hanumantha Rao Group. During the first two years, the State has not made any efforts to operationalize the concept. During 1987-88, the State selected three districts for the formulation of district plan. Even for the three districts, the State Government could not appoint the nucleus of district planning officers/staff due to administrative difficulties. The provision of 'untied' funds for the districts was also only very nominal – Rs. 15 lakhs per district for 1987-88.

The measures taken by Tamil Nadu so far, are not likely to make any significant development towards decentralized district level planning in the State in the remaining two years of the Seventh Plan. No attempt has been made to disaggregate the State Plan outlay into district-wise outlays and demarcate the district sector activities. The political authority does not seem to have evinced any interest in the decentralized planning, and even the basic requirement of establishing planning cells in the districts has not been accomplished. The quantum of 'untied funds', provided in the Annual Plan is too low to enthuse the district authorities to take up district planning with any seriousness and with a semblance of associating the District Development Councils. In other words, Tamil Nadu has not even fulfilled the pre requisites for decentralized planning envisaged for Stage I of the stages' approach recommended in the Seventh Plan.

District Planning in Karnataka: A Big Leap Forward

Karnataka had set up a separate Planning Department in 1975 and organized it on functional lines. The technical wing has six functional divisions like Project Formulation, Manpower and Employment, Perspective Planning, Plan Monitoring, District and Regional Planning and Special Studies. The District and Regional Planning Division is responsible for work connected with district planning.

Progress During Sixth Plan

Karnataka has taken up the district planning exercise in a systematic manner in 1978-79. As part of the preparatory measure for introduction of district planning, the State Planning Department organized a three-month training programme jointly with the Institute for Social and Economic Change, Bangalore. For each district- a nucleus planning team was constituted. An economist drawn from a University/College, located at the district headquarters, Deputy Director of Agriculture and the District Planning Officers constituted the nucleus team : after six weeks training the entire team went to the district, toured intensively in the blocks to understand the problem and came up with an approach paper for each district. This was utilized in the second half of the training programme to give a very realistic approach to training in the preparation of district plan. After the training was over each team was charged with the responsibility of preparing a perspective plan for the district. To facilitate formulation of programme based on local needs and taking note of the handling capacity of the planners at the district level, the State Planning Department demarcated the sectors for State level and district level planning. Broadly the demarcation was based on the principle that an individual scheme is demonstrably beneficial to the district and would promote socio-economic interest of the people in the district. Another important consideration was whether such an activity could be planned and implemented at the district level. For distribution of plan funds among districts, the State has evolved an objective criterion : the district sector outlay is distributed among the districts on the basis of 50 per cent weightage to population and 50 per cent to backwardness of the district. Backward districts got a relatively higher outlay in the distribution scheme. The State Planning Department worked out the share of each district (in the total district sector outlay) and communicated the same to the district for formulating district plan. A District Planning Committee with Deputy Commissioner as Chairman and consisting of six other officials has been constituted for each district for formulation of district plan. The plan prepared by the committee with the help of other district level officers was considered by District Development Council (DDC) consisting of MLAs, MLCs and MPs, Presidents of Taluka-Development Boards. The district plan as approved by DDC is then sent to the Government for final approval. At the State level the district plans are scrutinized by the concerned Heads of the State Departments and final allocation determined. In this process, the district plan, as approved by the DDC, underwent drastic changes. This was mainly due to the fact that the State's Annual Plan was formulated independently of district plans. Hence, the sectoral priority determined at the district level did not exactly tally with the priorities at the State level. There were also other administrative and budgetary problems, choice of location of certain projects, lack of clear understanding of the State sector/district sector schemes among the heads of departments and district level functionaries, etc. These problems were overcome in the preparation of district plans for 1983-84 and for subsequent years by way of certain new/revised guidelines prepared by the Planning Department for demarcation of district sector schemes and giving freedom to the DDC to evolve new schemes best suited to the district, subject to certain ceiling of outlays for specified sectors. Discretionary outlays were also provided to the District Development Councils to take up programmes of local importance and to enlist public participation in development activities. Thus, during the Sixth Plan, the State had taken concerted efforts to operationalize the concept of district planning. The experiments with different approaches between 1978-79 and 1984-85 have brought to light several problems in implementing the decentralized planning process. The absence of an executive body with elected representatives at the district level, the restriction within which the District Development Councils have to formulate the district plans, the areas of disagreement between district and State priorities were some of the major impediments in the implementation of decentralized planning noted during the Sixth Plan.

Progress during the Seventh Plan

The experiences gained by Karnataka in implementing the district planning concept ever since its introduction in 1978-79 have emboldened the State to embark on a more ambitious scheme of decentralized planning. The close interaction between district planning machinery and the State planning department has helped in clearly demarcating the district level schemes from the State level schemes. Above all, the political authority displayed its determination to launch the scheme of "democratic decentralization" and established a three-tier *Panchayat Raj* set-up in 1987 under the Karnataka *Zilla Parishad, Taluka Panchayat Samitis, Mandal Panchayat* and *Nyaya Panchayat Act*, 1983. A major hurdle in operationalizing the district planning concept has been the absence of an executive body with elected representatives at the district level and this deficiency has been overcome with the establishment of *Zilla Parishads*. The main objective of establishing these local institutions (*Zilla Parishad* and *Mandal Panchayats*) was to decentralize decision-making process to the district and *mandal* levels. The Act envisages greater devolution of powers to these local institutions. A High Power Committee set up by the State for implementing the Act had identified the schemes that can be transferred to *Zilla Parishads* and *Mandal Panchayats* and recommended a scheme for delegating powers – administrative, technical and financial. With this, the areas for planning at the State and *Zilla Parishad* levels have been clearly demarcated. For formulating an integrated development plan based on local resources, the *Zilla Parishad* should have freedom to determine priorities and also the required financial resources. For this purpose the State Government has made a lump sum allocation for *Zilla Parishads*. This lump sum allocation includes not only the outlay from State Plan scheme but also the outlay from Centrally-sponsored and Central Sector Schemes. To ensure that district priorities in respect of important programmes, like Minimum Needs Programme (MNP), are consistent with overall priorities envisaged at the State level, the *Zilla Parishads* are required to earmark outlay for MNP, Special Component Plan, Tribal Plan, etc. For the purpose of distribution of outlay among the *Zilla Parishads*, the State has adopted the same criterion which gives 50 per cent weightage to population and 50 per cent to backwardness in agriculture, irrigation, etc. A Finance Commission for *Zilla Parishads* and *Mandal Panchayats* has also been constituted to go into the problem of income and expenditure of these bodies. This Commission will look into the aspects relating to revenue sharing and will suggest a formula for allocating funds covering both plan and non-plan expenditures of *Zilla Parishads* and *Mandal Panchayats*. The criterion mentioned above will be followed till the Finance Commission makes its recommendations.

The decentralized planning process implies that the State Plan is formulated on the basis of plan proposals from *Zilla Parishads*. In order to keep pace with the existing procedure for consideration and approval of Five-Year/Annual Plans at the State/National level, the *Zilla Parishads* have to begin the exercise of plan formulation, much earlier than at the State level. To accomplish this, the State has proposed to adopt a reasonable outlay for the State even before the Planning Commission holds discussion with the State and on this basis a tentative allocation will be intimated to each *Zilla Parishad* against which they will formulate their plan proposals for the succeeding year. According to the calendar for planning proposed by the State, the exercise commences in the middle of July with the adoption of a tentative size for the State Annual Plan of the next year and intimation of financial ceiling to *Zilla Parishads* within which the annual plan should be formulated for the next year. The *Zilla Parishads* are required to send the draft plans to the Government in the Planning Department and concerned Heads of the Departments at the State level by 20th September. During October the Planning Department would hold a series of discussions with *Zilla Parishads* on their draft district plan for ensuring consistency and integration of district sector with State sector scheme/plan. On the basis of the discussion, the Government/Heads of Departments would consolidate these proposals, build them into State plan and send them to the Planning Commission by middle of November. The Planning Department has been designated as the nodal department for effectively implementing the process of decentralized planning under the *Zilla Parishad* set up and to ensure the much needed co-ordination among the various agencies involved in planning : A separate division – District and Regional Planning Division – in the Planning Department performs the functions like determining the size of district sector outlay and its distribution among districts on the basis of objective criterion, guiding the district planning units in plan formulation, co-ordinating the matters relating to district sector schemes, at the State level, finalization of district plans and bringing out a link document to the budget giving district-wise and scheme-wise outlays, etc.

Though the *Zilla Parishad* and *Mandal Panchayats* were established in April 1987, they had no opportunity of formulating their own plan proposals for 1987-88. The plans already prepared by the State level heads of departments and approved by the Government were adopted by the *Zilla Parishad* for 1987-88. This has given them an opportunity to understand the programmes of different sectors, procedures for implementation and form their own views about these programmes. 1988-89 marks a milestone in the decentralized planning process in Karnataka, for, it was for that year and for the first time the State's Annual Plan was formulated on the basis of plans formulated at the *Mandal Panchayats* and *Zilla Parishads.* A Committee of officers with Planning Commissioner as Chairman considered the draft district plans and held discussions with the officers of *Zilla Parishads* for finalizing them. The objective of this discussion with the representatives of *Zilla Parishads* was :

(i) to ensure that the *Zilla Parishads* have provided adequate money for Minimum Needs Programme, Special Component

Plan, Tribal sub-plan and for staff component;

(ii) to understand the reasons for reduction or increase in the outlays for particular programmes or deletion of any programme, and

(iii) to provide an opportunity for the State Heads of the Departments concerned with the *Zilla Parishad* sectors to express their technical opinion on the *Zilla Parishad* and *Mandal Panchayat* proposals.

In all these discussions the philosophy of decentralized planning wherein the function of plan formulation has been delegated to the *Zilla Parishad* and *Mandal Panchayat* was kept in view. Subject to the financial ceiling indicated by the Government, the *Zilla Parishads'* plans, tentatively finalized, have been integrated into the sectoral plans of the State for 1988-89. The State has proposed an outlay of Rs. 1,000 crores for 1988-89 Annual Plan. Of this a sum of Rs. 245.5 crores has been earmarked as the outlay for *Zilla Parishads* and *Mandal Panchayats*. This accounts for 24.5 per cent of the States plan outlay. The *Zilla Parishad* plans have given priority to primary and secondary education, roads and bridges, and rural water supply and schemes under MNP. This is reflected in substantial step up in the outlay for these sectors in 1988-89 compared to the previous years. According to the State Government, "with the establishment of these institutions the spread of information about the plan programmes has percolated down to the *Mandal Panchayat* level. All the *Mandal Panchayat* and *Zilla Parishad* members have now become conversant with plan programmes implemented in the State and are actively involved in the plan formulation and implementation. This is the single biggest gain that has been achieved through the decentralized planning process.

Karnataka's achievement in operationalizing the concept of district planning is noteworthy. It is the only State in India, which has made rapid strides in decentralized planning. The Working Group on District Planning, while recommending the stages approach for decentralized planning had also suggested that "as far as possible, the States should try to reach the goal even before the time span indicated here (i.e. 2000 A.D.). For instance, the Stages I and II could be compressed and completed by the end of Seventh Plan itself".

Karnataka has done precisely this and has made a quantum jump towards achieving the goal of decentralized planning.

Why District Planning did not Take Off in Tamil Nadu

Even though Tamil Nadu formulated district plans for all the districts in the State in 1974, these plans have not been translated into action plans, nor they have been meaningfully integrated into the State's Five-Year/Annual Plans. The district plans were dubbed as academic exercise indulged in by the State Planning Commission. The State had not pursued the concept of district plan afterwards. Decentralized planning at district level has not made any headway in Tamil Nadu largely due to :

(i) lack of clarity on the concept of district planning,
(ii) organizational inadequacies, and
(iii) lack of political commitment.

The district planning exercise encompassed all sectors and the district planning teams have not been given any indication of financial limits within which they have to formulate the plan. No attempt was made to demarcate clearly the areas of planning within each sector relevant to district level planning. The short orientation given to the district planning officers and the guidelines provided by the State Planning Commission were found to be inadequate to make the district planning officers understand the whole concept of district planning and formulate plans. In such circumstances, the district planning team made an inventory of resources, studied the on-going development schemes, collected the proposals for development from various district level officers concerned with developmental activities, consolidated them and presented it as district plan. Many schemes were hastily prepared. Projects which have not been examined from the point of view of techno-economic feasibility found a place in the plan. The financial resources required for implementing the district plan turned but to be a staggering amount.

The District Planning Cells were disbanded after the formulation of the plan. The State Planning Commission was reconstituted in 1974 but commission did not have any separate division to deal with district planning. At the district level, there was no elected executive body to take follow up action on the plan. The District Development Council is only an advisory body so it cannot exert pressure on the government to implement the district plan, even in a revised form. In short, there was no machinery, both at State and district levels, to scrutinize the district plans, revise them consistent with priorities of the State's Five-Year/Annual Plan and to take effective follow-up action on the district plans.

The political commitment to decentralize planning was also found to be lacking, which perhaps seems to be the main factor responsible for the failure of this concept to gain acceptance and take roots in Tamil Nadu. The Government which initiated the district planning in early '70s, itself did not evince keen interest in taking any follow-up measures to translate the district perspective plans into action plans. The State witnessed political changes in the mid-'70s and the new government which came to power retained the State Planning Commission, but did not introduce any major reform in the planning process. The views of the then Chief Minister of Tamil Nadu, found in his dissenting note to the Ashoka Mehta Committee on Panchayati Raj Institution, give an indication of the Tamil Nadu Government's thinking on the district planning. The Chief Minister has not accepted the concept of *Zilla Parishad* and *Mandal Panchayat* advocated by the Ashoka Mehta Committee. Instead, the Chief Minister commended block level planning (Panchayat Union) as may be seen from the extracts given below :

> While I am in broad agreement with a major number of recommendations in the report, I have to record my differences of opinion on the concept of the *Zilla Parishad* and *mandal panchayat* envisaged in the report. Basically I am guided in this regard by the views not only from the people of Tamil Nadu but also my own experience and analysis of the situation in various parts of the country. I am convinced that the *Zilla Parishad* with its head as a non-official chairman elected by indirect election and ultimately functioning with the objective of having to bring the Collector also under the control of the *Zilla Parishad* will result in dangerous complication of a dyarchy and it will become difficult for the Collector to function under the circumstances under the two masters, viz., one his government authority and the other elected *Zilla Parishad* chairman and this will lead to, I am convinced, to a situation brought with serious consequences so I am not subscribing to this concept.
>
> I would also commend the idea that there may be a planning cell at the level of the Panchayat Union. It can be presided over by a representative from the State Planning Commission or a State Government officer who could guide and finalize the block planning, sub-

ject to the Government objectives. This plan can be got reviewed by the District Development Council at the district level under the Collector and can be passed on to the Government for approval.

It is clear from the above, that the political authority, which ruled the State for nearly a decade from 1977, has shown a preference for block level planning rather than district level planning. It may be noted that the block level planning was also not pursued vigorously and in fact the Panchayati Raj Institutions remained dormant without the elected representatives and election to local bodies had not been conducted for more than a decade. It was held only in 1986. Therefore, in the absence of any clear directives from political authority, the bureaucracy is hesitant to initiate any action which will lead to decentralized district level planning. Discussion with some officials and non-officials in the State revealed that Tamil Nadu witnessed centralizing tendencies since the beginning of '80s. Several functions (primary education, primary health, water supply) were taken away from *Panchayat Raj* bodies and entrusted to the State level departments under the scheme of provincialization.

Factors Responsible for Success of District Planning in Karnataka

Karnataka has made rapid strides in decentralizing its planning process to the district level. Though the first systematic effort was made in 1978-79, within a decade the State has achieved considerable success in operationalizing the concept of district planning. Sustained interest shown by the State Government building up an organizational structure and the political commitment are the main factors behind the success.

The State Government had set-up a Planning Department comprising seven functional divisions and professional expertise was inducted at different levels in the Planning Department. The department itself was headed by an economist who took keen interest in the district planning experiment and guided it continuously. In its first stage of evolution, the disaggregation of State plan outlays was considered rather mistakenly as district planning. The Planning Department soon realized the shortcomings and allocated lump sum provision to districts which gave a measure of freedom at the district level in taking decision regarding some schemes of local importance. The Planning Department strived hard to demarcate the areas of planning at district and State levels with a view to improving the effectiveness of district level planning. A separate division in the Planning Department – District and Regional Planning Division constantly interacted with various agencies connected with district planning and helped in solving the problem in administration co-ordination.

With the establishment of *Zilla Parishads* and *Mandal Panchayats* in 1987, under the "democratic decentralization" scheme, Karnataka has ushered in a new decentralized planning era. The Karnataka *Zilla Parishad* Act, under which these local institutions have been created, envisages transfer of functions and resources from the State level agencies. *Zilla Parishads* have also been assigned a greater role in planning and implementation of a large number of development and welfare schemes of local importance. Karnataka's experiment in democratic decentralization has been variously described as bold, revolutionary and innovative. Creation of new institutions at district level, with power and resources, lead to a considerable extent erosion of powers of the ruling elite at the State level. Such wholesale transfer of functions is possible only if there is a commitment to decentralization and political will to implement it. In this respect it must be said Karnataka Government had displayed the political will which made the district planning or grass-roots planning a reality.

Teething Troubles in the Karnataka Experiment

Any major politico-administrative reform would naturally have its transitional problems and Karnataka's launching of 'democratic decentralization' scheme also had its own share of teething troubles during the initial stages of implementation. The most important objective of the new experiment was the transfer of power to the *Zilla Parishads* and *Mandal Panchayats* and this resulted in the change of power equations at the district level and below. Prior to the establishment of *Zilla Parishad*, only Members of Legislative Assemblies, Legislative Council and Parliament and Presidents of TDBs belonged to the group of people's representatives who wielded considerable influence in the decision-making process at the district level. In the emergence of the new rulers of rural Karnataka, i.e., the Presidents and Members of *Zilla Parishads*, *Pradhans* of *Mandal Panchayats*, many MPs and MLAs feared, to some extent rightly so, that their powers were likely to be eroded. In fact, with the decision-making powers and resources at their command, the President of *Zilla Parishad* and *Pradhans* of *Mandal Panchayats* are in a much better position to redress the grievances of the local people and decide on the implementation of welfare and development programmes, choice of location of projects, etc. The rulers of local self-government also posed a threat to some vested interests in the district who held sway over the rural mass because of their political connections at the State and higher levels.

There were also some discontentment among Government officials belonging to various cadres. A large number of government functionaries at the district and field levels have been transferred to work under *Zilla Parishads*. These officials were accustomed to working under the vertical chain of command from Head of the Departments. In the new dispensation, school teachers, public works engineers, doctors in primarily health centres and a host of other functionaries have to work under the watchful eyes of the people's representatives. In fact, in some services, the officials showed their disinterest to work under the *Zilla Parishads*. School teachers in some part of the State have gone to the extent of demanding withdrawal of primary and secondary education from the purview of *Zilla Parishad*. Though such a demand was the result of their dissatisfaction over their transfer to *Zilla Parishads*, they justified their demand in the interest of uniformity in the implementation of education policy in the State. There were also reports that some persons who were appointed as Chief Secretaries to *Zilla Parishad* were not willing to continue in their posts and wanted repatriation to their parent department. At the *Mandal* level also several persons who were appointed as *Mandal Panchayat* Secretaries have shown initial resistance to join duty and adopted all sorts of delaying tactics for avoiding posting in *Mandal Panchayats*. The Deputy Commissioner/District Collector enjoyed the pride of place in the district administration until the establishment of *Zilla Parishads*. They found that their role and responsibility have considerably been reduced and downgraded with the creation of *Zilla Parishads*. First, major part of the development administration is now outside the control of Deputy Commissioner. Secondly, the persons appointed as Chief Secretary to *Zilla Parishad* are invariably senior officers who had already served as Deputy Commissioner in one district or other. This also led to some peculiar situation involving protocol between two important district functionaries and this aspect has been pointed out in an article on this subject in *The Hindu* (dated 21st Oct.1987).

Though reduced in rank, responsibilities and status, the Deputy

Commissioner still ranked senior in the district in the matter of protocol since he represented the State Government. Though high in hierarchy, the Chief Secretary of the *Zilla Parishads* could at best represent the district government only and not the State Government. How would the two functions and what would happen in the event of lack of rapport between the two?

The problem inherent in the system of diarchy at the district level found expression rather succinctly when the State was called upon to counter drought for the fifth year in succession. Instead of a single agency to tackle the phenomenon including the identification of the relief measures, as it used to be in the past, every district was now faced with two agencies for the same work. While the Deputy Commissioner continued to be the authority to identify and report on the area afflicted, the responsibility of planning for the relief works and implementing the same had been entrusted to the *Zilla Parishads*. Co-operation and understanding between the two officials became a vital input for efficient drought management.

The problems arising out of the implementation of the new scheme prompted the Chief Minister to undertake an extensive tour of the districts to get personally acquainted with the nature and magnitude of problems faced by *Zilla Parishads*, hurdles in the implementation of schemes, etc. The problems were also discussed in a conference of Presidents of *Zilla Parishads* held in Dharwar towards the end of 1988.

While addressing the Conference, Mr. Nazir Sab, Karnataka's Minister for Rural Development and *Panchayat Raj* also referred to the problems faced by the Government and the efforts being made to sort them out. "We don't say that we are foolproof and that we have done well." He began and went on to relate his own experience of the difficulties. He referred to the confusion prevailing and how in some areas the new rulers, without realizing the powers conferred on them awaited sanction from the top. Until the formation of a service commission for the *Zilla Parishads* it was not possible to recruit staff. Staff from the Government departments was unwilling to opt for *Zilla Parishad* service and as a result about 370 posts of assistant engineers and 400 posts of junior engineers were vacant. Efforts were under way to simplify both the finance code and the administrative manual and it was taking time. He was on the lookout for a suitable officer who would undertake the job. He admitted that some of the Chief Secretaries of *Zilla Parishads* were not willing to continue in their posts and wanted repatriation to their parent departments. More than 100 *Mandal Panchayat* secretaries had not reported for duty and some others had gone on leave and all this affected the working of *Mandal Panchayat*. Some were even prepared to get suspended rather than report for duty. He was sorry that the importance of the institution of *Gramsabha* provided for in the Act had not been properly realized. This was a forum which could be a training ground for future leaders and for people to take an active part in planning at the grass-roots level. (reported in *The Hindu*, dated 6-12-88).

8

DECENTRALIZATION OF MANAGEMENT AND ADMINISTRATION*

AN APPROPRIATE structure and effective co-ordination among its components are the basic ingredients of successful multilevel planning. The adoption and implementation of multilevel planning run into several operational issues of organization and management. Basically they relate to the problem of how best to structure a multilevel planning system and to link up its component parts, including its people. The main issues dealt with in this chapter are: task adoption among various area levels in the hierarchy; institutional arrangements for the organization of the planning process, including planning machinery establishment and capability development co-ordination and implementation management and public participation.

Task Adoption

Multilevel planning is a complex task. An effective way to organize its performance is to decompose it into various components to be adopted by different levels. This implies a clear delineation of the major tasks to be performed at each level, agency responsibilities, activity scheduling and personnel deployment. There is no hard and fast rule for sorting out the various responsibilities and finding the best way to assign

* Reprinted from *Toward Improved Multi-level Planning for Agricultural and Rural Development in Asia and the Pacific*, FAO Economic and Social Development Paper 52, FAO Rome, pp.71-92. It may be noted that Dr. Sundaram played a crucial role in the preparation of this report.

them. It varies according to what is being decided, present circumstances, past experience and the capabilities of the executives involved at the various levels. Tackling the division of responsibilities realistically in each country context is perhaps the best way.

The multilevel planning structure, as visualized in this document, at the sub-national level includes an intermediate level and a local level, besides the village level. Task adoption will have to be approached in this context. Certain organizational mechanisms and a planning infrastructure are necessary for effective performance.

At the national level, while the structure will differ the effectiveness of the planning and development system will be determined by the extent and strength of its political linkage and multi-disciplinary capabilities. Apart from this machinery, a high-powered advisory council is necessary where policy-matters may be discussed and harmonized with the policy decisions of the government. For the agricultural and rural development sector this could be a national advisory council for agricultural and rural development in which some enlightened farmers could also be represented.

At the intermediate level, the tasks involved are both planning and co-ordination. The planning function includes tasks such as resource inventory and analysis; the specification of a regional strategy, thrusts and priorities; determination of the intra-regional allocation of funds; budgetary control; inter-agency co-ordination; the utilization of the findings of research bodies in planning; the preparation of special programmes (where necessary) for target groups and problem areas; and the monitoring of plans/programmes' projects. The mechanism to facilitate these tasks at the intermediate level may be a task force/committee for inter-agency co-ordination in agricultural and rural development set-up within the organization for overall planning established at this level. In this task force/committee, all sub-sector departments and then agencies should be represented. This task force/committee would have a secretariat of its own with essential multi-disciplinary technical staff.

The local level comes close to the people, where plans must be prepared to reflect local resources and potential as well as the needs felt by the population; extension services have to be organized and directed and the operations of various agencies in the delivery of agricultural and rural services and inputs have to be co-ordinated. Close supervision and control over the functioning of the various agencies must be exercised at this level. The organizational structure for this purpose could be in the form of an Agricultural and Rural Development Council (ARDC) which would be an arm of the local-level planning body. Various interests relating to agriculture, food, specialized commodity agencies (e.g., for cereals, cotton, tobacco, coconut, sugar, etc.), nutrition agencies, banking institutions, irrigation and public works departments, fertilizer and pesticides agencies, rural industry organizations, representatives of labour organizations, local government and accredited farmer organizations should be represented on the ARDC. The Council would have its own technical team which would be assisted by the staff of the line departments and agencies in performing various tasks.

Planning Machinery

The allocation of planning and decision-making tasks at the various sub-national levels must be matched by a capacity to plan and co-ordinate. This calls for the establishment of a suitable planning machinery at the different levels.

At present in most countries agricultural and rural development activities are being handled by several departments, each with its own hierarchy. The important departments concerned are: agriculture, irrigation, animal husbandry, dairying, fisheries, forestry, rural industries, public works, co-operation, education, medical and public health, social welfare, local government, etc. Besides, there are some autonomous agencies which perform certain special functions, e.g., the Land Development Corporation, the Input Supply Corporation and credit agencies. In some countries there are also other special agencies set up for particular programmes like the Small Farmers' Development Agency and Integrated Rural Development. Thus, agricultural and rural development functions are highly fragmented among numerous departments and agencies. In most countries, the sectoral departments/agencies have their regional offices at the intermediate level which plan for their sectors. But the essential task of co-ordinating these plans and bringing them into a consistent regional framework, elaborating priorities, time sequence and locations, would have to be done by a planning machinery located at the intermediate level.

To carry out these tasks effectively, a multi-disciplinary technical team is needed at the intermediate level. In most countries, wherever a separate intermediate level planning body exists, it consists of a small team with a generalist, assisted by lower-level staff which is deficient both in expertise and strength. While the actual number and composition of a technical team must be decided by each country for its specific context and judging purely from job requirements, the planning team at this level could consist of a core staff assisted by specialized staff. The core staff of this team might consist of an economist, specialists in agriculture, livestock, forestry and fisheries, a civil engineer, a rural industrial planner and a credit planning officer. Wherever necessary, the core staff may be augmented by a few consultants/specialists during different phases of the planning exercise, according to area needs. The planning team may also obtain additional technical support from sectoral functionaries in the line departments. The planning team should be co-ordinated by an area co-ordinator who could be the economist of the planning team.

At the local level, *action planning* becomes the major thrust. In the agricultural and rural development sectors, this would consist of activities such as project planning; farm/household-level planning; organization and arrangement for the timely mobilization and efficient delivery of inputs and credits; group organization and planning for the target groups and the communication of skills. In terms of planning/implementation personnel, it would need an agricultural planner/project economist, a sociologist and other staff, as required according to the special requirements of the area. At the local level, the emphasis should be on upgrading the skills of existing functionaries through on-the-job training. Where some supplementing of planning skills is required for short periods, it would be possible to obtain necessary assistance from the intermediate level planning body. For this purpose, the intermediate level planning body should be conceived as an experience bank which can readily come to the rescue of the local level as needed. Such working relations for the optimal deployment of available personnel resources must be encouraged and developed in a multilevel planning structure among the different hierarchical levels. This is necessary because in most developing countries today local levels are greatly handicapped either in finding suitable talents or in engaging full-time specialists on their teams.

It is also possible to envisage the same kind of mutual arrangement between the local level and its lower levels (the district and the subdistrict levels, for instance). A working group set-up in India echoes this idea when it talks about establishing a 'peripatetic planning team' at the district level to assist in block (sub-district) level planning.[1] Such a movement of planning personnel from higher to lower levels also ultimately helps in the harmonization of plans at various area levels, as it facilitates an easier flow of information among different levels and permits effective forward and backward linkages to be established among programmes/projects at various levels with informed understanding.

Training

For those functionaries engaged in development work, multilevel planning implies a major transformation. It means giving up some of their powers or command, adjusting to complementary roles and getting used to participatory procedures in planning. The only effective way that this can be accomplished is by repeatedly exposing functionaries to intensive training in multilevel planning principles and procedures as well as to their operational content. Many success stories in rural development have demonstrated that people are more critical than programmes. If this has any message it would be that greater importance should be attached to the training of personnel, particularly when the transformation envisaged is vital and revolutionary.

Training has to be considered at various levels and for various groups of functionaries. For this purpose, suitable institutions should be identified at the apex and other levels. To ensure that the training programme in multilevel planning is communicated as an intensive practical orientation, such training should preferably be seen as a research-cum-training programme. For the research component, the training institution may adopt an area as its laboratory and conduct various investigations and experiments in that area with alternative strategies and simulations of various kinds on a continuous basis so that enough practical experience will be accumulated. This may constitute valuable training material in the form of case studies and illustrative material. Using this material, trainees could be encouraged to perform various exercises based on the method of learning by doing.

Although there is quite a bit of experience with training programmes in every country and some specialized institutions for training have also emerged, there are not yet sufficient insights as to the best ways of integrating training with applications in the regular departmental functioning of governments. Two methods are occasionally advocated.

One method is a comparatively long programme, ranging from four to six months in which trainees receive both theoretical and practical training. The practical training would be in the nature of a planning exercise in area development conducted jointly by the trainees for an area adopted by the training institution as its laboratory and for which investigations and data already exist. The practical constraint faced in this kind of training programme is its length. Many governments find it difficult to release functionaries for such long periods.

Alternatively, a method of discontinuous training – 'a repeated contact approach' – is advocated, in which trainees are brought to the training institution for shorter periods at repeated intervals. They are exposed to analytical techniques and to their practical and working applications. Then they return to the field (i.e., to their offices), apply this knowledge in their field area and go back for a second round of exposure and so on. The constraints in this method are the difficulty of establishing extended continuity of association with the trainees (some are transferred from the area) and the heavy demands for preparation and follow up made on the faculty of the training institute. Thus, the problems inherent in establishing appropriate training methods suited to multilevel planning are to be tackled in a more concerted way. Further experiments are necessary in this direction and the role of international organizations is also important.

Since 1983, Food and Agriculture Organization (FAO) has been assisting the Government of Nepal in strengthening its planning and implementation capacity at local levels (i.e., regional, district and sub-district) in line with the Decentralization Act passed by the national legislature in September 1982. For this purpose, a three-year training programme (1983–86) has been launched and is presently being implemented in collaboration with the Agricultural Project Services Centre (APROSC) of Nepal to provide on-the-job training to concerned government officials in two regions and eight districts within them. In addition, a self-instruction training manual has been prepared for use in training courses and seminars as well as for dissemination to concerned agencies.[2] The training method followed here is the repeated contact approach with two contact periods together lasting four to six weeks. It is hoped that the experience gained through this programme will help to improve training methods for sub-national level planners.

In addition to formal training programmes, other methods may also be tried for staff development in multilevel planning. One of them is a strategy of rotating technical staff among the different levels and training them on the job on an exchange basis. Though methods of this kind may entail many problems of their own, including cadre, placement and similar problems a change-over to a multilevel planning system demands several innovations and tactics, both of an orthodox as well as an unorthodox nature. It would demand great ingenuity on the part of governments to get a multilevel planning process started and their staff attuned to this new process. It cannot be over-emphasized that training (well handled), imparts a decisive momentum to a movement toward multilevel planning.

In the end, it is not merely officials who require training, but also those non-officials holding responsible public office at various levels, such as elected representatives, co-operative members and workers in voluntary agencies, etc. Multilevel planning seeks an integration of political authority with administration at the various levels. This integration would be greatly facilitated by training which can pave the way for attitudinal changes. Many governments are already thinking along these lines and are instituting training programmes/seminars to educate non-officials.

Data and Information Needs

The preparation of a macro-level plan at the *national level*, a regional plan at the *intermediate level* and a local plan at the *local level* constitute the chain of planning activities in a multilevel planning system. The planning cycle includes the tasks of resource inventory and analysis, identification of projects, formulation of plans/programmes/ projects, and monitoring and evaluation. Each stage of the planning exercise involves the collection and analysis of data. These data should be minimum, meaningful and relevant. Experience in developing countries shows that as one goes from the national to the sub-national levels, the data available decrease both in terms of quantity and quality. As a rule, the data at the sub-national levels in many countries are quite weak and inadequate for the planning needs at these levels. The changes in the orientation of development planning that have recently taken place call for new kinds of disaggregated data of great reliability and authenticity. Country experiences reveal that there are several sources of data in each country such as the national statistical office, the central planning agency and its regional offices, sectoral ministries, and research and various other institutions, e.g., universities, farmer associations, co-operatives, rural industrial organizations, credit agencies, etc. There is a need to integrate available data from these institutions and agencies at each territorial level of decision-making and assess their usefulness, relevance and reliability. On the basis of such an assessment gaps should be identified and a Comprehensive Information System (CIS) that is valid, reliable, relevant, sensitive, specific and simple should be designed for each country. This is an urgent task for successful decentralized planning efforts in developing countries. International agencies could greatly assist developing countries in this regard, with both technical inputs and the physical infrastructure required for data handling.

Organizational Design and Co-ordination

In the decentralized management of agricultural and rural development sector, two sets of problems usually arise and call for careful thinking about alternatives to organizational design. One of these relates to the choice of organizational structure for a new programme, where the question is one of either setting up an administratively different system focussed on the particular new function, or merging the targeted emphasis into the larger system. Usually the temptation to set-up new organizations and create new instruments to perform tasks is strong among both administrators and technocrats. But there is a cost – in terms of resources and time – to be considered in adopting such a policy. New structures give greater independence but entail additional costs in duplicating infrastructures and time to produce an impact. Further, there is no guarantee that over time the deficiencies noted in an existing general administration system may not also appear in the new autonomous system as well. Also, when an unit is placed in an existing hierarchical system, it may not be able to function with flexibility. Potential alternatives are shown in Figure 8.1 arranged in order from those involving minimal change to those requiring a complete break, calling for the establishment of a parallel hierarchy.[3] In terms of the degree of independence for action, it may be seen that the alternatives range from low to high.

The great operational problem in multilevel planning, however, regards effecting horizontal inter-agency linkages. This is a particularly important issue in agricultural and rural development planning because field enterprises in this sector often require more than one kind of technical support and weaknesses of horizontal co-ordination will

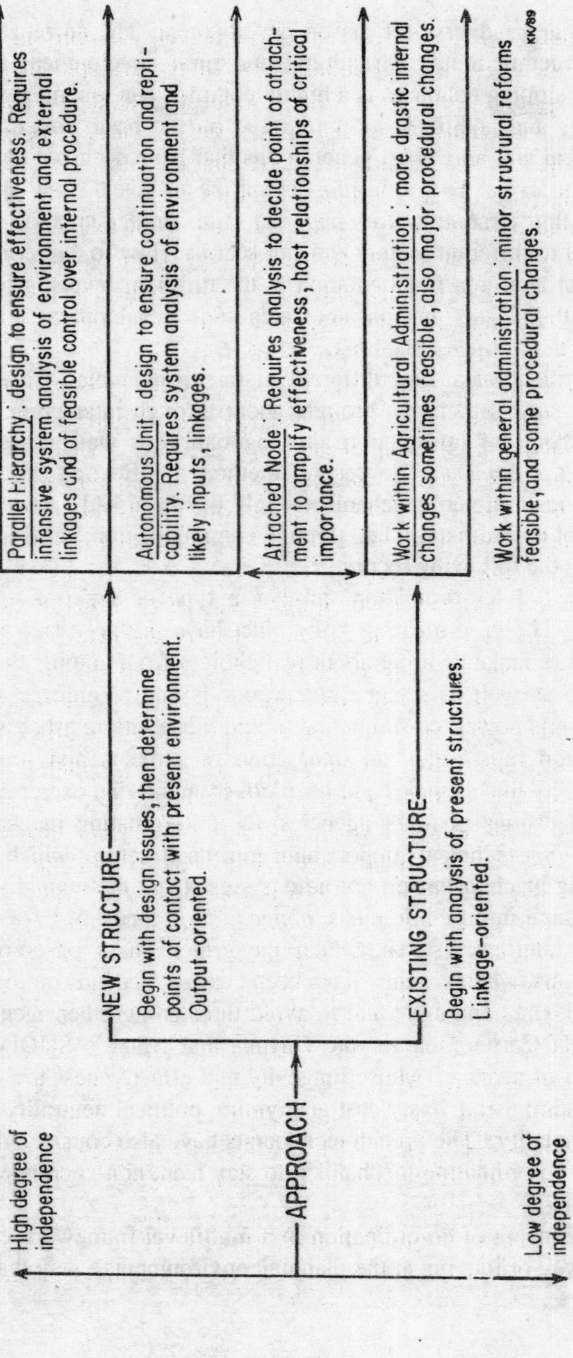
High degree of independence
APPROACH
Low degree of independence
NEW STRUCTURE
Begin with design issues, then determine points of contact with present environment. Output-oriented.
EXISTING STRUCTURE
Begin with analysis of present structures. Linkage-oriented.
Parallel Hierarchy: design to ensure effectiveness. Requires intensive system analysis of environment and external linkages and of feasible control over internal procedure.
Autonomous Unit: design to ensure continuation and replicability. Requires system analysis of environment and likely inputs, linkages.
Attached Node: Requires analysis to decide point of attachment to amplify effectiveness, host relationships of critical importance.
Work within Agricultural Administration: more drastic internal changes sometimes feasible, also major procedural changes.
Work within general administration: minor structural reforms feasible, and some procedural changes.
KK/89

have strongly adverse effects on development. The current organizational structure in the agricultural and rural development sectors in most developing countries is a highly complex one, owing partly to the variations and additions super-imposed on the basic structure and to the vertical and horizontal penetrations that have occurred between institutional levels. Today, in most countries all levels show an array of interlocking structures for planning and implementation that are restricted to different sectors and sub-sectors. How to overcome the institutional and area fragmentation at the different levels, effect cross-functional linkages and promote area-wide development is a crucial question in multilevel planning.

Co-ordination among different hierarchical levels in a multilevel planning structure can be brought about through interaction dialogue, and exchange of information and negotiation as well as through organizational devices. The second method of effecting co-ordination through institutional mechanisms will be discussed here. The first method of co-ordination, i.e., through communication and flows, is discussed in the following section.

The word 'co-ordination' implies a type of superior-subordinate relations. The co-ordinating body must have the necessary degree of authority to make or bring about real choices from among alternatives, to merge as well as select from proposals and to enforce decisions. Without this power, co-ordination would mean only a process of loose aggregation rather than an integration of projects and programmes proposed by line agencies and local governments. To exercise leverage on the decisions of other agencies, the co-ordinating mechanism requires strong technical support built into its structure, which most co-ordinating mechanisms do not now possess (e.g., the regional development council in the Philippines, *bappeda* in Indonesia). Experiences in several countries also show that the effectiveness of co-ordinating mechanisms, wherever they have been created, depends on their ability to stay flexible and agile and to avoid threatening other agencies. The Venezuela Corporation for the Guyana and Brazil's SUDDENG are examples of agencies whose longevity and effectiveness are attributed to their administrative style of anonymity, political neutrality and non-controversiality.[4] The French technocrats have also considered it an asset for a co-ordinating mechanism to stay lean, non-coercive and non-threatening.[5]

The concept of co-ordination in a multilevel framework calls for a special way of looking at the planning environment, a way that is comprehensive and yet capable of delineating the relationship of each part to other parts and of each part to the whole. This is often called the systems' approach. It means being able to identify and relate the various parts of the planning area. Operationally, it means being able to create a relationship among various institutions, public and private, where each institution's effort complements the others, and where total efforts contribute to the attainment of certain planning goals. This means making the departments of agriculture, natural resources, rural industries, infrastructure and social services of government work together. It also means making the public and private sectors work together to achieve common development goals.

The mechanisms of co-ordination suggested earlier for agricultural and rural development planning at the intermediate and local levels – namely, task forces/committees or councils – are in fact part of the larger co-ordination mechanism at respective levels and derive their power and authority from the way the overall co-ordinating mechanism has been constituted and its politico-administrative linkages designed. Apart from the administrative powers, finances and functions devolved from higher levels to this co-ordinating body, the presence of a political authority is an equally important consideration. Some observers hold that the design of a political-territorial framework is essential to the strategy of implementation and co-ordination. According to one, 'in order for the regional level to exercise legitimate powers of co-ordination over districts, regional assemblies would have to be created with membership drawn by indirect vote'.[6] Another remarks that 'a major issue that is raised in any approach where only administrative powers and functions are devolved from the national level (in this case the region), but not the political authority over major and substantive functions, is that it does not develop fully the capability of the regional and the local governments to perform functions crucial to their jurisdiction'.[7]

The design and management of co-ordination functions should be effected at an early stage in the planning process and should involve all planning and implementing ministries and departments in order to preserve continuity. This means that co-ordination should be effected at the stage of plan formulation itself, i.e., when projects are being formulated by the various departments, so that it will be possible to create backward and forward linkages for projects and to ensure full inter-dependencies and complementarities. To seek co-ordination after plans or projects have been prepared is a futile effort.

Having stated some of the essential principles of co-ordination in multilevel planning, attention may now be drawn to some possible alternative models for this purpose.

Governments in developing countries have generally chosen from among four organizational design patterns for rural development planning, execution and co-ordination.[8] These include:

Pattern A – Parallel programming and implementation by separate sectoral organizations that are weakly orchestrated by a national co-ordination body (Figure 8.2).
Pattern B – A strong co-ordinating body with its own implementing arm (Figure 8.3).
Pattern C – A strong co-ordinating body without its own implementing arm (Figure 8.4).
Pattern D – A system based on a decentralized integrative executive framework (Figure 8.5).

In Pattern A the co-ordination of rural development activities is assigned to a single ministry which ensures co-ordination through exchange and negotiation at the field level. Also, at the national level, co-ordination would be achieved by a high-powered co-ordinating body.

Figure 8.2: Pattern A: Parallel Programming and Implementation by a Separate Organization

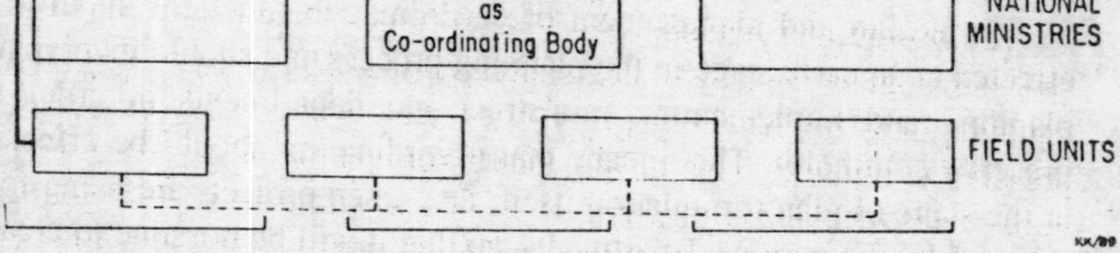

Figure 8.3: Pattern B: Strong Co-ordinating Body with Implementing Arm

National Executive

Co-ordinating Body

Alternative Ministry as Co-ord. Body

National Ministries

Field Units

Note: Solid lines represent formal lines of command; broken lines represent informal contacts between units.

Figure 8.4: Pattern C: Strong Co-ordinating Body without Implementing Arm

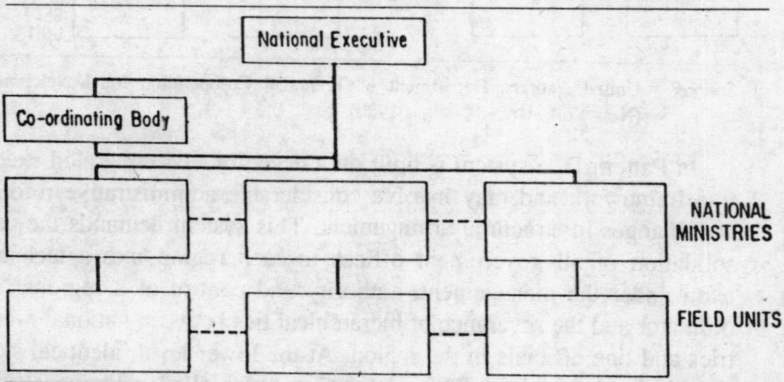

In Pattern B, co-ordination is multiple. Along with the assigned ministry, a central co-ordinating body would also carry out the co-ordinating function. Therefore, the field units would be under a three-dimensional review, i.e., from their ministries to the ministry assigned to co-ordination and to the field offices of the central co-ordinating agency. Such multidimentional co-ordination, however, might create confusion, duplication and misunderstanding.

In Pattern C, a central co-ordinating body ensures co-ordination from the centre as a directing and controlling authority, without having field-or regional-level offices. In most countries, such a pattern is widely practised.

Figure 8.5: Pattern D: Decentralized Integrative Framework

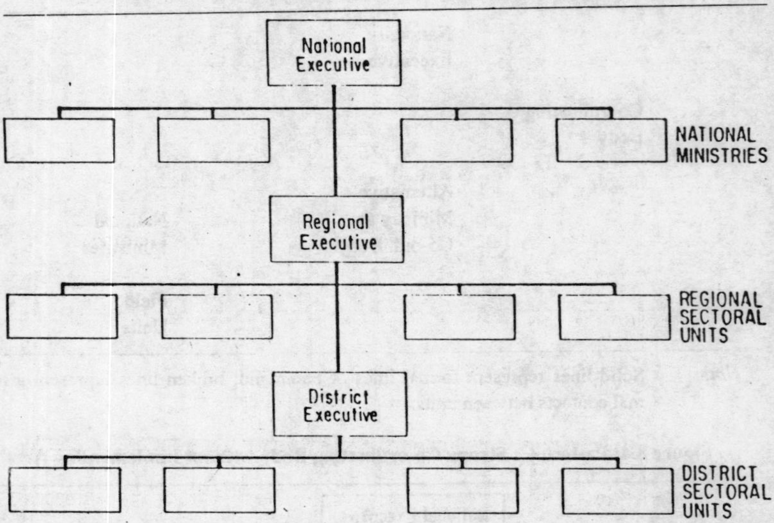

Source: United Nations, Department of Technical Co-operation for Development, (New York: United Nations,1980).

In Pattern D, a system is built on a decentralized integrated executive framework and may involve considerable administrative reforms and changes in structural arrangement. This system demands the consolidation of all government offices in each region into a technical team under the management, authority and control of a regional co-ordinator and the severance of hierarchical ties between national ministries and line officials in the region. At the lower level, identical steps would also be devised. This pattern integrates all development functions into one authority at certain levels under a single leadership which is duly accountable to the higher level authority. Pattern D has been applied to Tanzania.

Notably, co-ordinating structures are in the nature of a pathological response. The context is a determining factor – perhaps the overall determining factor – which designs, shapes and modifies the structure of any organization. But within these contextual limits, there are some opportunities for choice and variation. The alternatives discussed earlier indicate the range of variations possible for co-ordination mechanisms. Broadly speaking, the problem of co-ordination can be seen in two perspectives: the first through political re-orientation and re-organization where a regional/local political structure is suggested; the other aspect is merely administrative or structural. The latter can be accomplished by designing a structural arrangement whereby an official at the level of programme execution is given appropriate authority, control and command over line officials. This approach is relatively easy to achieve and has been followed in several developing countries. The main limitation of this approach, however, is that it virtually ignores the dynamics of politics in the development process and emphasizes the role of administration. The first approach appears more democratic in its nature and content, while the other seems to be a mere administrative re-ordering. Choosing any of the approaches would depend on the existing politico-economic, cultural and administrative conditions of a country, as well as upon the political philosophy of the government in power.

Linkages, Communication and Flows

Multilevel planning involves the use of a system's approach. If the organizational structures devised at various levels constitute its skeleton, the planning activities are its flesh, linkages, communication and flows constitute its blood and guts. Without the latter, the system cannot function. Thus the planning process in a multilevel planning structure proceeds in a system of flows and interactions among the hierarchical levels. In fact, the efficiency of a multilevel planning process is determined by the intensity of these flows and interactions. Organizing these flows effectively implies multiple interactions and communication among levels which take on the character of an interactive process. For maximum effectiveness, it is better to use more than one communication net, such as the hierarchical group, the expert group, status group and friendship group. Most formal communication goes through one of the first two methods. The informal nets through status group, friendship group, etc., help considerably in preparing the ground for formal communications. Thus the exchange in a multilevel planning framework has to be through both formal and informal methods of communication. An immense amount of data transfers and estimation revisions on various matters can take place in this manner, e.g., an information exchange relating to output targets, material quotas, manpower requirements, financial allocations, preferred priorities, etc. This communication is two-way, so that the recipient is encouraged to intervene in the message for clarification or to ask questions. In this way, assumptions and plan magnitudes can be developed at both ends with mutual understanding. Such understanding will pave the way for consistency in planning. If the end product is to be successful, the participants in the planning process must operate in a highly flexible manner – i.e., far from a neat and simple arrangement of systematized and routine inter-actions. The institutional mechanisms devised at the various hierarchical levels must, therefore, be designed for such flexibility.

Administrative Decentralization

While the organizational structures designed at the various levels provide the essential planning and mediating links in a multilevel planning system, the extent of the delegation of administrative powers to these levels determines the relative success of performance. How much administrative decentralization or deconcentration should be provided to the different levels is a crucial question. While the central government should retain its 'command', the extent of supervision and control should be optimal. Sometimes this is called 'co-ordinated decentralization'. While decentralization promotes initiative, responsibility, the development of personnel, decisions close to facts, and flexibility, coordination results in efficiencies and economies. The extent of control has to be determined very carefully, as increased efficiency does not necessarily occur with increased control. The kind of control that is advocated in this context is sometimes termed 'broad' or 'overall' control rather than detailed control. But, at the same time, the accountability of sub-national-level bodies in the responsibilities' devolved to them must be fully ensured. The various aspects of administrative decentralization that deserve consideration in a multilevel planning context are itemized below:

Administrative and Technical Sanctions

The procedures for administrative and technical sanctions should be streamlined and simplified so that the usual procedures of referring a project repeatedly to various ministries and finance/planning departments for approval would be avoided. For the purpose of administrative sanctions, the plan should be considered sacrosanct. Once any project is included in the approved plan, the financial sanction would be presumed. Since no project may be included in the plan which does not have prior technical sanction, a separate technical sanction is not needed. This would mean that the departments at the sub-national level must always keep a shelf of *approved* projects on hand, ready for incorporation in the plan at any time. Sanctioning procedures can be simplified further by permitting marginal powers to the sub-national-level bodies to effect any changes in the project either in terms of design or costs by a certain percentage. If it is within the prescribed ceiling, no further reference need be made to higher levels. In this way, it would be possible to overcome the many delays that normally afflict project implementation.

Release of Funds

A problem creating great difficulty in many situations is the long lag between the preliminary commitment of funds and their actual receipt in the field. The length and complexity of the funding chain are formidable in some countries. When multilevel planning procedures are adopted, arrangements may be made so that allocations reach the local level directly, bypassing all intermediate layers. For this purpose, the budgetary methods may need suitable alteration, as, for example, by introducing an area spatial budgeting system and ensuring accountability at the sub-national level.

Intersectoral Transfers and Powers of Re-appropriation

No implementation machinery can be considered perfect. There are always lagging projects and leading ones contributing to either shortfalls or an overfulfilment of targets. Taking note of the performance of projects, the authorities at sub-national levels should be empowered to make any midstream changes needed as long as they do not upset plan priorities. This means that intersectoral transfers and powers of re-appropriation should be permitted within certain limits. National governments should indicate such limits in their guidelines so that blockages do not occur during the plan implementation stage.

Personnel Control

This is always a complicated problem in multilevel planning. Depending on the administrative set-up and personnel system of a country, there may be at any particular level more than one stream of personnel to be controlled. One of these may be a set of personnel which is appointed by the area level and is controlled by it, both technically and administratively. There may also be a second stream consisting of staff belonging to the line agencies/departments seconded to the subnational level. This category of personnel is supposed to be administratively under the sub-national-level authority, but may technically fall under their respective departments. In a situation like this, it is desirable to ensure the answerability of these officers to the co-ordinating bodies instituted at the intermediate and local levels. This is best done by considering these officers as being 'on transfer' to these bodies and vesting all their daily control in the organizations at the horizontal levels. This would also mean that their performance would be assessed by the co-ordinator at the sub-national level. In this way, the horizontal co-ordination mechanism could be greatly strengthened.

Monitoring and Evaluation

The decentralized management of agricultural and rural development also implies that effective arrangements should be made to assess the progress of implementation and to take timely decisions to ensure that progress is maintained according to schedule. Monitoring assesses overall project effects, both intentional and unintentional, and their impact. One of the important functions assigned to the planning machinery at intermediate and local levels in the present scheme of multilevel planning is the effective monitoring of projects at their respective levels. Thus, monitoring is a decentralized function, particularly since it is linked to improved management efficiency. It must, therefore, be integrated with the project management structure. While evaluation will draw on the data generated by the monitoring system it need not be decentralized to all levels. Because it would demand professional skills to interpret evaluation data and would also seek wider horizons requiring comparative information, it may be envisaged as a centralized activity, with analytical capabilities pooled either at the central level only or also at regional levels, depending on country requirements. For instance, in countries with a federal set-up, evaluation may have to be organized at each sovereign level. The performance of the monitoring function at either the intermediate or local levels of planning would be the responsibility of the respective planning teams recommended for these levels which can quickly collate, summarize and present the information to decision-makers.

Many United Nations agencies, including Food and Agriculture Organization (FAO), International Food and Agriculture Department (IFAD), International Labour Organization (ILO), United Nations International Children's Emergency Fund (UNICEF), the World Bank, have issued monitoring and evaluation guidelines, handbooks, etc.[9] The IFAD has prepared and the ACC Task Force on Rural Development of the United Nations has adopted Guiding Principles for the Design and Use of Monitoring and Evaluation in Rural Development Projects/Programmes. This is an attempt to pull together common principles based on the monitoring and evaluation guidelines, handbooks and practices of the various United Nations agencies and organizations engaged in agricultural and rural development.

Monitoring and evaluation should not only be restricted to discovering the impact, effects and benefits of particular projects. While this is important, it is necessary in the context of multilevel planning to broaden the perspective of evaluation by inquiring into the impact of decentralized planning on the whole in bringing about social and economic change in the area, and particularly as to whether the processes of development have percolated evenly across rural areas.

While designing, monitoring and evaluation systems for agricultural and rural development projects, the crucial issue of the variables or indicators to be measured within these systems should be tackled. The range of these indicators in the agricultural and rural development sectors may fall in three broad groups, namely:

(a) Output indicators
(b) Economic indicators
(c) Quality-of-life indicators

National governments may issue detailed guidelines specifying appropriate indicators, indicating the sources of data from which they may be compiled as well as the kind of data handling and analyses necessary for their meaningful presentation to decision-makers.

People's Participation

Multilevel planning marks a departure in the style of development from what is essentially a bureaucratic approach to an increasingly participatory approach. It provides an important channel for private sector participation. People's participation, therefore, constitutes an essential element of its software aspect. Participation can be spontaneous or induced, direct or indirect, complete or partial, organized or unorganized and intensive or extensive, depending on who organizes it, the level at which it is organized, how it is organized and the purpose for which it is organized. The planning process itself consists of several components or stages such as the formulation of objectives, research and survey, plan formulation, plan acceptance, implementation and evaluation. Participation at any particular level may be confined to any one or more aspects of this process, or it can encompass all aspects. In this way it may be partial or complete.

At the higher levels, like the national or even the intermediate level, participation will be more indirect, while at the local level, it will be more direct. Again, at the national and intermediate levels, participation would be of a consultative nature, whereas at the local level, participation should be seen both as the *tool* and *goal* of development, as it serves as a medium of social transformation and as a pre-condition for authentic development.

Like multilevel planning, people's participation is also a two-way process. While a government's willingness to permit and encourage public participation at different levels is no doubt important, this is not the only important pre-condition to ensure such participation. The people must also be willing and able to participate. People's willingness to participate will depend on whether they have the capacity to undertake the task, whether they consider that such participation will benefit them and whether – in terms of certain sacrifices that they have to make such as time and energy – it will be worth it. The Nepal experience of associating people in agricultural planning at the different tiers shows that participation cannot be assumed simply because the government has decided that it should occur. In this case, participation was not forthcoming, probably because the people did not have the necessary capacity to undertake the tasks expected of them and also because they felt that this was another top-down imposition. Thus, it should be noted that interest and competence are relevant factors to be taken into account in public participation.

In recent years, another important dimension to participation has been added. This is the participation of the rural poor, arising from the realization that low-income, disadvantaged families are the neglected entities in the normal channels of public participation provided by governments. It is believed that the MLP approach will actually improve the effectiveness of all types of development, leading to greater efficiencies of effort and to increased social equity. This has led national governments and international bodies to devise new approaches to the participation of the rural poor in plan formulation and other stages of the planning process.

The Food and Agriculture Department is supporting pilot projects in several countries which help the rural poor to obtain loans, learn new skills and identify and use government services so that they can raise their incomes and improve their living standards. These projects operate by helping the rural poor form their own organizations, which are sometimes known as 'trust groups'. Initially these groups are informal, without any official or bureaucratic status. They are small, usually with about 10 to 15 members, and homogeneous, with all members from similar backgrounds or economic levels. To ensure that the project reaches the least-advantaged people, membership is often restricted to people living at a subsistence level, producing at least enough for their families, but without a surplus. To assist governments and implementing agencies, FAO has also prepared 'Guiding Principles for People's Participation Projects' covering design, operation and monitoring, and on-going evaluation.[10] Although written specifically for pilot projects, the guidelines are useful in incorporating the participation of beneficiaries in any types of development project.

Food and Agriculture Department has emphasized the need for developing and strengthening the receiving/utilizing system among small farmers and peasants at the grass-root level to enable them to take advantage of the facilities and services being made available by local delivery systems. Methods, like decentralized field-level consultations, direct dialogue between concerned agencies and multilevel task-oriented communication, devised for the purpose are discussed in the 'Small Farmers Development Manual', which may be usefully consulted by National Governments.[11] In various countries, several new approaches are also being introduced to give representation to the rural poor in various forms.

Country experiences indicate that the following modes of people's participation are possible:

(i) participation limited to elites only (mostly elected representatives);

(ii) participation in which the people or beneficiaries are asked to legitimize or ratify projects identified and formulated by the Government, but they do not actively participate in the detailed planning and management of the project;

(iii) participation in which the people are consulted from the very start and also actively participate in the planning and management of projects;

(iv) participation in which the representatives from different strata of society/occupation groups/beneficiaries find their places in all planning/co-ordination/evaluation mechanisms devised at the various levels, including the highest policy-making level; and

(v) participation in which the representatives enumerated in (iv) actually control the decisions at all levels.

Experience in the various countries shows that the modes of participation mentioned in (iv) and (v) above have not effectively materialized.

Other issues in the context of public participation are: On what issues should public participation be sought and when should they be sought. A round-table organized by ESCAP in 1978 has observed that the people can make a significant contribution to the planning process only if they are presented a well-articulated and feasible framework of approaches, objectives, analyses and alternatives.[12] Some areas identified on which the public could be consulted with advantage are :

(a) assessment of the benefits and cost-effectiveness of on-going programmes;
(b) effective measures for the further development of the area;
(c) suggestions on assigning priorities in the plan;
(d) location decisions for different programmes;
(e) the identification of beneficiaries for a programme; and
(f) the role to be assigned to different groups in implementation.

It appears from several experiences relating to participation that the development of *readiness* and *skills* for participation by the people in itself demands a 'participatory education strategy'. National Governments should pay attention to this aspect of training intended to develop

(a) skills in group work;
(b) readiness for identifying one's own problem with those of the community and understanding community problems as his own;

(c) focus on community thinking; and
(d) skills in problem-solving and action-planning.

The kind of public participation at various levels demanded of a multilevel planning framework cannot be institutionalized overnight, nor can it be obtained through legislation. For workable and stable model for people's participation in a multilevel planning framework, it has to emerge in each country through a process of experimentation or trial and error.

Costs

As discussed in this chapter, the decentralization of decision-making in multilevel planning would imply the establishment of appropriate institutional and administrative mechanisms and a suitable planning machinery with multi-disciplinary talents at the sub-national level. It may even involve the strengthening of the planning machinery at the central level. The need for training and the requirement for data will increase with successive decentralization. The streamlining of coordination and communication among various levels will require more resources. Therefore, each stage in multilevel planning will generally need additional funds. The cost involved is, therefore, an important consideration in the kinds of decentralization aimed at a particular time in a multilevel planning system.

REFERENCES

1. Government of India, Planning Commission (1978). Report of the Working Group on Block-Level Planning, p. 8
2 FAO/APROSC (1983). *Planning Training Manual: District and Sub-District Level*, Kathmandu, Nepal.
3 J.R. Moris (1981). *Managing Induced Rural Development.* International Development Institute, Indiana University, Bloomington, Indiana.
4. J.R. Dinkelspiel (1969). "Administrative Style" in L. Rodwin et al. (eds.). *Planning Urban Growth and Regional Development.* MIT Press, Cambridge, Massachusetts, pp. 301-14.
5. S. Cohen (1969). *Modern Capitalist Planning: The French Model.* Harvard University Press, Cambridge, Massachusetts.
6. J. Friedmann (1980). *The Active Community — Towards a Political-Territorial Framework for Rural Development in Asia*, Regional Development Dialogue 1, 2, Autumn 1980. United Nations Centre for Regional Development, Nagoya.
7 G.I. Iglesias (1977). Political and Administrative Issues in Regional Planning

and Development. *Philippine Journal of Public Administration* 3 and 4 (July-October).

8. United Nations, Department of Technical Co-operation for Development (1980). Public Administration Institution and Practices in Integrated Rural Development Programme. New York.

9. A large number of publications exist. Some major publications are:
   (i) FAO: Monitoring Systems for Agricultural and Rural Development Projects. Economic and Social Development Paper 12, edited by E. Clayton and F. Petry (1981). Rome.
   (ii) IFAD (1979). *Operational Guidelines on Monitoring and Evaluation.* December.
   (iii) ILO (1981). *Procedures for the Design and Evaluation of ILO Projects.* II, Technical Co-operation. Bureau of Programming and Management, (Revised).
   (iv) United Nations, Department of Economic and Social Affairs (1978). *Systematic Monitoring and Evaluation of Integrated Development Programmes:* A Source-Book. ST/ES/A78, New York.
   (v) UNICEF (1983). *Improving Programme Monitoring and Evaluation.* EXD-2865. New York.
   (vi) D.J. Casely and D.A. Lury (1981). *Handbook on Monitoring and Evaluation of Agriculture and Rural Development Projects.* World Bank; Washington D.C. November.

10. G. Huizer (1983). *Guiding Principles for People's Participation Projects: Design, Operation, Monitoring and On-going Evaluation.* FAO, Rome.
    —, B. Van Heck, (1979). *Participation of the Poor in Rural Organizations. A Consolidated Report on Studies in Selected Countries of Asia, the Near East and Africa.* Rural Organizations Action Programme (ROAP), FAO, Rome.
    B.Van Hack (1983). *Training of Group Promoters in Field Projects of the People's Participation Programme.* FAO, Rome.
    DSE/FAO (1983). *Promotion of Self-Help Organizations of the Rural Poor in Africa: Problems of Implementation, Monitoring and Evaluation.* Feldafing.

11. Food and Agriculture Department (1978). *Small Farmers Development Manual.* I and II. Bangkok.

12. United Nations, ESCAP (1978). *Rural Development Administration in India: Some Emerging Policy Issues.* Report of a Round table on Adaptation of Administration to Rural Development held in New Delhi.

9

PREPARING DISTRICT PLANS*

THE FIRST objective of the formulation of district plans is to set forth a long-term perspective indicating the economic activities to be established in different sub-regions of the district and the measures to be taken over the next 15 or 20 years to develop (and conserve) natural resources, build-up infrastructural facilities and social services and foster the growth of towns and cities in a manner that would help the district to develop in the pre-determined direction. The second objective is to prepare an integrated programme of action for the next five-years or one-year period on the basis of a careful analysis of the existing conditions and a realistic assessment of the immediate problems, short-term priorities and available resources.

For the projection of a long-term perspective as well as the preparation of a short-term operational plan, it is necessary that a careful analysis should be made of the administrative situation and the existing socio-economic conditions in different sub-regions of the district. The lines of future action can thereafter be laid down on the basis of potentials, problems and lacunae discovered in the process. It has already been discussed as to how the district may be divided into homogeneous agro-climatic and economic sub-regions by the preparation and comparison of a number of maps and the analysis of available data. The manner in which the prevailing situation is to be assessed and a plan

* Reprinted from *Report of the working Group on District Planning*, Vol.II, Govt of India, Planning Commission, 1985, pp.166-82. Dr. Sundaram was the Member-Convener of this Working Group. The extrect provided here is from the widelines for District Planning issued by the Planning commission in 1969 and has been included here for its seminal ideas. Mr. Anand Sarup was instrumental for preparing these guidelines.

for development is to be formulated as has been suggested in the latter part of this chapter.

Even though considerable administrative and statistical data is currently being collected at the district level in the normal course, there are a number of activities in respect of which adequate and reliable statistical information is not available. Even where some statistical data may be available, it may not by itself be adequate for determining the lines of future action. In the planning for agriculture and allied activities, as also for village and small-scale industries it would be necessary to carefully take into consideration the attitudes, aspirations and preferences of the private individuals who are to provide the bulk of the investment for development and actually implement the programmes. Similary past experience gathered in connection with the running of various development schemes would also have to be carefully analyzed at the time of plan formulation in order to chalk out programmes or schemes which would yield adequate returns for the efforts and expenditure involved and avoid the kind of difficulties experienced earlier. It is, therefore, necessary that *district plans should be formulated on the basis of available statistical and administrative data, the advice of the knowledgeable farmers and entrepreneurs, the experience of the local officials and a systematic appraisal of the ongoing programmes.*

As a first step in starting the work of the formulation of district plan, the district officers in charge of the various activities should be asked to fill up the statistical tables and prepare notes on the guidepoints. These tables and notes will, it must be remembered, provide only the raw materials for the formulation of district plan. *Once these have been prepared, it would be necessary to study and integrate these into a broad statement listing the resources, problems and prospects and setting forth the priorities to be accorded to different activities in various sub-regions.* This broad statement or framework for the plan will form the basis for a series of discussions with the officials of various departments, knowledgeable farmers, entrepreneurs as also the representatives of the various institutions. A strategy of development will emerge from these discussions which will essentially be tentative to start with but the experience gained and with the availability of former data as the development process gets on, it will get modified, revised and eventually concretized.

This work of intergrating the views and statistics furnished by different departmental representatives, drafting the broad statement mentioned above and finally preparing a plan would have to be undertaken by the authority which would be unimpeded by narrow departmental loyalties and would also have adequate authority to bring together and determine the programmes of the government departments, local government authorities, co-operative and financing institutions.

In most parts of the country this responsibility will have to be borne by the Collectors of the districts. In the few States, where the *Zilla Parishads* have the necessary resources and enjoy considerable statutory powers, this responsibility would have to be borne by these institutions. Both these authorities will, however, have to associate the representatives of important institutions and functional groups such as co-operatives, local self government institutions, banks, knowledgeable farmers and progressive entrepreneurs, for the purpose of preparing comprehensive district plan. For obvious reasons, the staff provided in the district for planning and statistical work will have to play a very important role in assisting the Collectors or the *Zilla Parishad* in discharging this responsibility.

Once the district level officer has furnished the relevant statistics and his views on the guidepoints and these have been carefully scrutinized and integrated into a 'preliminary framework' of prospects, objectives and priorities. The formulation of the district plan will proceed through a series of meetings organized to obtain the reactions of officials and non-officals in respect of the different assumptions and hypotheses underlying the 'preliminary framework' mentioned above. It is assumed that a careful consideration of the different views expressed with reference to the preliminary framework will help in the evolution of a firm strategy for the development of the district around which specific operational schemes might be formulated.

Consultation with BDOs

The first meeting in this series may be held with the Block Development Officers and district level officers at the district headquarters. In this meeting, apart from discussing the preliminary framework for the plans an attempt would be made to determine the comparative position of different blocks in respect of the following items :

(a) availability of marketing facilities in different areas through regulated as well as unregulated rural *mandis*/towns;
(b) availability of communication facilities in terms of the length of

State or district road;

(c) linking of villages with *mandis* and with block headquarters, hospitals, veterinary dispensaries, etc.
(d) availability of irrigation by canal system;
(e) availability of irrigation by government tube-wells;
(f) availability of easily accessible sub-soil water and the extent to which this has been tapped by private parties;
(g) availability of power (spread of power lines, sub-stations, etc.);
(h) degree of urbanization (number of urban units such as town areas, notified areas, municipalities and villages with a population of over 5,000);
(i) extent of industrial activity;
(j) general assessment of the level of agricultural development attained and extent and type of industrial development; and
(k) overall economic condition of the area.

It will not be necessary to go into very specific details while determining the *inter se* position of different blocks in respect of the indicators mentioned above. The main idea behind this kind of categorization is to get an overview of the variety of conditions existing in the district. In the system of target distribution which has been prevalent up to now, these factors are usually taken into consideration when targets for fertilizers or seed distribution, loaning, collection of small savings, etc. are assigned. Therefore, district and block level officers would be in a position to give rough and ready answers for the tentative gradation of Blocks.

Besides eliciting information on the above points, enquiries might be made from the block/district level officers to elicit their views about the performance of co-operatives, *Panchayati Raj* bodies and other institutions in the matter of provision of services, participation in plan formulation and programme implementation and the raising of local resources. A general discussion on the problems of programme implementation in the preceding two or three years could bring to the fore some of the organizational problems which may have to be kept in view while evolving or implementing specific schemes of development. Because of their intimate knowledge of field condition, BDOs may also be able to give some idea of projections which could reasonably be made in respect of the latent demand for agricultural inputs such as fertilizers, seeds, pesticides, tractors and also for credit for the above items as well as for minor irrigation and rural electrification.

Since BDOs will be eventually involved with the mobilization of local resources, it would also be desirable to elicit their reactions regarding the possibility of raising local resources for village roads, school buildings, location and opening of high schools and colleges and the augmentation of medical facilities.

Consultation with Progressive Farmers/Entrepreneurs

No uniform procedure can be prescribed for ensuring public participation in the process of plan formulation, because of the variety of institutional set-ups existing in different States. It is, however, necessary that the views of the progressive farmers/entrepreneurs should be ascertained about the problems or activities which should be given priority in different blocks or areas. A simple device to obtain their views would be to constitute an advisory panel of selected farmers and entrepreneurs representing different classes and sub-regions. The preliminary framework of the district plan would be presented before this panel for a free and frank discussion. The idea of presenting the 'preliminary framework' to this panel is not really to obtain their endorsement but to stimulate them to articulate their perceptions about the problems and prospects of development of various sub-regions and to obtain their views about the feasibility of approaches set-forth in the framework. During discussions with progressive farmers or entrepreneurs, it would be useful to start with the presumption that many of these people would have the experience and the capacity to make a critical appraisal of the conditions in which they live and suggest measures of improvement which could be taken up in the plan. It would also be worthwhile finding out as to what concrete measures are being taken by them to increase their productivity. A correlation between the practices adopted by them and the schemes already in operation could provide a basis not only for the modification and improvement of new schemes specifically oriented to the needs of the different areas or strata in the district.

At the grass-roots level, the development of infrastructure and social services is still at a rudimentary level. In practically every area, people are experiencing difficulties on account of the paucity of link roads, medical facilities, irrigation channels and educational institutions. It is, therefore, difficult for people to be objective with discussing proposals which would affect their villages/towns or their sources of livelihood. In spite of this, an attempt has to be made to obtain some idea of the local needs and aspirations from the panel of farmers and entrepreneurs. The list of demands which would be drawn up in the process should, however, be used only as raw material for the Plan. It would not be much use arranging these haphazard demands in an order of priority. The arrangement of infrastructural and other programmes of needs in an order of priority should be attempted only on the basis of an objective view of the functional importance of individual items derived from the strategy of development adopted for the different sub-regions of the district.

After holding discussions with the block and district level officers and the panel of selected farmers and entrepreneurs, the next round of discussions will have to be arranged with the representatives of co-operatives, local self-government bodies, banks and Panchayati Raj Institutions in order to obtain their views about the ideas contained in the 'preliminary framework' and assess the quantum of resources likely to become available for the district plan from within the district.

After these discussions have been held, it would be necessary to pause for a while and re-appraise, revise and enlarge the preliminary 'framework' in the light of these discussions. This revised framework would form the basis of detailed and more specific discussions with individual district level officers for the purpose of defining the lines of approach to be adopted for the solution of the problems posed by them or the representatives of different institutions and functional groups. The discussions with individual district level officers would generally cover the following points :

(a) level of development already reached in the different sub-regions of the district in respect of his sphere of activities;
(b) under the various programmes administered by him the existence of marked differences in the quantity or quality of essential facilities or services available to different sub-regions or communities in the district;
(c) marked variations in the response from different areas to the different development programmes run by his department;
(d) performance of different programmes/schemes and the emergent trends of behaviour or preferences shown by the people with regard to these;
(e) relation of earlier programmes to local needs;
(f) their views about the needs mentioned by the local representatives;

(g) proposed programme objectives for the forthcoming plan;
(h) specific activities or inputs which will have to be arranged for their fulfilment; and
(i) the *inter se* priority to be given to programmes and specific activities.

In addition to getting specific information on the above points, it would be useful to discuss with them the problems of inter-departmental co-ordination, the scope of economy in government expenditure and the possibility of mobilizing local resources for the various activities falling within their sphere of action.

Laying down Guidelines

After the completion of detailed discussions with individual officers, meeting of all district level officers would have to be called to lay down the long-term perspective of development as well as the integrated strategy to be followed in the short-term plan under preparation. In addition, the objectives and guidelines to be adopted for different programmes would also have to be laid down in these meetings to furnish a basis for the drawing up of detailed schemes for inclusion in the plan of the district. This will be the most crucial stage in the process of district plan formulation. It would, therefore, be desirable to involve all such people in the meetings who would be playing a significant role in the formulation or the implementation of the district plan.

These guidelines would indicate firm inter-sectoral and intra-sectoral priorities, specify sectoral and programme objectives, stipulate the lines on which new schemes should be drawn up, existing schemes should be modified and clarify the manner in which the development of backward areas or communities would be undertaken. These guidelines would obviously have to be prepared on the basis of careful consideration of the different alternatives available for achieving specific programme objectives. Supposing one of the programme objectives adopted is to bring about a substantial increase in agricultural production, it would have to be laid down as to how far and in which sub-regions this would be achieved mainly by the intensification of agriculture on irrigated land and in which areas efforts would be concentrated mainly on raising the productivity of dry areas. Similarly, in respect of the objective of increasing the area under irrigation, a choice will have to be indicated in respect of particular areas, between the extension of irrigation through canals, State tubewells, private tubewells, percolation wells, etc. The nature or the choice will, in each case, depend upon the evaluation of the potential, the resources required for its development and the benefit expected from each of the alternatives.

Contents of Concrete Schemes

Once the guidelines have been drawn up, the district level officers should be asked to concretize the guidelines into different schemes, specifying in each case :

(a) the objectives;
(b) the activities envisaged;
(c) the financial, physical and personnel inputs required;
(d) the physical results expected from year to year;
(e) the quantum of private and institutional resources likely to become available towards its execution; and
(f) the manner in which the scheme would be reviewed, co-ordinated and synchronized with other schemes and evaluated from time to time.

Though the development plan will be put together in stages, the inter-relationship between its various parts will have to examined very carefully so as to maintain internal consistency and order. The production, demand and the supply implications of particular inputs and resources for plan implementation will have to be aggregated and checked well in advance in order to determine the feasibility of different programmes. The schemes thus drawn up by the district level officers will eventually have to be presented in the form of an integrated and operational plan in a meeting of the district level officers and representatives of various institutions by the Collector/Chairman, *Zilla Parishad* with a view to ascertain whether:

(a) the *inter se* priorities laid down in the guidelines have been adhered to;
(b) the objectives laid down under a particular sector are in consonance with the objectives in other inter-related sectors;
(c) steps have been taken to ensure co-ordination between specific

schemes at the local level;

(d) an attempt has been made to identify and plan for the exploitation of unutilized potentials available at a given time;

(e) the specific interests and requirement of different areas/classes have been kept in view;

(f) the estimated financial and physical inputs for plan schemes are reasonable and feasible; and

(g) the criteria for gauging the success of different schemes have been laid down and a programme for periodical physical reporting has been drawn up.

In case it is discovered that the plan drawn up for the coming year or five years at the district level is very ambitious in financial and physical terms, an exercise at pruning would have to be undertaken. It is very important that this exercise should not be undertaken at the State level in a mechanical fashion without consultation with the departmental officials and others who have participated in the formulation of the guidelines for the district plan. The main idea of laying down inter-sectoral and intra-sectoral priorities in these guidelines was to provide an objective basis for the allocation of resources between different programmes and also for the reduction as well as the expansion of the plan on the basis of the availability of resources. In most cases, the cutting down of programme in one sector will lead to a corresponding cut in some other programmes also. For example, if the programmes for the distribution of co-operative credit or fertilizers are cut, it would probably be necessary to reduce the outlays proposed for minor irrigation or for the extension of the High Yielding Varieties Programme also. It will, however, not be possible to apply this rule universally. Certain schemes within a sector may not have to be cut even though, for the sector as a whole, financial availabilities have been considerably reduced. If the plan has been formulated in a systematic manner and care has been taken to lay down the long-term objectives as well as the *inter se* priorities between sectors and progrmmes the process of pruning will not lead to distortion of the plan. If, however, an effort has not been made to set forth a long-term view of development, pruning of the plan will have to be undertaken in an *ad hoc* manner.

In drawing up the district plan, attention will necessarily have to be focussed mainly on those aspects of development which are to be planned and implemented at the district level. It is, nevertheless, desirable that an attempt should be made in the course of plan formulation to identify the manner in which the schemes adopted for the development of the district will require to be supported by suitable action at the State level, particularly through the extension of the superstructure, the provision of essential inputs and the modernization and modification of administrative or policy frame-work. It would also be desirable that some of the issues which may have emerged in the course of plan formulation and for which no rough and ready solution could be found because of lack of adequate data should be specifically pinpointed with a view to take up, subsequently, suitable surveys and studies to discover the nature and magnitude of the problems and the lines on which solutions would have to be attempted.

Levels of Development

It is anticipated that the formulation of a district plan will start with the preparation of a set of at least four maps, the first, showing the basic physical or topographical characteristics of the district, including elevations by suitable contours, rainfall, rivers, forest area, predominant soil types, depth of underground water strata and area liable to flooding/waterlogging/soil erosion/alkalinity, the second describing the cropping patterns and industrial activities, the third depicting the communication system and the irrigation and power distribution work, and the fourth showing location of administrative centres, rural and urban *mandi* towns, storage godown, primary health centres, human and veterinary hospitals/dispensaries and educational institutions. A comparative study of these will give a fairly good indication of the level of development in different parts of the district and also help in dividing the district into homogeneous sub-regions on the basis of the physio-geographical conditions and the pattern of agricultural and industrial activities. Proper demarcation of sub-regions is of great importance chiefly because the pattern of economic activities as well as the requirements of infrastructure are determined by the character and the basic potentials of the sub-region. If significant variations between different areas within the district are ignored and development programmes are taken up on a uniform basis, the result would not be commensurate with the resources expended for development.

Since the maps will bring out mainly the locational aspects and the broad pattern of development, it is necessary that these should be supplemented by a critical and detailed assessment of the existing socio-economic situation. It is further necessary that an appraisal should be made of the development programmes taken up in the recent past with reference to the conditions and the response in the different sub-regions of the district. Far too often, new programmes are formulated without a careful appraisal of the past experiences and the techno-administrative milieu within which these would have to be operated. Because of certain budgeting procedures, development schemes have to be grouped into plan and non-plan sectors. This, however, does not justify the tendency to ignore the part played by the non-plan development schemes in the process of development. As has been indicated earlier, in any annual or Five-Year Plan, the schemes taken up would largely have a corrective or a supplemental character. It is, therefore, necessary that the entire framework of plan as well as non-plan development schemes should be carefully examined at the time of formulating a new plan.

Assessment of Infrastructural Development

While assessing the existing situation, an important factor to be taken into consideration would be the manner in which the framework of infrastructural facilities and social services are spread over the different sub-regions of the district. The main items of infrastructural to be taken into account would be :

(a) the communication system;
(b) the pattern of marketing facilities;
(c) the storage and processing facilities;
(d) the irrigation and power distribution net-work; and
(e) the structure of banking and credit facilities.

Communication System

The adequacy of a communication system should not be estimated only in terms of kilometres per lakh of a population or per 100 square kilometres of Area. A meaningful study of it would be possible only in relation to the volume and the pattern of movement of agricultural, industrial and consumer goods, the trends in the growth of marketing facilities, the spatial distribution of population and the livelihood pattern of the people living in the area. A rough and ready method of assessing the adequacy of the communication system in different sub-regions will be to find out :

(a) the extent to which villages have been linked with the marketing centres; administrative towns and places catering to educational, medical and veterinary facilities; and
(b) the extent to which smaller centres of marketing and administrative activities have been joined with larger trading or industrial administrative centres.

An efficient communication system ensures that marketing, credit, storage and processing as well as educational and medical facilities are easily accessible in the *integrated* fashion to all the villages in the sub-region or the district and thereby facilitates the development of every area in accordance with the nature of its potentials. The weaknesses of the system would, therefore, have to be judged by identifying the areas where people are not being able to take full advantage of available resources, facilities and services because of the inadequacy of communication of *marketing*.

Marketing Facilities

The adequacy or otherwise of marketing facilities has a very significant effect on the development of an area for, it is through the market that an area is economically integrated with the rest of the economy. Intensification of economic activities cannot be brought about in an area unless it is first linked with appropriate marketing facilities.

In assessing the adequacy or otherwise of marketing facilities, it is best to think of these in terms of a hierarchical structure in which villages are linked with small marketing towns, which in turn are connected with larger marketing and processing centres. Where any tier of this structure is ill-organized or is not well-linked with the next higher level by appropriate means of communication the development of the area gets retarded.

Though the adequacy of marketing facilities at a particular place can really be assessed only with reference to the productive pattern of the area, a general assessment can be attempted on the basis of the availability of the following facilities:

(a) quality of linkages with the villages lying in the hinterland as also with the larger marketing and processing centres;
(b) variety and volume of products handled;
(c) type and capacity of storage space;
(d) availability of banking facilities;
(e) existence of the appropriate grading and quality marketing arrangements; and
(f) existence of regulatory bodies such as marketing committees, etc.

Experience has shown that centres of marketing activities tend to emerge not only as multipurpose servicing centres but also as convenient centres for the dissemination of new ideas as well as for the organization of administrative, educational, medical and veterinary facilities. It is, therefore, important that market centres should be classified in terms of district level markets, sub-regional marketing centres and village markets so as to determine the type of facilities to be provided at various places. If it is sought to accelerate the growth of some of the smaller marketing centres which are already showing signs of development as nodal points of economic activity, the factors responsible for this trend will have to be identified and deliberate action will have to be taken to support the factors playing their part in the process.

Storage Facilities

Existence of storage and processing facilities is often an index of the development of an area. Wherever sizable surpluses are generated as a result of agricultural development, transit as well as long duration storage facilities have to be provided at different marketing centres. Serious problems are likely to arise wherever storage facilities are outstripped by the volume of marketable surpluses or supplies coming in for distribution. The experience of Punjab, Haryana, western U.P. and some of the coastal districts of southern India has given ample proof of the significance of this aspect of infrastructure. There is also the need for looking into the qualitative aspect of the storage facilities in order to plug the considerable losses which occur during storage through destruction by insects, rodents and pests of various kinds. Different crops such as rice, wheat, cotton, potatoes, tobacco, etc. require different types of storage facilities. Therefore, while assessing the adequacy of these facilities in different sub-regions, it would be desirable to examine the position with reference to the productive pattern in the area and the quantum and variety of inputs to be handled on seasonal/annual basis.

Processing Facilities

Quite often the nature of processing facilities determines the direction of agricultural development in an area. It is, therefore, necessary to study the situation in this regard with reference to the points mentioned below:

(a) nature of the existing and the projected pattern of primary production;
(b) quantum of raw products exported;
(c) nature and capacity of the existing processing facilities;
(d) scale of operations and volume of investment required for the processing units in vogue;
(e) technological efficiency and economic viability of the existing units; and
(f) pattern of ownership of processing units.

Canal Irrigation System

Normally the distribution system in respect of irrigation is not taken into account while assessing the nature of infrastructural development in an area. However, when underground water resources in some parts of the district are scarce or are unsuitable for irrigation. It would be necessary to take a view of the irrigation potential, the extent of actual utilization and the spatial distribution of the canal system in order to determine the lines on which canal irrigation facilities should be extended in case of additional availability in the different sub-regions of the district.

Power Distribution

The alignment and capacity of the power distribution network has to be carefully kept in view in order to decide upon the areas in which concentrated efforts should be made in the immediate future to intensify the development of underground water resources or to step up agro-industrial and other industrial activities. In this connection, (a) the alignment and capacity of the existing network for power distribution; (b) the existence of non-reticulated areas; (c) the incidence of over-loading or under-utilization of the power system; and (d) the emerging trends in the demand for power for agricultural, industrial and domestic use in different sub-regions have to be carefully examined.

For the mobilization of private resources and the development of productive or commercial activities the existence of adequate and well distributed *banking and credit facilities* are an important prerequisite. These facilities are being provided by scheduled and non-scheduled banks, branches of co-operative banks, private bankers and money-lenders. In order to make an assessment of the banking and credit structure. It would be necessary to study the spatial location of the various types of facilities and their performances in terms of the volume of business handled, the number of persons covered either through deposits or advance of credit, the integration between credit and marketing and the variety of services provided by them to fulfil the needs of the different sub-regions and marketing/processing centres. Such of the sub-regions which are at present not so well served with these facilities will have to be identified so that steps may be initiated under the plan to provide these.

In the case of private bankers and money-lenders it would be necessary to make some sort of an estimation of the credit needs supplied, the interest rates charged and the business practices followed by them.

Structure of Social Services

While economic infrastructure has a direct bearing on economic development, social services have a significant effect not only on the quality of day-to-day life but also indirectly on the long-term development of the area. It is, therefore, necessary that an assessment should be made of the (a) accessibility, *(b)* adequacy, *(c)* quality, and (d) quantity of social services available in different sub-regions of the district. The main items of social services to be taken into consideration in this connection are:

(a) primary, middle, secondary and higher levels of educational institutions, elementary teacher training institutions and Adult Education Programmes including libraries and reading rooms;
(b) institutions for vocational education including craftsmen train-

ing facilities;
- (c) indoor and outdoor medical, family planning and public health facilities;
- (d) tapped drinking water schemes; and
- (e) veterinary hospitals, stockmen centres, artificial insemination and natural services centres and various types of cattle breeding and up-grading facilities.

Physio-geographical Conditions and Natural Resources

While infrastructural facilities provide the essential prerequisites for the development of an area, the nature and scope of development is determined mainly by physio-geographical or agro-climatic conditions and the availability of natural resources in the area. In view of this, it is necessary to make a careful assessment of the extent to which the natural resources available in the district have been identified and the extent to which effective action has been taken to conserve and to make optimum utilization of these resources.

A realistic assessment on the lines suggested would be possible only if the potentialities of the available natural resources are viewed in the context of the physio-geographic conditions in different sub-regions of the district. As is well-known, land and vegetation resources have a different potential and scope in the hill areas as compared to the plains. Similarly the technology and investment required for the exploitation of water resources in different agro-climatic regions also varies greatly from one area to another.

The main elements of the physio-geographical situation which need to be kept in view are:

- (a) elevation and drainage patterns;
- (b) seasonal variations in temperature and wind velocity and direction;
- (c) pattern of seasonal variations in rainfall;
- (d) areas of poor drainage and areas subject to seasonal flooding; and
- (e) quality and quantity of water in mainstreams.

For the assessment of the potentials and the actual utilization/ conservation of natural resources, the following items would have to be taken into consideration:

(a) *Land* – its qualitative classification, the pattern of its use, its classification in terms of the units of various sizes; its distribution in terms of ownership, its per acre productivity in irrigated and unirrigated conditions and the incidence of soil erosion, waterlogging, high acidity and alkalinity in different sub-regions of the district;

(b) *Water* – availability of surface and underground water for drinking and for irrigation and the current practices in respect of its conservation and optimum utilization in different sub-regions;

(c) *Minerals* – quantitative and qualitative assessment of the variety of minerals available, their accessibility, the existing level of their utilization, the investment structure and the technological and other problems relating to their fuller exploitation and the scope for their primary and secondary processing in the district;

(d) *Vegetation* – the area and productivity under various categories of forest, fuelwood and horticultural plantations and grasslands; the patterns of ownership or management and the level of efficiency in the utilization and replacement of this very important resources; and

(e) *Livestock* – quantitative estimation of the various categories of livestock (including fisheries and poultry) available in the various sub-regions and their qualitative assessment in terms of per unit yield of milk, meat, eggs, wool and draught-power, the existing management and breeding practices and the extent to which the livestock products are being skilfully and efficiently exploited.

Nature and Scope of Economic Activities

From the point of view of a planner, the main aim of studying the existing infrastructure and the available natural resources is to understand the scope for the development and diversification of economic activities to a given area. However, before the future direction and scope of these activities can be determined, it is necessary to study the existing pattern of primary and secondary economic activities in different sub-regions of the district.

Among primary activities, the main items to be kept in view are agriculture (including horticulture), animal husbandry (including dairying, pisciculture and poultry), forestry and mining. All types of agro-industries and other manufacturing industries such as traditional crafts, cottage and small industries, modern small-scale industries based on machinery and power as well as large-scale industries would be taken into consideration in connection with the assessment of secondary activities.

Some of the points to be considered in connection with the assessment of the various economic activities are:

(a) range in the size of the units of production;
(b) variety in the technologies of production;
(c) variety and volume of products and the extent to which these are meant for local consumption;
(d) per unit productivity in terms of land/capital/labour;
(e) employment generated;
(f) the nature and source of raw materials and other inputs required; and
(g) economic activity.

While assessing the scope of the development of economic activities in the district, it is desirable that the incidence of underutilization or the inadequacy of natural resources, infrastructural facilities and productive capacities should be carefully identified. It is also necessary that the problems and scope of future development of a particular economic activity should be assessed especially and separately for the different types and sizes of units in existence. Developments in communications, technology and the nature of demand have quite a different impact on the small farmers, village craftsmen and small entrepreneurs than on their counterparts operating on a much larger scale. Moreover, smaller entrepreneurs/farmers find it very much more difficult to adjust to changes in demand or technology than their more substantial counterparts. Because of this, it is necessary that the measures to be adopted for the development or rehabilitation of different units operating on different scales or with different technologies should be worked out in the context of their specific problems and conditions.

Labour Resources and Employment

Having studied the pattern and scope of economic activities, it would be necessary to take stock of the *labour resources* in an area not only because of their obviously decisive role in socio-economic development but also because their gainful employment as one of the most important objectives of economic planning. While assessing these resources in each sub-region of the district, it is desirable to take a view of:

(a) the population between 15 and 59 years;
(b) its distribution by sex;
(c) the number of workers amongst men and women between 15 and 59 years;
(d) the occupational distribution of workers by type of classification of employment;
(e) the level of productivity per worker and wage structure in different occupations;
(f) the incidence of overcrowding and under-utilization of the available skilled or unskilled labour in certain occupations or community groups; and
(g) the shortages of skilled and semi-skilled craftsmen and workers for different economic activities.

While studying the existing conditions in respect of labour resources and their utilization, it would be desirable that particular attention should be paid to the number of agricultural labourers and the conditions under which they are functioning. In this connection, it would be necessary to examine the caste/class composition of this labour force, their mobility, the wage rates for different agricultural operations, the mode of payment of wages, the incidence of share cropping, the nature of customary practices affecting their relationship with land owners and the extent to which land reforms have stabilized their position as sub-tenants or conferred upon old sub-tenants a title to the lands cultivated by them. It is also necessary that some kind of estimation should be made of the problem of educated unemployment so that steps necessary for their absorption may be taken under the plan.

Institutional Structure and its Performance

In a developing society where a myriad of tasks have to be undertaken to foster a quick enough rate of development, statutory, professional and voluntary institutions of the people have to be assigned many important responsibilities. However, the exact nature and scope of these responsibilities has to be determined on the basis of a careful study and correlation of:

(a) the statutory or constitutional structure;
(b) the objectives;
(c) the coverage and volume of activities;
(d) the representative character;
(e) the financial and administrative resources;
(f) the economic viability; and
(g) the past performance

of the institutions functioning in the area. In this context the *Panchayati Raj*, local self-government and co-operative institutions have a special significance because of the statutory roles already assigned to these and also because these organizations have been made the channels for the flow of sizable resources and inputs for most of the development programmes launched under the plan. These institutions have been organized in a hierarchical pattern. To get a correct idea of the scope of operation of these institutions, it would be desirable to evaluate each tier for its functional efficiency. One of the criteria which should be applied in the course of the assessment of the institutional structure pertains to the self-reliance exhibited by these bodies and the quantum of resources which are locally mobilized by them to supplement the resources provided to them by government or their apex organizations.

Condition of Backward Communities

Since the amelioration of scheduled tribes and other backward communities has been adopted as one of the important objectives of the Fourth Plan, it is necessary that a systematic study should be made of the condition and the problem of these people. For this purpose it would be necessary to identify the areas in which particular community groups have been concentrated and then to analyze the reasons which are responsible for their present condition. In this connection, it is very important to recognize that most of the backward communities and tribal groups have distinctive socio-cultural traits and livelihood patterns because of which generalizations about the problems and the possible lines of development of these groups as a whole have very limited validity. For a meaningful assessment, therefore, it is necessary to take a view of the following aspects of each community group within the spatial context of the area in which they are concentrated:

(a) the availability/ownership and access to natural resources such as land and forests;
(b) livelihood pattern, wage structure and security of tenure;
(c) level of educational and technological development;
(d) quality of housing, medical and public health, water supply, communication, craftsmen training, credit and marketing facilities generally enjoyed;
(e) the degree of integration with the existing institutional structure; and
(f) the framework of cultural mores and social organization and its implications in relation to the development goals envisaged.

In addition to the study of the present situation and problems of certain specified backward communities indicated in the Constitution, it seems desirable that the condition of unskilled labourers in urban areas, traditional craftsmen and other backward groups should also be studied in the manner indicated above.

Assessment of the Existing Schemes

From time to time general schemes have been initiated by the government to meet the diverse problems which have been coming to its notice now and then. Experience has, however, shown that schemes to changing their character have a tendency to go on indefinitely because of the vested interests which develope around them and also because of the failure to institute a regular critical and objective appraisal of the performance of various schemes in the context of the existing needs and circumstances. In view of the limitations of resources under which development plans have to be formulated and implemented, it is necessary that all the schemes whose benefits are not commensurate with the resources expended on them, should be identified so that action should be taken for their modification or replacement. In this connection, it would be desirable to look at all the development schemes irrespective of whether these are operating as plan or non-plan schemes. It would also be necessary to make a special effort to look for the inherent inter-relationships and inter-dependence between schemes and pin-point incidence of both duplication as well as lack of coordination. Moreover, the appraisal of each schemes would have to be made in the light of the local experience. A study of the existing schemes would require as a first step, a critical analysis of their explicit or implicit objectives and the relevance of these in the context of the local priorities. The type of assessment contemplated here will become very much easier if an attempt is made to examine the impact of each scheme in its functional framework, i.e. in relation to the contribution expected from it by way of the fulfilment of a specific role in relation to a community or an economic function. It would have to be examined as to whether appropriate mechanisms exist in each scheme for proper co-ordination with relative schemes in the same or in other sectors of development. It will also have to be ascertained if the phasing of schemes has ensured the synchronisation of events and availabilities required for the successful and smooth implementation of various programmes. Besides all this, the procedures and indicators for periodical reporting of physical progress as also for the systematic and objective evaluation of individual programmes would have to be looked into.

Assessment of Resources

Since plans are formulated essentially to get the maximum benefits from the limited resources available, it is essential that a realistic estimation of the financial, physical or material resources, likely to become available for the district, should be made before laying down the priorities for development and formulating specific programmes/ schemes for their implementation.

In regard to the assessment of physical or material resources, it would be desirable to take into consideration the volume of the existing and the projected local availabilities in terms of minerals, agricultural products, irrigation and power, construction materials as well as certain essential industrial products such as cotton, woollen, yarn, man-made fibres, etc. The specific items whose availability from within or without the district is to be estimated will have to be determined on the basis of the requirements of the predominant pattern of economic activities being carried on in the district.

While estimating financial resources, it would be necessary to assess the likely availability of these from within as well as outside the district. How often, while estimating local area plans, there is a tendency to take into account only those resources which, through government, co-operative or institutional channels, are likely to flow from outside the area. This naturally leads to the formulation of wholly unrealistic plans, since in most of the economic activities, the resources expended by private citizens and their institutions form the bulk of investment. When these private or institutional resources are taken into account, there is a tendency to exclude from the plan the measures required for augmenting the rate of savings and for channelling available investments into productive activities. Once the significance of local resources is realized and their planned utilization is made an integral objective of local plans, the role of *Panchayati Raj* co-operative and local self-governments and other local institutions will also come to be adequately appreciated and every effort will be made to involve them in the process of planning as well as programme implementation. It is, therefore, desirable that the emerging trends in respect of savings and investments by private individuals, co-operatives as well as banking institutions should be studied and carefully articulated.

In order to ensure that the process of planning at the district level is undertaken on a rational and realistic basis, it is necessary that an element of flexibility and resources consciousness should be introduced at the district level. Unless this is done, district plans will remain compilations of unintegrated and impossible demands. To achieve this, State governments should classify schemes and allocate funds on the basis of their nature and advisability in the matter of planning as well as execution. This, however, is not to be done in a mechanical fashion merely by the allotment of funds for pre-determined schemes already included in the State plan. The very idea of formulating district plans really is to ensure that the character and approach to the State plans would be determined by the potential problems and priorities identified in the district plans. The district plans would, therefore, have to set forth a long-term perspective of development as well as the immediate requirements for the next five-year or one-year period. The State governments would examine the short- and long-term requirements of the districts for drawing up integrated State plans and thereafter they would indicate the quantum of resources which would be available to each district during the next five-year or one-year period. On the basis of these indications, the expectations of private investment and the resources likely to be raised by local bodies, Panchayati Raj Institutions and co-operatives, the districts would have to finalize their five-year and one-year operational plans.

So far as the annual plans are concerned, the formulation of these would be a two-way process, both at the State and district levels. Each district would report to the State headquarters the estimated expenditure and progress of work in the current year as well as the requirements for the next year and this will form the basis for the formulation of the annual plan of the State. After the State plan is finalized on this basis, the State government would indicate the availability of resources to the district for the coming year which would, in their turn, work out the phasing and priorities of various programmes for the annual plan of the district in the light of available resources.

PLANNING FOR DEVELOPMENT

The purpose behind the formulation of a district plan is to lay down an operational framework of future action. For this, it would be necessary to make a critical assessment of the existing situation and thereafter to formulate integrated strategies for further development for each sub-region and for the district as a whole on the basis of the available resources and potentials, the nature of local needs and problems, the trends of development already in evidence, the priorities assigned to different socio-economic activities and the framework of basic objectives adopted for the State or the country as a whole.

The lines on which a given sub-region could be developed is determined by the study and co-relation of the following factors:

(a) Physio-geographical characteristics such as elevation, location, general topography, climatic conditions, rainfall, drainage etc.;
(b) quality, quantity and variety of natural resources available in the area;
(c) level of development and coverage of infrastructural facilities;
(d) nature and variety of primary and secondary economic activities;
(e) availability of human resources, technological skills and entrepreneurial talent;
(f) quantum of financial resources locally and externally available, and
(g) the organizational and institutional framework in existence in the area.

Marked variation in respect of potentials pertaining to anyone of these factors necessarily result in the emergence of different patterns of economic activities and, therefore, requires a different type of infrastructural development and a different distribution of investment resources. If a particular area has a lot of valuable and easily accessible mineral resources, the strategy for its long-term development will have to be substantially different from the strategy for an area which has a preponderance of natural vegetation. Similarly, for an area which has a highly developed urban infrastructure, the development prospects will have to be conceived differently than for another area which has poorly developed infrastructure combined with a surplus of labour resources. The most difficult task faced by a planner is to decide as to what broad strategies of development should be adopted in respect of each sub-region in the district and how the different activities and measures to be taken up in the immediate future should be organized to subserve the long-term strategy adopted for an area.

While determining the specific strategy for each sub-region, four inter-related objectives have to be kept in view. These are:

(a) increase in the per unit productivity;
(b) better utilization/conservation of natural resources;
(c) more equitable distribution of the benefits of development between different areas and communities through more rational location of facilities and services; and
(d) the expansion and diversification of employment opportunities.

In order to work out the details of the development strategies for different sub-regions, the first step to be taken is to identify the economic activities such as agriculture, forestry, pisciculture or small industries which would occupy the central position in the plan of development of the area. The subsidiary economic activities to be undertaken and the organization and provision of infrastructural facilities and services depend largely upon the nature of basic activities which would be developed in an area. In a sub-region where agriculture would be the main economic activity, greater attention would have to be paid to the provision of irrigation and the establishment of storage, credit, processing and marketing facilities whereas these factors would have quite a different significance in an area whose development is likely to depend more substantially on the establishment of mining and manufacturing activities. The simplest procedure for working out the basic strategy and the development plan for an area would be on the following steps:

(i) Identify the main economic activities to be developed;
(ii) list the subsidiary, supplemental additional activities to be promoted;
(iii) determine within a scheme of priorities the needs of the main economic activities in terms of infrastructural facilities, inputs and services;
(iv) lay down in order of importance the specific requirements of the subsidiary, supplementary or additional activities;
(v) work out the measures to be taken for the proper utilization/ conservation of natural resources;
(vi) indicate the minimum requirements of backward areas and communities;
(vii) compare the requirements listed under items (iii), (iv), (v) and (vi) above, with whatever is already available on the ground and thereafter work out the additional facilities, inputs or services to be arranged for various activities, areas or communities;
(viii) correlate the requirements listed under items (vii) and determine the manner in which these may be located, integrated and organized spatially and functionally with the least cost and the largest coverage; and
(ix) determine the *inter se* importance of the measures or activities to be undertaken in accordance with the locational and organizational plan worked out under item (viii).

Once a locational and organizational plan of the main and subsidiary or additional activities to be promoted and the facilities, services and inputs to be provided therefor have been worked out within a scheme of priorities, the next step to be taken could be to re-cast the plan in accordance with the departmental structure by allotting responsibilities to various departments and suggesting the order of priorities and time schedule to be followed in the implementation of the various programmes.

While drawing up a programme for the development of specific activities, it would be desirable to keep two things in view. The first is always to look at specific activities, not as unrelated or individual items by themselves but in terms of their inter-relationship with other related, subsidiary or supplementary activities and to draw up plans for all the related activities in an integrated manner.

The second point to be borne in mind is that an economic activity cannot be seen in its true perspective unless it is seen in a dynamic context, that is, in the context of a situation in which, for a variety or reasons, changes are constantly taking place in respect not only of other economic activities but also in respect of the availability of natural resources, infrastructural facilities and the administrative structure. The developments in respect of these factors will be influenced and will also affect the developments under various economic activities.

The idea of inter-action put forward here may be illustrated by the following examples:

(a) If a cold storage is established in an area, there may immediately be a sizable expansion of not only in the area under potatoes but also in the consumption of fertilizers and the area under irrigation;

(b) If there is a large scale expansion of sheep - rearing in a particular area, it might lead in the long run to an increase in the tempo of activity in carding, spinning as well as weaving industries;

(c) If the distribution network for power is extended to a new area, it may result very soon in a sizable increase in minor irrigation facilities and consequently in agricultural production which would in turn give rise to the demand for the improvement of facilities for communication, marketing, credit, etc.

(d) If a rural hinterland is integrated with the marketing complex by the construction of a bridge of a link road, the entire cropping pattern of the area might change and supplemental programmes like dairying, poultry etc. may also receive a considerable fillip.

Development of Agriculture

While planning for the development of agriculture, it is necessary first of all to take into account the basic conditions under which it is carried on in different sub-regions of the district. These are:

(i) General climate and the volume and seasonal distribution of rainfall;

(ii) elevation, general topography and the pattern of drainage;

(iii) availability and quality of land resources;

(iv) availability of easily accessible and suitable surface and underground water;

(v) pattern of local consumption;
(vi) availability of fertilizers and pesticides as also of communication, marketing, storage, processing and credit facilities;
(vii) proximity to centres of consumption of high value agricultural products;
(viii) patterns of tenure and size of holdings; and
(ix) availability of appropriate techniques for the production of various crops.

A careful consideration of the above-mentioned factors would give a reasonable idea of the appropriateness of the existing pattern of agriculture and also of the potentials which exist for the carrying out agriculture on a more extensive or intensive scale. In this regard, it would be useful to keep the following objectives generally in view with reference to the different sub-regions of the district:

(a) better utilization of facilities by (i) multi-cropping and (ii) introduction of better techniques of production such as high yielding programmes etc.;
(b) introduction of suitable cropping patterns in relation to the quality of soils, the agro-climatic conditions, the availability of irrigation facilities and inputs and labour resources and the nature of marketing and communication facilities;
(c) increase in the productivity of unirrigated land through better soil and water conservation practices as also through the introduction of more suitable cropping patterns; and
(d) improvement of the economy of small farmers through the liberalization of credit and other facilities and also through the provisions, where possible of irrigation facilities and other inputs specifically for this class of farmers.

Farm Forestry and Grassland Development

For Farm Forestry and Grassland Development planning programmes the main point to be kept in view relates to the availability of uncultivated wastelands. It is highly unlikely that the land which has already been brought under agriculture would under any circumstances be taken away from it and put up either under miscellaneous tree crops and fuelwood plantations or reserved for grassland development. In the case of farm forestry the basic constraints which have to be kept in view are:

(a) the pattern of ownership of wastelands;
(b) quality of wasteland;
(c) cost of planting and raising of fuelwood and scrub forest plantations and the return per acre accruing through sale of the products;
(d) technical assistance and financial and other incentives available to individuals, *Panchayats*, etc. in support of farm forestry; and
(e) organizational pattern for protection and utilization.

In the case of grassland development also, the regulatory measures and the incentives in the shape of suitable loans, subsidies and concessions would play a significant part. The return which would accrue from grasslands would be determined largely by the quality of milch cattle found in the area and the extent to which dairying and sheep rearing have become or are likely to become established as widespread commercial activities. It would be highly desirable to integrate the work of grassland development with the work of the Soil Conservation Department which, at present, is looking after the selection and extension of suitable grasses in area subject to soil erosion.

Horticulture

Horticultural activities are the important means of diversifying the pattern of production as also of gainfully combining an economic activity with soil conservation measures. The factors which influence the development of this activity are:

(a) the availability of suitable land and other agro-climatic conditions;
(b) distance from centres of consumption and quality of communication links with these centres;
(c) availability and quality of credit, marketing, storage and processing facilities;
(d) availability of reliable plant material, technical assistance (including training facilities) and plant protection services; and
(e) the nature of incentives by way of loans, grant-in-aid, etc., provided to encourage horticultural development.

Besides looking into the above points, it would also be necessary to examine carefully the relative economic benefits of various species of fruit plantations and their susceptibility to plant diseases before laying down the lines for the development of horticulture.

Other Supplemental Activities

The planning of other supplemental activities such as animal husbandry, dairying, poultry farming, pisciculture and sheep and pig rearing must be guided not only by the assessment of the economic returns expected from investment in these programmes but also by employment opportunities which are likely to be generated by these programmes. So far these programmes have not made enough headway either as supplemental (and part-time) programmes or as fully commercialized activities. This is partly because of the tendency to underestimate the technological and managerial problems pertaining to these activities, and partly because of the attempt to promote these in all areas and all classes of the people without making a comparison between the returns expected from these activities and the returns likely to accrue from agriculture and other economic activities in particular area. In order, therefore, to take a balanced view of the potentials of these supplemental activities, it is essential that the agro-climatic conditions, availability and productivity of land resources, the class, caste and vocational composition of local population, and the availability of surplus labour resources should be taken into consideration. It would also be essential to chalk out separate schemes for the promotion of these activities as supplemental or specialized commercial programmes and to take an integrated view of the support which would have to be provided for these in terms of appropriate transportation, credit, storage, grading processing, marketing and training facilities.

Secondary Activities

In the case of secondary activities, planning at the district level would usually relate to handicrafts, village and cottage industries and modern small-scale industries. These activities can play a very significant part in the economic growth of an area because of their capacity not only to provide essential inputs and services for primary activities but also to expand and diversity the employment opportunities for the people of the area. For these reasons, it is necessary to undertake special measures to rehabilitate languishing crafts and industries. The potentials for the development of an industry in an area are determined largely by the following factors;

(a) nature and volume of the local and external demand for agricultural inputs and equipment, housing prerequisites and consumer goods;
(b) availability of agricultural and other raw materials;
(c) availability of labour skills entrepreneurial talent and viable technologies of production on a scale feasible in a given set of local conditions;
(d) vocational mobility of labour engaged in traditional arts and crafts;
(e) availability of capital resources; and
(f) the nature of infrastructural facilities available in respect of communications, marketing, credit and banking, power and water supply and provision of common processing facilities.

It is very important that viability and the specific requirements for the development of each industry should be worked out before the potentials of its development and the programmes for its expansion are worked out at the districts level. The main objectives to be kept in view in connection with the development of industries are:

(i) greater and more efficient utilization of available physical, human and investment resources;
(ii) expansion and diversification of employment; and
(iii) location of industries in a manner which will lead to the dispersal of services and availabilities all over the district and help in arresting the trend towards the concentration of industries around metropolitan areas.

In order to ensure that the above objectives are achieved, measures indicated below would have to be taken:

(i) Identification and location of industries at growth centres where marketing, processing, credit, power and water supply facilities are already available;
(ii) demonstration of improved production techniques through pilot projects;

(iii) dissemination of improved technical and managerial know-how through short- and long-term training;
(iv) more equitable distribution of raw materials;
(v) liberalization of credit facilities; and
(vi) extension of grading, quality marking and marketing facilities.

Development of the Economic Infrastructure

While discussing the manner in which development of various economic activities should be planned, mention has repeatedly been made of the various items of infrastructure whose development would have to be taken into consideration while considering for the extension and the qualitative improvement of each of these infrastructural facilities. An integrated view should be taken of the development envisaged in respect of various economic activities and the measures contemplated under the plan in respect of other elements of infrastructure as well as other factors of development. To derive maximum benefits from investment, efforts would have to be made to avoid the duplication of these facilities for individual economic functions. Particular attention must be paid to the locational aspects of infrastructural facilities and efforts made to locate and organize them in such a manner that these would serve the needs of a large number or activities over as wide an area as possible. Care has also to be taken to ensure that the economic activities derive full benefits from available network of infrastructural facilities. While planning the development of infrastructure, it is necessary to take a dynamic view of economic activities and to initiate developments in infrastructure which would take care not only of the needs of the existing activities, but also of the activities which, it can be reasonably assessed, will come to be established in another five or ten years.

Special attention has to be paid to roads since these operate as the main integrative feature in the economic life of an area and have a decisive influence on the growth and location of marketing, storage and processing facilities. While planning for the improvement and the augmentation of the network of roads it would be necessary to take into account not only the already developed centres of economic, social and administrative activity but also the needs of areas or centres whose growth is being thwarted because of lack of adequate communications. In respect of other elements of infrastructure also, the nature of developments envisaged under the plan would be determined by the lacunae which may have been identified while assessing the existing economic situation and the requirements which might have emerged as a result of the developments planned in respect of the various economic activities, natural resources and backward areas/classes. The investments on infrastructural development would be most effectively utilized if as a result of planned efforts, the various facilities for marketing, storage, credit, processing and servicing come to be available in an integrated manner at certain focal points centrally placed with reference to their hinterlands. This will reduce the pressure on communication and transport facilities and will also help in the establishment of well-dispersed urban centres all over the area of the district.

Social Services

In the case of social services, such as general and technical education, medical and public health, drinking water and veterinary facilities, more attention will have to be paid to the qualitative improvement of the existing facilities, as also to the more equable distribution of whatever additional facilities might be provided under the plan, in determining the location of social services also, the objective must be to establish these at certain focal points of growth which are centrally placed with reference to the villages around them.

Education

Since educational facilities have a very important bearing on the economic life of an area or community, their development will have to be planned with particular care. For this it would be necessary to:

(a) assess the comparative backwardness of different areas or communities in terms of the availability of facilities for primary, middle, secondary and higher level vocational and adult education as well as libraries and reading rooms;

(b) take a view of the facilities available to educational institutions in terms of buildings, laboratories, play-grounds, school-farms, libraries etc.;

(c) study the problem of under-utilization of the existing institutions, facilities and equipment;

(d) relate the problems and trends of economic development and the consequent generation of employment opportunities with the availability of appropriately trained and suitably oriented young men and women and the existing structure and capacity of educational and vocational institutions (for students as well as non-student youth);

(e) indicate, on the basis of objective principles in respect of coverage as well as location, the areas and directions in which the provision of facilities for primary, middle, secondary, vocational and adult education and elementary school teachers training should be augmented/improved on a priority basis;

(f) evolve a pattern for the optimal utilization and sharing of available facilities and equipment through the development of school complexes;

(g) identify the institutional and other sources and assess the availability of local resources likely to become available from these for the provision of essential facilities and equipment and meeting non-teacher costs for formal and informal education/training;

(h) identify the ways in which the various types of educational institutions could provide services to the community (especially non-student youth) and thereby get organically integrated with the life of the community; and

(i) prepare a phased programme setting forth the *inter se* priorities between different tiers and types of formal and informal education and plan the measures for resources mobilization and the machinery and mechanics of implementation.

Since the resources available for social services are so limited, it seems desirable that an attempt should be made to evolve some principles for the proper location of all types of social service facilities and for the sharing of the more expensive equipment and facilities (such as gymnasia, playgrounds, laboratories, X-ray equipment, etc.) between different institutions located within a convenient distance. In the organization and maintenance of these social services, the voluntary efforts of the people can play a very significant role. Therefore, while planning for the expansion of these services, it would be desirable to set forth measures through which public support would be enlisted and financial resources would be mobilised.

Natural Resources

From this point of view of long-term development, it is important that suitable measures should be taken to ensure that the natural resources available in an area are not frittered away through negligence or misutilization. It has already been suggested that while planning for the development of economic activities, measures should be taken to bring about more efficient utilization of the natural resources. Some of these measures involve the changing of the cropping patterns as well as the introduction of better production techniques. In many areas adequate attention has not been paid, in the past, to the need for the conservation of top soil surface water and vegetative resources. Measures for the management/expansion of reserved forests, scrub forests, fuelwood plantations and grasslands would have to receive particular attention and suitable legislative as well as administrative measures would have to be taken to afford adequate protection to these dwindling resources. Above all, efforts must be made to co-ordinate the activities of various departments concerned with the promotion of development of economic activities, viz. agriculture or horticulture, with the work of the departments concerned with the development and conservation of natural resources so as to ensure that they would not operate at cross purposes.

Opportunities for Employment

From the point of view of distribution of economic resources, it is important that some attention should be paid to the provision of adequate and diversified employment opportunities in the districts. The problem of unemployment is quite complex in character because it covers a variety of groups whose educational and social background traditional role, skills and aspirations differ widely from one another. For the sake of convenience, it would be worthwhile devising measures separately in respect of the educated unemployed, the skilled craftsmen and the unskilled labour in rural and urban areas. So far as the first two categories are concerned, employment opportunities for them would largely be a function of the general tempo of economic development in an area which could be accelerated to some extent by the promotion of manufacturing, processing and servicing activities particularly on small-scale basis. So far as the unskilled labour in the rural areas is concerned, employment opportunities would be generated for them either in agriculture through more intensive cropping practices and multi-cropping or through taking up large-scale communication, irrigation and land development programmes. In areas which have an economic problem of natural calamities, it is not usual to take up relief programmes for providing employment for scarcity stricken people. These programmes have often to be taken up on an *ad hoc* basis which sometimes leads to inefficient utilization of financial as well as human resources. It is, therefore, desirable that for areas affected by natural calamities as also for other areas faced with an acute problem of unemployment and under-employment, a long-term view should be taken of the requirements of the communication and irrigation system as also of the need for soil and water conservation measures in order to prepare schemes which would ensure more optimum utilization of the human resources.

Institutional Structure

For the most part, the nature and performance of the institutional structure is at present determined by the statutory and administrative policies being followed at the State level. Both the *Panchayati Raj* and the co-operative bodies have been operating, by and large, as the agents of the State government and as the channels of financial, physical and administrative resources. As a result of this, the tiers closest to the ground level have not been given the importance they deserve. The quantum of resources raised at the local level and the managerial and administrative acumen acquired by the non-officals running these institutions have also not been adequate in some of the States. Adequate attention has also not been paid to the up-grading of the techniques for planning and programme implementation by these bodies. Therefore, perhaps, the first step in the development of the potentials of the institutional structure would be to work out in detail the specific activities which would be performed by these bodies over the next five-year or one-year period and, thereafter, chalk out the measures which would have to be taken to support these activities in terms of resources mobilization training of personnel and improvement in the procedures for decision-making, review and internal financial control. It is expected that in the course of this type of detailed planning for these institutions, the lacunae, if any, in their statutory, financial or administrative structure will also be properly identified and this would enable the States to take suitable action in this connection.

Backward Communities

While considering the measures to be taken for the improvement of the levels of living of the backward communities, it would be necessary to study:

(i) their occupational pattern;
(ii) their educational and technical competence;
(iii) the availability of economic means of production (such as land and forest rights) and infrastructural facilities and social services to them; and
(iv) the manner in which these resources and facilities could be augmented for their benefit.

In this context, particular attention will have to be paid to the formulation of appropriate procedures which would ensure easy flow of facilities, services and resources to the members of these communities. In case any schemes for the resettlement of tribal or backward communities and their involvement in specific agricultural or industrial activities are contemplated, these will have to be drawn up after full consideration of the cultural mores, the social organization and the existing livelihood patterns current amongst these communities. This is necessary because the backward and tribal communities find it much more difficult that other cultural groups to adapt themselves to new physical, organizational or technological situations.

It is expected that a number of supplemental programmes for the provision of additional facilities or services for the backward communities would have to be started in certain places. It is, however, not to be assumed that for this reason these communities are to be debarred from the benefits which would otherwise accrue to them from the normal programmes meant for everybody. While operating different schemes those responsible for their execution have been enjoined to give preference to the less well-to-do members of the community as compared to these who already have more resources at their command. It, therefore, follows that under the normal programmes also all these communities should receive priority.

Integration of Department and Institutional Plans

An important aspect of plan formulation at the district level would be the integration of the plans of local self-government bodies, *Panchayati Raj* institutions, co-operative organizations and government departments. Some attention has been paid in the past to the preparation of plans for Metropolitan Areas at the time of the formulation of five-year/annual plans of States. No attempt has, however, been made so far to get the municipalities, Notified and Town Area Committees to draw up integrated one-year or five-year programmes to coincide and dovetail with the activities envisaged in the State plans under different sectors or for different areas. As a result the process of urbanization, especially through the emergence of smaller townships, has been going on in a haphazard fashion. Most of the small town have been expanding in narrow strips along the roads which provide little scope for the provision of civic amenities and the development of industries and increase the burden on the communication and transport system. This has proved a hindrance not only in the dispersal of economic activities (especially industrialization) but has also led to the creation of bottlenecks in the provision of marketing, storage, credit, processing and servicing facilities for the orderly and even development of rural areas. Moreover, there have often been long time lags between the establishment of industries and the growth of cities and the production of agricultural raw materials and essential food, vegetable, poultry and dairy products in the hinterlands to serve the growing needs of these urban centres. It is, therefore, desirable that a deliberate attempt should be made to correlate the needs and the development programmes of the rural and the urban areas.

In the case of *Panchayati Raj* bodies generally, there has been adequate involvement in the planning process. However, in those States in which *Panchayati Raj* bodies have been given substantial powers to raise resources and set-up new services and facilities, it would be necessary to ensure that there is no duplication between them and the State sector. It will also have to be ensured that the plans of co-operatives as well as local units of various financing departmental institutions are also drawn up keeping in view the projections in respect of economic activities envisaged under district plans. This will be possible only if there is considerable consultation not only after the plans have already been framed but also before and during the process of programme formulation. Without this kind of consultation, it is possible that unduly ambitious programmes will get drawn up for Agriculture, Minor Irrigation, Dairying, Small Industries, etc., which would assume the provision of resources on the part of these institutions far in excess of their capability either to mobilize on the local level or to attract and channellize externally.

Even though a great deal has been done in recent years to strengthen the existing institutional or organizational structure, there are still many aspects of development which could be given greater support by the organization of suitable voluntary or statutory institutions. For instance, in the identification and promotion of technological innovations, voluntary organizations of artisans, craftsmen and small scale entrepreneurs can play a very significant part. Similarly, the organization of land and water development boards in river valley areas could prove very beneficial in organizing the integrated and optimum utilization of these resources. These illustrations have been given mainly to stress that the scope of organizational innovations has by no means been exhausted. As time passes and new problems come to the surface, innovations and modifications in the existing structure of institutions and developmental organization will have to be introduced. It is, therefore, desirable that while formulating district plans, the weaknesses and lacunae in this respect should be carefully identified and suitable measures taken to strengthen the existing structure.

SUGGESTIVE FORMAT FOR DISTRICT PLAN

Section I: Assessment of the Existing Situation

Chapter I. Introduction – Giving a brief account of the physio-geographical conditions in the different sub-regions of the district in terms of elevation, general topography, rainfall, rivers and streams, drainage, soil structure, vegetation, flora and fauna, the composition and distribution of population in terms of rural/urban habitations and vocations, the special economic, social or cultural characteristics of the district and the level of development in different sub-regions of the district.

Chapter II. Infrastructure and Social Services – Describing the variety, coverage and performance of the facilities and social services available in the various sub-regions of the district, with particular reference, in the case of economic infrastructure, to communication, marketing, credit, storage, processing and servicing facilities as well as to the distributive network of power and irrigation system, and in the case of social services, to the facilities for education, vocational training, medical, public health and veterinary assistance and the propagation and demonstration of new ideas about agriculture, industries etc.

Chapter III. Natural Resources – Describing their availability in the different sub-regions of the district, indicating the extent to which these are being properly conserved and efficiently utilized.

Chapter IV. Administrative and Institutional Structure – Giving an account of the administrative structure and the interrelationship between different departmental wings and the situal in respect of the delegation of authority in the planning and execution of various programmes. Also describing the functions, structure, financial viability and record of performance of the important statutory and voluntary institutions, particularly *Panchayati Raj* bodies, local self-government, institutions and co-operatives.

Chapter V. Economic Activities – Describing the variety of primary and secondary economic activities going on in different sub-regions of the district and bringing out their present level of development, their technological efficiency and the problems faced by them particularly with reference to marketing, credit, storage processing, servicing and input-supply facilities and the availability of requisite raw materials, skilled labour and entrepreneurial resources.

Chapter VI. Problems of Employment – Analyzing the position regarding the present availability and the emerging trends of employment in primary and secondary sectors in relation to the number of people (particularly landless labourers, craftsmen and unskilled urban labour) available for employment, their level of technological sophistication and the adequacy or otherwise of their real or monetary wages.

Chapter VII. Problems of Backward Communities – Describing the peculiarities of their socio-cultural organization, their livelihood pattern, their rights to use of land and forest resources, the level of educational and technological proficiency attained by them and their access to the facilities and services provided by the Government and other developmental institutions.

Chapter VIII. Critical appraisal of the on-going development schemes – Plan and non-plan, in the context of economic and social objectives/activities these are to subserve, with a view to determine which of these should be continued/enlarged with or without modifications.

Chapter IX. Local Mobilization of Resources – Estimating the local resources likely to be available from the private and institutional sources for different programmes during the next five-year/one year period.

Chapter X. Programmes for Backward Communities – Indicating the measures proposed for the accelerated and integrated development of the backward communities, scheduled castes and the landless or unskilled labourers inhabiting the district.

Section II: Planning for Development

Chapter XI. The Long-term Perspective – Indicating the prospects for different sub-regions based on the present trends of economic development, the availability of natural resources present and the projected availability of infrastructural facilities and inputs, the emerging trends in the technologies of production particularly with reference to unit-size of production. Also a tentative identification of the large villages/towns/cities which are likely to emerge as the centres of trade, commerce, transport network and manufacturing activities.

Chapter XII. Priorities for the District Plan – Stating the *inter se* priorities to be accorded in various sub-regions of the district to the promotion of different economic activities in the long-term as well as the short-term perspective.

Chapter XIII. Programmes for Development –Describing the integrated strategy for different sub-regions to be followed during the plan period, indicating the interaction of various factors or programmes envisaged and setting forth the specific steps to be taken to promote the development of various economic activities and the welfare of backward areas/communities, by way of:

(i) extending infrastructural facilities;
(ii) promoting better utilization/conservation of natural resources;
(iii) providing, re-organizing or re-locating specific social services; and
(iv) strengthening the administrative and institutional structure.

Chapter XIV. Resources for the Plan – Giving the year to year phasing of the physical, financial and specialized labour requirements for the measures envisaged under the plan and the manner in which these would be mobilized internally or externally.

Chapter XV. Issues for the State Government – Indicating the action required at the State level to promote the development of the district, with particular reference to the State superstructure and the statutory, fiscal and administrative policies regulating various economic activities, institutions, land tenure and employment.

10

DETERMINING THE SECTORAL-MIX FOR INTEGRATED DEVELOPMENT

K.V. SUNDARAM

Introduction

THE MOST important problem in all planning activities is how to ultimately integrate the various projects and programmes in the different sectors. Not only the projects and programmes within each sector have to be integrated but such integration has also to be brought about between different sectors. While there is no standard way of achieving such integration, certain general guidelines could be given.

Usually it is stated that the sectoral priorities in an area development plan should, by and large, conform to the overall pattern envisaged at the State level; but in practice it is possible that due to diversified local conditions, each individual area may not necessarily follow these broad sectoral allocations and may have to evolve their own pattern to suit their local conditions. This may result in some distortion of the overall pattern envisaged in the State plan. Some deviation from the overall pattern cannot be helped and must be deemex inevitable. All that can be done is to see that a maximum synchronization of sectoral priorities are achieved in the planning exercises at different area levels.

Integrated Approach

Basic Principles

Integration is a complicated task. It is necessary in the first instance to comprehend the full meaning of integration and the basic principles underlying the integrated approach to area development. These principles may be broadly stated as follows:

1. The very nature of the process of area development and the size of the problem of framing economic and social progress in rural and urban areas in a particular area, say a district, requires that action be taken on several fronts simultaneously and not independently of each other. Hence, programmes of agriculture, minor irrigation, soil conservation, grass land development, roads, education and training, health and nutrition, community development, etc., should not be planned and implemented each in isolation and without consideration of the implications that development programmes for one area might have for the others.
2. The concept of the integrated approach in the context of area development means an "integral" approach in the sense that it is a highly structural and systematic exercise in which each of the components in the system of development can be understood as important and appreciated for the part which they play individually and collectively. In this sense the concept of integration differs from the "harmonization" of plans or the "co-operation" of various agencies or even the "administrative co-ordination" of existing plans and programmes.
3. Integration is not something which could be manipulated at a final stage by pruning something here or increasing something there, but must come as a conscious exercise carried on right from the time of inception of an idea/scheme and must be carried through to completion.
4. The concept of integration implies establishing proper linkages, complementarities and sequences among various programmes and sectors and envisaging development in its totality.

Types of Integration

Multi-level Integration

This would mean that the plan at any area level has to be integrated with the plans at the higher and lower area levels. Thus, when a plan at district level is prepared (as is the case for the drought prone area programme), the district plan should be dovetailed into the plans at the higher area levels, i.e., the regional plan (if there is one), the State plan and the National plan. The district plan should also dovetail the plans at the lower area levels, i.e., the block and village levels. Such integration would be effective only if there is considerable consultation among the planning bodies at different levels both before and during the process of programme formulation.

Sectoral and Inter-sectoral Integration

Socio-economic development is more or less an organic process and different sectors, sub-sectors and schemes have to be consistently adjusted in a cohesive and unified manner to attain a structural balance of the plan. For this purpose, several consistency checks will have to be introduced. Three main types of consistency checks may be mentioned in this connection.

1. *Consistency in Financial Outlays and Physical Targets*: For major schemes, it must be checked to see that the financial outlays arrived at are in accordance with standard unit cost norms evolved in the various departments. It is also necessary to see whether the physical targets mentioned in the plan are also in accordance with the cost norms.

2. *Internal Inconsistency of the Various Physical Targets and the Sectoral Programmes*: It would be necessary for instance to see if the requirements of the inputs for a targeted output are properly provided as per norm. The physical inputs and outputs and the various programmes should also be inter-linked properly. For example, the supply of improved seeds, fertilizers and irrigation should be linked up quantitatively with the additional production targets of different crops. This can be done for instance by using the yardsticks prepared by Agriculture Department. Similarly, the credit requirements should be linked up with the cropping pattern that is suggested. The warehousing, marketing and road development programmes should be linked up with the additional production potential. In the same manner, the establishment and development of processing industries should be linked up with the local production levels. In social services too there is a necessity to maintain consistency in planning. For example, in any programme of universalization of primary education care has to be taken to ensure that sufficient intake capacity or facilities are available

in the secondary education to absorb larger off take from primary schools. Thus, the programme of increasing primary education cannot be taken up in isolation or without considering the development of secondary education. Similarly, if intake capacity in the secondary schools is increased, it logically leads to the fact that such capacity in higher and technical education is also adequately provided for with consideration to due time lag. Moreover, in primary education, if the number of schools is to be increased, steps will have to be taken to ensure that adequate number of trained teachers are available. This would mean that the programme of training of teachers will have to be given equal priority if real results for universalization of primary education are to be achieved.

3. *Sector to Sector Consistency*: The above examples deal with problem of consistency within a single sector. Consistency *between* sectors is equally important. Non-agricultural development, for instance agro-industrial development, has to be closely related to agricultural development. Similarly, industrial development has to be related to he provision of infrastructure like transport and communications, power, etc., and both non-agriculture and agricultural developments have to be supported by social services. In this way proper inter sectoral linkages have also got to be established.

Sectoral-Spatial Integration

This implies horizontal integration of sectoral programmes in which location of specific activities are given due and proper attention and spatial overlaps are avoided. Achieving spatial integration requires analysis of location related to the distribution of production and population. Land-use considerations become important in such integration.

Rural-Urban Integration

The concept of integrated area development pre-supposes the recognition of a rural-urban continuum, and implies that the rural areas cannot be considered in isolation, but in relation; to the urban counterpart, for it is in this sense that problems of rural-urban migration, rural exodus and agricultural and industrial development can be tackled. Development must be harmonious in such a manner that both the rural and urban sectors can complement each other. This would need that the plans of urban local bodies have to be integrated with those of the Panchayati Raj Institutions. Very little attempt has been made so far to get the urban local bodies to draw up integrated five-year programmes to coincide and dovetail with the activities envisaged in the State plans under different sectors or for different areas. Thus, urban growth and the requirements for the provision of marketing, storage, credit, processing and servicing facilities for the orderly and even development of rural areas have never matched.

Avoiding Overlapping among the Programmes

It must be understood that the schemes proposed under area planning have been conceived only as an additive to the other plan and non-plan schemes proposed in the district. Hence, in this case the programmes envisaged under Drought Prone Area Programme (DPAP) have to be integrated with other relevant programmes in the districts. Among these other programmes there are certain other similar central programmes/schemes which are operating in all or some of the drought prone areas. Among them, mention may be made of (a) desert development programmes; (b) pilot projects on dry land farming; (c) research programmes of Central Arid Zone Institute; and (d) All-India Co-ordinated Dry Land Farming Research Project. Integration of all these programmes in this context would mean ensuring that the schemes do not overlap but mutually complement and supplement each other. Thus, for example, if it is found that adequate outlays have already been provided for certain sector under other schemes, it may be desirable to use funds under DPAP for augmenting infrastructure and extension programmes different from the one for which the funds have already been provided.

Determining the Sectoral-mix in Area Development Planning

The planning for drought prone districts is a specialized kind of area planning and here the pattern of sectoral allocation has necessarily to be different from the overall pattern of outlays in the State sector. The sectors which should be of crucial significance in these areas would be minor irrigation, roads, soil conservation, afforestation, pasture development, rural water supply and animal husbandry (which includes development of cattle, sheep husbandry, dairying, etc.). An analysis of the sectoral-mix of programmes undertaken in drought prone districts in the various States between 1970 and 1972 show the following pattern of outlays:

Sectors	*Percentage of outlays*
Minor irrigation	56.5
Roads	23.5
Soil conservation	7.6
Afforestation	7.6
Others	4.8

The analysis further reveals that minor irrigation constituted between 62 to 97 per cent of outlays in the States of Haryana, Maharashtra, West Bengal, Uttar Pradesh and Madhya Pradesh. Roads constituted a high proportion of outlay ranging from 46 to 57 per cent in Jammu & Kashmir, Tamil Nadu but in Haryana and West Bengal there was no outlays on roads. Soil conservation accounted for 33 per cent of outlays in Mysore and between 10 and 12 per cent in the States of Maharashtra, Andhra Pradesh, Orissa and Tamil Nadu. Afforestation programmes accounted for 8 per cent of total outlay in Rajasthan and Mysore and between 1 to 2 per cent in Bihar, Gujarat, Madhya Pradesh, Maharashtra, Orissa and Uttar Pradesh. There was no outlay under this programme in Jammu & Kashmir. Pasture development, rural water supply and animal husbandry programmes accounted for relatively smaller proportion of outlays. This was partly restricted to a few schemes. However, pasture development and drinking water supply programmes accounted for a sizable proportion (22%) of the approved outlay in Rajasthan.

The picture at the district level shows still further variations in the sectoral allocation of funds.

From all these it is obvious that there is a wide diversity in the content of the programme both at the district and State levels. However, these discussions tend to give some idea of the kind of sectoral-mix that one should aim at in planning for drought prone districts. Obviously it would be difficult to provide any blanket formula for sectoral allocations since various drought prone areas do not represent a homogeneous land and water resources situations. Notwithstanding this difficulty, the above examples provide some general guidelines regarding the ingredients which should be put into integrated areas development plan for drought prone districts.

Check List for Economic Scrutiny of the District Plans

Agriculture

1. Requirements of improved seeds and hybrid seeds are to be checked with seed rate for the proposed area under different crops.
2. Fertilizer requirements are to be checked with the standard dosages for the areas for different crops.
3. Additional agricultural production estimates are to be checked as per yardsticks adopted by the Agriculture Department.

Minor Irrigation

4. Number of additional wells to be linked up with availability of water-table as per underground water survey in different parts of the district.
5. Per well and per other minor irrigation project cost provided by the district plan.
6. Per hectare cost of additional irrigation potential under the well programme.
7. Per hectare cost of additional irrigation potential under other minor irrigation programmes.
8. Area irrigated per well to be checked with the observed potential in each district.

Agricultural Credit

9. Per hectare and per *khatedar*, short-, medium- and long-term agricultural credits provided in the plan. This is to be checked with the standard norms.

Warehousing and Marketing

10. Present level of warehousing and godown facilities available in the district to be linked up with the additional marketable surplus likely to be produced in the district.

11. The existing number of marketing centres and number of additional marketing centres to be developed are to be linked up with the additional marketable surplus to be produced in the district.
12. The rural electrification cost per village and per well.

Road Development

13. Per kilometer construction cost for different types of roads such as major district roads, minor district roads and village roads.

Soil Conservation

14. The total soil conservation programme to be linked up with total bundable and terracable areas in the district.

Animal Husbandry

15. Additional number of veterinary dispensaries, intensive cattle development blocks, etc., to be linked up with the total livestock population in the district.
16. Number of artificial insemination centres to be linked up with the total population of cows and she-buffaloes.
17. The number of sheep-breeding farms to be linked up with the total sheep population in the district.
18. Number of government poultry farms to be linked up with poultry population in the district.

Forest

19. Outlay on forest to be linked up with the total area under forest.
20. Value of major and minor forest products per hectare of forest area.
21. Unit cost of respective forest development programmes in different districts.

Fishery

22. Number and unit cost of different fish seed production projects in different districts.

Agro-based Industries

23. The number of agro-based processing and manufacturing units to be linked up with the existing and the additional production of the base material. For example, number of sugar mills to be linked up with area and production programme of sugarcane. Number of cotton ginning, weaving and spinning mills to be linked up with the cotton production programme.

Water Supply

24. Per village cost of water supply measures in simple and difficult villages.

Education

25. Present and targeted intake capacity in educational institutions to be linked up with the respective age groups and the qualifying students' population.

Health

26. Number of beds and unit cost per bed in hospitals in different districts. The bed-population ratio.
27. Number and unit cost per primary health centre and sub-centre.

Housing

28. Number and unit cost of tenements to be constructed in urban area under different housing schemes.
29. Rural housing programme under the minimum needs programme to be linked up with the population of landless agricultural labourers in each district.
30. Number and unit price per household site in different districts.

Backward Areas

31. Number of backward class people in the district and the per capita plan expenditure proposed to be spent on backward class population such as scheduled castes, scheduled tribes, nav-Buddhas and

nomadic tribes, etc.

Rural Employment

32. The allocation under employment guarantee and special employment schemes to be linked up with total number of people who have registered for seeking manual jobs in the district. Number of persons likely to be given jobs under these schemes in different districts to be checked up with the allocation.

11

SPATIAL PLANNING

R.P. MISRA

THIS CHAPTER is designed to introduce the concept of spatial planning. The need for this chapter arises from the fact that planning as conceived and practised the world over has, until very recently, been essentially sectoral. Most planning documents – the Five-Year Plans for example – discuss the existing conditions of various sectors like agriculture, industry, social services, etc., set certain objectives and targets for development of each sector within a given period of time and state the resources – financial and others – needed and earmarked for achieving the objectives and targets.

A realistic planning should have three dimensions i.e., economic, social and spatial. It is not enough to say which sectors should develop and to what extent. What is equally important to tell is who benefits from the development and to what extent ? In other words, planned development should lead not only to an improvement in the per capita income measured in average terms but also to progressive reduction in the disparities in per capita income of individuals and areas. Wide differences in the earning capacities of urban and rural populations, industrial and agricultural populations, and socially privileged and under-privileged populations must be progressively reduced.

More often than not, there is close association between low productivity, traditional agriculture, poor health and educational facilities, low urbanization, poor accessibility to transportation and communication network, poverty and so on. They together form a vicious circle. It is also seen that such conditions are more prevalent in some areas and regions than others. Such a situation gives rise to what is generally known as social and spatial imbalances in national economy. Sectoral planning in its traditional form emphasizes economic efficiency of investment in a particular sector; the distributive aspects of investment are of secondary importance. The task of spatial planning is to emphasize the equity aspects of planning, without at the same time, neglecting the efficiency aspects altogether. It measures returns to investment both in economic and social terms.

The equity and distributive aspects of planning did not receive the attention, they ought to have in the developing countries in the early stages of planning largely because of the desire of these countries to catch up with the developed countries in average per capita income or GNP, as fast as possible, and the implicit assumption that economic growth automatically benefits all the people in the long run. Experience of these countries, however, indicates that the conditions under which the less-developed countries are developing their economies are not the same or even similar under which the present day economically advanced countries developed their economies. They now realize that economic history does not repeat itself. In many countries, notwithstanding the high rate of economic growth, disparities in income and production capacities increased because modern technology and production processes tended to favour those who had the intellectual, organizational and financial capacity to utilize them best. Those who were illiterates, had poor economic base and were slow in adapting themselves to the changing circumstances and modern methods benefited least.

Had such under-privileged people been few, the developing countries could ignore them. They could have rationalized this by saying: 'the society must pay for economic growth'. It, however, so happens that such people form a large group in the developing countries. In some countries they form a great majority; in Iran they constitute about 50 per cent of the total population. If this group is ignored and not taken care of by planners, national development would have no meaning to them. A small minority would reap the fruits of development; economic differences would widen; social tensions would increase; and the orderly development of the national economy would be jeopardized. It is, therefore, important that planning should aim at not only rapid economic growth but also better distribution of the fruits of economic growth inter-personally as well as inter-regionally and areally.

Disparities in socio-economic development manifest themselves in two ways: inter-personal and inter-regional (or inter-areal). More often than not, it is, however, seen that the two go together. The inhabitants of the poorer areas are relatively poorer than those of the richer areas when we measure their incomes in average terms. It is, however, true that even in the poorer or richer areas, there are inter-personal disparities in income and earning capacities.

Spatial planning attempts to create conditions for the poorer areas and regions to catch up with the richer areas and regions. Where inter-personal disparities in economic and social development are significant, spatial planning is oriented to the poorer sections of the society within the framework of overall areal or regional development. Special institutions, such as small farmers development agency, are created to handle such problems.

Spatial Organization

To understand spatial planning, one should first understand the spatial organization of national economy and human activities. Spatial organization means the order in which a given set of activities are organized in space. We see this organization when we fly at an altitude of say 30,000 feet. From that elevation, we see a number of nodes (cities, towns, villages, etc.) – urban and rural settlements. These nodes are linked with each other by a network of communication lines radiating from the nodes. The networks consist of railways, highways, etc. If we fly at a still lower level, we observe more details of the nodes and networks. The larger nodes specialize in activities which are not space consuming factors, i.e., commercial establishments, etc. The small nodes specialize in space consuming activities such as agriculture.

The intermediate nodes, such as small towns, have a mixed activity pattern. We also notice that network linkages weaken as the size of nodes decreases so much so that some of the tiny nodes inhabited by a few people and located in resource-poor areas have no or extremely poor linkages.

What binds the various sizes of nodes with each other is the flow of people, goods and services through the network linkages. Larger nodes attract goods consumed by the people such as food and those consumed by industries such as raw materials. They, in return, send out finished products and a variety of other services to the smaller nodes in their hinterland.

The interaction among the various sizes of nodes depends largely on productive capacity of each node and the surplus of goods and income they generate. The nodes which have no surplus have a very small area of interaction. Those which have more surplus have relatively larger area of interaction. This area of interaction of a node is often referred to as hinterland or the zone of influence. When we refer to interaction for social services, we can call it service area and when referring to economic activities alone we can call it economic hinterland. Urban geographers call it urban field.

The nodes and the activities associated with them and the interaction among them through the networks are called spatial organization. It must be noted here that the spatial organization as seen at a particular time cannot be seen in the same state again. It is always changing. Each birth of a baby, each investment in the factory or farm, each improvement in communication and each new input in transportation changes the organization. These changes are not perceptible to us at a particular moment of time because, taken individually, they are minute. Cumulatively, they however, force the spatial system to re-adjust itself to a new situation. New cities come into being, villages are transformed into towns, many communities disappear, small farms become large, crop patterns change, new communication lines give a new pattern of linkages. All this happens in response to the decision of the people to locate themselves and their activities at some but not other places.

Spatial Structure

The arrangement of nodes and networks in space in relation to each other is called spatial structure. Each country or region has its own unique spatial structure. It has resulted from the past decisions of individuals and governments. Economically developed countries have one type of spatial structure; the under-developed countries have another type; and those in between have a third type. The typology is, however, not as simple as given above. In fact, one can think of a continuum of spatial structures from highly polarized to highly dispersed. Each country or region can be placed on this continuum and categories could be made then.

A close study of this continuum reveals that the highly developed countries have evolved spatial structures which have many similarities. The less-developed countries are also marked with a similar, if not the same, spatial structure. It is not accidental. It happens because of the inter-dependence between socio-economic development and spatial structure. They are two sides of the same coin. For a particular type and level of socio-economic development, there is a particular type of spatial structure.

The above analysis leads us to some very significant conclusions.

(a) Planning has to be sectoral-cum-spatial so that a disfunctional spatial structure does not hinder planned growth of the economy;
(b) Each country or region has to evolve its own organization and structure of space to meet the specific goals and objectives of planning; and
(c) Developing countries with a highly polarized spatial economy have to evolve a spatial structure which carries the benefits of planned development also to those who have been bypassed by history.

Spatial Planning

Spatial planning is the sum total of the concepts, approaches, methods and techniques of evolving a desired spatial organization and structure. It is often used as co-terminus with regional planning. Theoretically speaking, the concepts of space are more dynamic and open than the concepts of region. Space cuts across regional boundaries. It is a process which is continuous, temporally, vertically and horizontally. In practical terms, integrated regional planning can be considered to be an important dimension of spatial planning.

Spatial planning is an exercise to determine the allocation of sectoral resources in places and areas in a way that:

(a) Sectoral investments give highest social and economic returns and maximum support to each other,
(b) Productive activities and social facilities are available to all those who need and deserve,
(c) Differences in incomes and welfare among the people and areas are reduced, if not eliminated, and
(d) A spatial structure conducive to planned development of the country or region is evolved.

It may be recalled that spatial organizations and structures of human activities are determined by the nodes, the networks and the flows linking the nodes through the networks. The efficiency of the spatial structures depends upon the location and density pattern of the nodes, the shape and density of the networks, and the quantity, quality and direction of the flows. The task of spatial planning is to analyze the spatial structures, evaluate the efficiency against the needs of the national and regional economies, and to generate structural changes to meet the objectives of planned development.

How are the structural changes brought about? To answer this question let us take a hypothetical example of a country which has decided to invest rials 1,000 billion on health services to make these services available to all the people. Let us also hypothesize that this country has 10 urban centres and 1,000 small villages spread over in space rather randomly. The economic condition of the rural population is rather poor and is based on subsistence agriculture. The links between the urban and rural places are weak which is apparent from a very inefficient communication network development. The linkages are maintained by a set of intermediaries who collect the surplus rural products in small bits at a subsistence price and transport the same to the urban centres. They also carry the basic necessities of life produced at the urban centres to the tiny villages and sell them at a predetermined price.

Now the question is: How and where to invest the health funds and in what form to carry the benefits of investment in health services to the rural population? It is obvious that the health plan should attempt to develop rural health centres with resident doctor and supporting staff. Where should such health centres be built? It has to be based on certain criteria of distance, doctor-population ratio, etc. The health centre should be easily accessible to people. The spatial planner develops distance norms or standards for each region of the country. He also prescribes the number of health centres required to serve all or a maximum number of people of the region. While prescribing these norms or standards he would keep in view what is feasible given the constraints in development in the region, then he would suggest the vertical linkage between the health centres and better equipped hospitals so that specialized medical advice can be secured and to which serious cases can be sent. He may recommend that such higher medical centres should be within, say 25 km from each health centre. He may further recommend that there should be at least one large general and specialized hospital at the apex of the hierarchy where chronic and more serious cases can be handled.

The spatial planner would thus tell: Where to locate these various levels of health services? What norms or standards about distance and population should be adopted? But his problems would not be over with these. If it were only the question of health services, the problem would have been easy. He has to carry out the same exercise for so many other sectors simultaneously. For example, educational services, agricultural services, cultural services, economic activities and so on. If he decides to locate each facility independent of the other, he would be diffusing the resources at so many places, and would find it difficult to evolve a spatial structure conducive to autonomous development of the regional economy. Further, he would create tremendous strains on the time and resources of the people, so that the facilities would remain unutilized or under-utilized and interactivity linkages which create conditions for further development would not evolve.

Thus, one of the important tasks of spatial planning is to integrate the spatially dual economies through successive locational decisions leading to the development of a spatially balanced social and economic structure. The second task is to identify the economic activities, given the local, regional and national resources – physical, human and financial – and needs which can be located at various places selected to help fill the gaps in the settlement hierarchy and generate greater flow of goods and services among the places. And, thirdly, spatial planning attempts to evolve a system of transportation and communication network which facilitates the expected flow. And, finally, spatial planning specifies the institutional infrastructure including administrative and planning which can effectively implement the spatial plan.

Problems in Spatial Planning for Rural Areas

The spatial organization of any national economy manifests a clear dichotomy between urban and rural areas. This is now a well known phenomenon. Here, an attempt is made to enunciate certain principles which underline the methodology and methods of solving the problems emanating from such a situation.

Setting the Distance Standards

Locating a large industrial plant has now become an easier task as the methods and techniques of location analysis for such plants are now well standardized. For the location of social services and non-export-oriented local economic activities and services, however, the industrial location theories are of little use. For these activities one has to rely heavily on the old theories of Von Thunen and Christaller which offer general principles of location of agricultural activities[1] and social facilities[2].

Taking these formulations as the base, we can say that the services and activities which are basic to the people and which are to be used most intensively should be located closest to the users' residential places. Those to be used less frequently should be located at some longer distances.

For different services and activities, there should be different distance standards. Establishing distance standards which are realistic in the light of the local and regional conditions is an essential step in spatial planning specially for the rural areas. This must be done for every area or region to be planned with respect to each kind of service or activity which is to figure in the planning.

Let us take the example of education. What is the range of distance from which children can be drawn for primary schooling. One may say that the school should be located where the children live. But, what to do if the rural settlements are small and none of them can singly provide enough children for the school? Or, if enough resources – financial or human – are not available to provide a primary school for every village? One of the several small villages would have to be selected. If the school is so located that most of the children would have to walk for, say, 10 km to reach it, it would not be efficient in social terms. The objective is to provide primary education to every child within a walking distance.

It is the goal of every developing country to provide primary education to each child of school-going age without impairing the effective functioning of the school, i.e., the school is viable. Let us say that two km radius can be taken as a standard for primary school. If possible it should be less, but, barring very exceptional situations, it should not exceed two km. Now we will call two km as the distance standard for primary schools. We would then take up each activity and set distance standards, remembering that within a given activity, say education, we have to set distance standards for nursery, primary, secondary, college, etc., levels, separately.

The procedure for setting distance standards has to be evolved by planners.

Setting Population Threshold Standards

Besides distance standard, a population standard has also to be evolved. For each activity, there should be a minimum population in its catchment area carved out by the distance standard. For example, a primary school should have at least 100 children, i.e., 20 children in each class. If we take 15 per cent of the population being in the age group of 6 to 11, and if we assume that every child in the primary school age group should or would attend school, there should be at least 800 persons in the catchment area of the school. The required population will increase, as the strength of the school in terms of children enrolled increases. Thus, we arrive at population standard.

Conflict between Distance and Population Standards

After distance and population standards are set for different levels of each activity, the two should be empirically tested to determine their applicability in different situations. Population density in some areas or regions may be so low that sufficient number of people may not live within the distance standard to make the offering of a particular service feasible. Or, there may be too many people within the radius of the standard distance. In such circumstances, necessary adjustments would have to be made between the conflicting standards. The nature of this compromise will depend on considerations such as future development possibilities, transport impediments improvements, mobile service availability, even on a selected basis, etc.

The conflict between distance and population standards raises the question of equity versus efficiency in spatial planning. If equity expressed as a maximum travel distance is the governing factor, then the efficiency question is: What is the minimum number of places required to put all places in the area of operation within that distance of a centre and where should the services be located ? If efficiency governs in terms of minimum population base, then the equity question is: Where should a given number of services be located so that the maximum level distance from all the places selected to the most remote villages they serve is least but that around each place the minimum number of people necessary to support the facilities are present ? Spatial planner has to resolve these conflicts.

Setting the Hierarchy of Services and Activities

Another problem needing attention in spatial planning is the hierarchy of services and activities. Certain services are needed by the people too frequently, for example, primary school, health clinic, extension agent, grocery store, agricultural marketing, agricultural inputs, etc., and some are not needed so frequently, such as specialized hospitals, colleges, wholesale market, etc. When we set the distance and population standards for various services and activities, we have to keep the hierarchy of services and activities in view.

It is, therefore, important that the services and activities to be located to meet the equity and efficiency criteria are classified and standards for each class is worked out.

Each class of the educational service mentioned above requires a separate set of standards. It should be emphasized here that the classification mentioned above is illustrative. For each country and region, different hierarchies would have to be worked out for each service.

Determining the Hierarchy of Settlements

Another problem to be resolved in spatial planning is given the standards and hierarchy of services, where to locate the services to meet the standards? The methodology for settlement analysis and the selection of places for locating various services and activities is not gone in detail here. Suffice it is mention here that the hierarchy should be so conceived that it integrates the national or regional space both vertically and horizontally.

The hierarchy of settlements have to be matched with the hierarchy of services and activities and vice versa before a spatial development plan is prepared

Making the Spatial Plan Dynamic

It has to be realized that planning and development are dynamic processes. As population change, the standards or norms change. As economy develops, better facilities may be needed. The spatial plan should be so devised as to absorb changes. The service centres selected for rural areas, for example, reflect the realities of the present needs and constraints. It should correct the gaps in the present structure, yet should provide a blue-print and guidelines for an evolving system as resources permit its development. It should neither be a time-bound plan nor a plan tied to rigid notions of ideal sets of distances and populations. It should avoid the latter because of the impossibility of constructing hierarchy of settlements that meet arbitrary distance standards and because of the danger that, in attempting to meet such standards, the suggested plan would appear unrealistic. It should not be time-bound because it is unlikely that an ideal set of distances will remain unchanged as a settlement system develops, mobility of population changes, needs of the people change, new facilities are introduced, new resources are available, etc. At any point of time, to be useful ideal standards must themselves compromise between fundamental ideals and ends that can realistically be achieved. They should, therefore, change and the most that any service centre plan can offer is a range of options from each village to centres that form the nuclei of ever larger groups of places. The principal virtue of the plan is to ensure that all villages are connected to a hierarchic system. So long as the process of plan implementation proceeds in each area down the hierarchy from top to bottom, the ultimate connection of every settlement to every facility type is guaranteed.

Problems of Implementation

Implementation of a spatial plan is always problematic specially because governmental machinery operates sectorally and co-ordination among sectoral departments is always difficult, if not impossible. There is, however, one welcome feature in governmental organization which lays greater emphasis on spatial integration and location of sectoral investments. It is the political organization.

The elected representatives of the people represent areas and regions, and not the sectors. Since the political institutions – parliament, councils and municipalities – set the policies and goals and are often in the position to over-ride the sectoral bureaucracies, there is every chance of a well formulated spatial plan being implemented. Further, even the administrative machinery cannot remain for long insensitive to the policies laid down by the policy-making bodies, like the parliament in India. It is in response to this 'political pressure' that the concept of integrated area and regional development catches the attention of the administrative machinery in every country.

Innovations take time to be adopted and to percolate down. Every system tends to stabilize itself because system in continuous change is painful to many. From the changes in the attitude of the administrators in India, seen during the past few years, one can foresee a major breakthrough in planning mechanism and organization in not too distant a future leading to better appreciation of the spatial planning process.

REFERENCES

1. Von Thunen, *Der Isolierte Staate.*
2. W. Christaller, (1966). *Die Zentralen Orte in Suddeutschland*, Jena Fisher 1933; translated by C. Baskin as *The Central Places of Southern Germany*, Englewood Cliffs: Prentice-Hall.

PART - II

DISTRICT PLAN OF CHITRADURGA

12

INTRODUCTION

SETTING REALISTIC goals and objectives is the first requisite of a successful planning exercise. After all, planning is only a means to achieve a given set of goals and objectives. If we are not sure about these, then planning can serve no useful purpose.

It would be pertinent to mention here that the types of goals and objectives and the degree of clarity with which they are stated and defined depend largely on the ideological and socio-political bases of the society, specially of its ruling classes. More clear-cut the ideology of the class or party in power, greater is the clarity of the goals and objectives.

In situations where socio-economic goals and objectives are hazy, undefined and liable to be interpreted in different ways at the implementation stage, planning can play only a limited purpose and development must remain a slow and uncertain process. One is then tempted to ask: Are we clear about the goals and objectives of Chitradurga Plan ?

Goal setting in a Multi-level Planning System

We are set on the task of formulating a development plan for Chitradurga district. The task at hand is not as comprehensive as its counter-part, let us say, at the national or State level. We are functioning in a multi-level territorial planning framework which places certain specific responsibilities at each level.

Seen on a macro-scale, there are three tiers in territorial planning in India today these are:

1. National,

2. State (regional) and
3. District (sub-regional).

At the sub-regional (district) level, we again have or should have four tiers:

1. District,
2. Block,
3. Sub-block *(mandal)*, and
4. Village *panchayat*.

There are specific functions to be performed at each of these levels. One should be fairly clear about the purpose and functions of planning at the level one is set to plan. Otherwise, there is every chance of a plan becoming a dysfunctional and overlapping exercise.

A district development plan should:

1. Provide for an over-all district development design or framework within which block and sub-block plans could be prepared.
2. Set the goals and objectives including the targets which the blocks must achieve.
3. Set the limits of the external assistance within which block plans are to be operated.
4. Give details of projects and schemes which have to be implemented by district level development authorities.
5. Give details of the programmes and projects which are to be implemented at the block-level, but can be planned only at the district level because of their implications for more than one block.

Now, it has to be noted that the goals, objectives and targets to be set at the district level have to conform to three conditions:

(i) goals, objectives, and targets set at the State level;
(ii) capacity to implement the district plan; and
(iii) capabilities of the blocks and villages to achieve the objectives and targets set at the district level.

In other words, in a multilevel planning set-up, there must be a vertical integration of territorial plans, and no plan should be prepared in isolation of the plans prepared at the top and bottom territorial levels. This does not, however, mean that planning for, let us say, a block cannot be done unless it is simultaneously also done for the district and village. It means that the plan for a block should not involve execution programmes and projects which can be better executed at the district and village levels for the obvious reason that neither the block level development administration has the capacity nor the resources to execute such projects.

The contents and focus of the district development plan would, therefore, be determined by:

(i) the development policies of the State/Nation,
(ii) the local resources – physical, human and fiscal, and their development potentialities; and
(iii) special problems, if any, of the district such as poverty, ecological imbalances, high rate of unemployment, low productivity, etc.

Developmental Goals for Chitradurga District

The plan for Chitradurga district given in this volume is for a period of 25 years from 1977 to 2001. It is perspective plan with the break-up of the targets for a medium term of 15 years (1977 – 1991).
There are certain assumptions which are at the back of all the goals, objectives, targets and programmes included in this plan. If these assumptions do not hold good, the plan will become inoperative. It must be restated here that the assumptions are not derived from what the drafters of this plan think to be right or wrong, but from what they think is likely to happen given the past happenings, present tendencies and future prospects.
The assumptions are:

1. The existing constitutional and political set up and power structure of the country would not undergo any revolutionary change.
2. Greater emphasis will be laid on eradication of poverty and distributive justice through a series of welfare measures.
3. There will be no major natural calamities affecting the area, except the recurring droughts.

4. The powers, that be, will be willing to make certain institutional changes more drastic than done hitherto, involving natural resources, development administration; and popular participation.

Given the above assumptions the following are the development goals of Chitradurga district set for the next 25 years:

1. Optimum use of land and water resources, so that every piece of land is used for the purpose for which it is best suited ecologically.
2. Diversified economy of the district to provide employment for all with an average per capita income of Rs. 2,500 per annum at current prices.
3. Restructured human settlement system to offer all social and economic services at a place and cost within the reach of the people.
4. Elimination of abject poverty through a vigorous Basic Minimum Needs Programme, agrarian reforms and rural industrialization.

Objectives and Targets

To accomplish the above goals, the plan for Chitradurga district has the following objectives:

1. To re-design the land-use pattern on the basis of known ecological principles and people's needs and aspirations.
2. To change the land tenure system for effective land-use control.
3. To bring down the dependence of rural population on agriculture from 67 per cent in 1971 to 50 per cent by 2001 A.D.
4. To increase agricultural production by 100 per cent by 1990 and 200 per cent by 2001 A.D.
5. To provide gainful employment to at least 20 per cent of people in agro-based industries and 30 per cent in tertiary, small-scale and manufacturing sectors.
6. To increase the per capita income of the district from present Rs. 700 (1976) to Rs. 2,500 by 2001 A.D.
7. To eliminate poverty in the sense that the three basic needs of all the people – food, clothing and shelter – would be ade-

quately met and the three basic socio-economic needs – **health,** education and employment – would be met adequately.

8. To provide adequate health and educational facilites so that all the people above the age of 15 are literate and all the school-going children are in schools of quality, comparable to those found in urban centres today.
9. To build up organizational structures enabling the people to initiate and manage planning and development of their own future.
10. To change the role of development administration from that of initiator and manager of development to that of promoter and participator in development.

It is apparent that the above objectives are interdependent and can be met only as a package.

Resources for Development

It is presumed that progressively more funds would be made available for district, block and village *panchayat*-level development. While at present district is the only micro-level areal unit accepted for planning, the time is not far off when the realization will dawn on the planners and decision-makers that unless planning is brought down to the block and village *panchayat*-level, people cannot be expected to take responsibility of their own development.

At present (1976) total annual public sector investment in Chitradurga district amounts to approximately Rs. 5 crores or Rs. 25 crores during the Fifth Five-Year Plan. Assuming that public sector investment in the district would increase at the rate the Central and State investments increase in years ahead, it is expected that total investment by the turn of this century would be about Rs. 750 crores. The trend of increase would be 1978 to 1983 – Rs. 50 crores, 1984 to 1989 Rs. 100 crores, 1990 to 1995 – Rs. 200 crores and 1996 to 2001 – Rs. 400 crores. Of this amount three-fifths would be in the district sector and the remaining in the State sector. However, the presumption is that the present inflationary trend would not continue during 1978-2001.

According to the Fifth Five-Year Plan of the district, total allocation for various development schemes amounts to Rs. 97.77 crores, i.e., Rs. 19.55 crores per annum. Of this, no more than Rs. 3 crores per annum has been earmarked by the State government for actual expenditure at the district level. Even of this amount, only a part is utilized effectively. Fairly good amount of expenditure does not generate development.

It is presumed that development administration in the district would be improved during the next 25 years to make it more responsive to the discipline, the development planning requires. If it happens, then the expected investment of Rs. 750 crores would put the district's economy on sound footing.

13

APPROACHES AND STRATEGIES

Watershed Planning

SCANTY and erratic rainfall lies at the roots of most of the problems in drought prone areas. The highly irregular nature of rainfall, characterized by occasional downpours and long dry spells, sets in a chain effect. It causes reduction in the moisture available for plant growth, which, in turn, results in reduction in vegetative cover. The scanty vegetative cover fails to absorb and check the flow of rain water during torrential rains. This, in turn, results in soil erosion, which leads to silting of river valleys and tank beds.

Reckless use of the natural resources over the millennia has brought about an imbalance in the eco-system. The harmonious relationship between the abiotic physio-cultural environment and the biotic life is disturbed. Unless this imbalance is corrected the situation will only worsen. In fact, such imbalances have more telling effects on human life now than ever before. It is natural in such circumstances that restoration of ecological balance has attracted global attention. The management of slopes, according to the ecological principles, holds the key to restoration of ecological balance. The adoption of watersheds as the planning and development units for the Drought Prone Area Programme is a concrete example of the growing realization of the need for ecological planning.

Watershed management envisages optimal utilization and conservation of natural resources, particularly land and water, restoration of ecological balance, and improvement in the quality of human life. Every piece of land and the associated environment from the valley bottom to the hill top has a definite role to play in the ecosystem. Watershed planning helps to identify this specific role and allows the planner to use the biotic and abiotic resources in such a way that the ecological balance is restored and maintained. Thus, watersheds provide the ideal spatial units for intervention in the ecological problems and for scientific resource management.

Adoption of watersheds or river basins as planning units is not new in India. As early as 1930, Visveswaraiya advocated the use of river basins for development of water resources in the erstwhile Mysore State. Under his stewardship, the resource potential of different watersheds was thoroughly studied and development of irrigation and hydro-electric power in the State was based on such studies. Elsewhere, the constitution of River Basin Development Boards, like the Damodar Valley Corporation, are examples of such efforts in the recent past.

Objectives of Watershed Planning

The specific objectives of watershed planning, apart from restoration of ecological balance, could be enumerated as below:

1. To conserve soil and water in agricultural fields, pastures, forests and other land.
2. To protect and enhance the water regime in the drainage basin for irrigation, power, drinking water supply, fishery, pasture development, forestry and wild life promotion.
3. To slow down silting of tanks, reservoirs and river beds.
4. To reduce flood hazards.

Watershed Profile

A watershed or drainage basin may be defined as the area which drains into a single stream or tank. The tank or steam may finally drain into a larger tank or a stream system. The stream system is a network of rivers with branches and sub-branches, resembling, in some respects, a tree with numerous branches of various sizes.

The stream is the most dominant element in the watershed. It symbolizes the flow of water to lower elevation in a linear channel and can be easily distinguished from sheet run-off, which is a thinly spread layer of water pouring down a slope during a heavy and long continuous rain. If a small stream is followed to its very head, it will be found to have a distinct upper end where the narrow channel is replaced by a smooth slope reaching up to the divide or watershed between it and another stream valley. It is on the divide slopes, above the end of the streams, that sheet run-off occurs, supplying water and waste to the stream. It follows that if the upper ends of a stream system are fed only by sheet run-off, their channels will be dry most of the time between the rains.

In humid regions where vegetation is thick, much of the rainfall is absorbed by the vegetation cover and soaked into the soil and bed-rock without running down the slope. The water slowly seeps into the stream channels, supplying a relatively steady flow of water which permits small streams to flow continuously throughout periods between rains. In dry regions, where vegetation is thin or lacking, stream flow is intermittent. Brief periods in which the channel flow swiftly alternates with a long period in which the channel is devoid of any water, over larger part of the drought-prone areas in India, the stream-flow happens to be only intermittent.

Analysis of the effect of land-use on the loss of soil, extensively carried out in the west, indicates that vegetation cover is one of the most important elements that influences the amount of erosion. It is also the most variable one. A plot, that loses soil at the rate of 100 tonnes (about half an inch of soil) a hectare under fallow or up-and-down-hill cultivation, might lose only 10 tonnes if it is planted to small grains, two tonnes if it is in good pasture and less than one tonne if it is in good forest cover.

The vegetation cover in upper reaches of the stream has, thus, a direct bearing on soil erosion and run-off. In case the vegetation cover is removed by deforestation, over-grazzing, or farming operations, surface run-off becomes rapid, sweeping large volumes of soil and mantle material into flooded stream channels. Once the fertile soil layers are gone, it becomes difficult to restore the fertility of the soil.

Delineation of Watersheds

In order to delineate the watersheds in a district, one should have a detailed topographic map showing the drainage network in the area. Such a map could be prepared on the basis of Survey of India topographic sheets of scale one inch to four miles or of scale 1 : 250,000. It is advisable to have the drainage network for the adjoining areas also so as to develop the perspective of stream systems of higher orders. The delineation of watersheds within the region should start with the highest order stream and should come down to the lowest order desired.

After the broad framework of watersheds at the district level is ready, one could proceed to demarcate the watersheds at the *taluk*-level. For demarcation of watersheds at the *taluk*-level, it is necessary to have a map of drainage network on a larger scale. Such a map could be prepared on the basis of Survey of India maps of scale one inch to 1 mile or of scale 1 : 50,000. The watersheds in the *taluk* should be demarcated under the broad framework already available from the district map. Here again, one should start with demarcating the watershed of the highest order stream and go down to the lower levels as required.

While delineating watersheds in a district or a *taluk* for watershed planning, the administrative infrastructure available for executing development programmes in the area should be thoroughly examined. These could include the personnel, machinery and equipment, transport, credit and other facilities. Existing and on-going development programmes in the field of irrigation and hydro-power generation should be kept in view while demarcating the watersheds. In areas of rugged terrain, where tank irrigation is important, attempt should be made to delineate the watershed of important tanks and reservoirs. Equally important are the physio-graphic characteristics of the land. The efforts required for watershed management will differ according to the nature of land – its parent materials, slope, relief, drainage, density, etc. In areas where problems of land and water management are severe, the size of watersheds could be kept small for efficient handling of the problems.

Watersheds in Chitradurga District

A series of three maps have been compiled to show the watersheds at the regional, district and *taluk*-levels. The drainage network in the region covering Chitradurga district and the adjoining areas was mapped on a scale of 1 : 1 million. The master stream in this area is the Tungabhadra which forms a tributary of the larger stream system – the Krishna. All the streams in the area drain to the Tungabhadra. An important tributary of the Tungabhadra is the Vedavati or Hagari river which drains almost three-fourths of the area of Chitradurga district. Thus, two watersheds of the highest order in this region can be identified:

(a) Tungabhadra basin (right bank), and
(b) Vedavati basin.

The Tungabhadra basin can be divided into three ma cro-watersheds:

1. Tungabhadra right bank between the Bhadra dam and the confluence of the Chikka Hagari.
2. The Chikka Hagari.
3. The Tungabhadra right bank between the confluence of the Chikka Hagari and the Vedavati.

These three watersheds can again be divided into watersheds of still lower order.

The Vedavati basin can be divided into five macro-watersheds. The two large tributaries of the Vedavati, the Chenna Hagari and the Swarnamukhi, warrant separate identity by dint of their size. The main Vedavati basin could be divided into three watersheds – the upper, middle and lower reaches. This division is made convenient by the presence of two big reservoirs – the Vanivilas Sagar and the Bhairavuntippa reservoir. The entire catchment area of the Vanivilas Sagar could be demarcated as one watershed and the catchment of the Bhairavuntippa reservoir, excluding the Swarnamukhi basin, as another watershed. Thus, the five macro-watersheds of the Vedavati basin are:

1. The Chenna Hagari basin.
2. The Swarnamukhi basin.
3. The upper Vedavati basin.
4. The middle Vedavati basin.
5. The lower Vedavati basin.

These macro-watersheds can again be divided into watersheds of the lower order.

Figure 13.1 shows the drainage network of Chitradurga district on 1 : 250,000 scale. The two major watersheds – the Tungabhadra right bank and the Vedavati basin – have been marked and have further been divided into macro and meso watersheds as described earlier in the regional context. It will be seen that the district boundaries cut across so many watersheds of different orders.

Figure 13.1

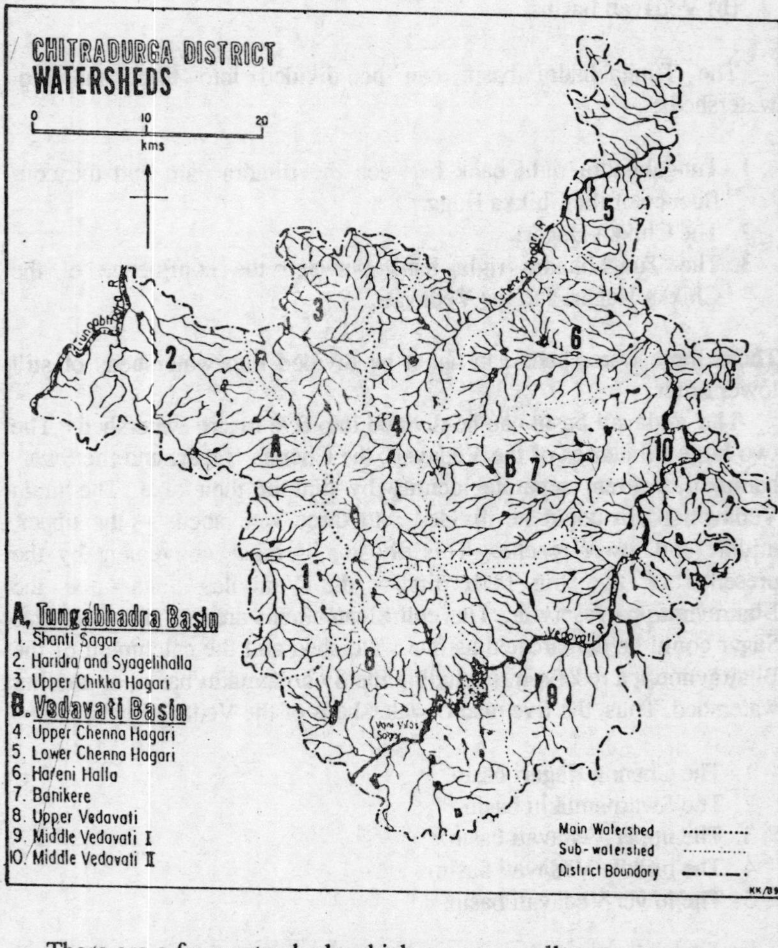

There are a few watersheds which are too small to warrant separate identity at the district level. Similarly, there are certain watersheds which are too large and need sub-division for effective resource planning. Taking into consideration all these points, the district can be divided into 10 watersheds of almost comparable size. These are :

A. The Tungabhadra basin (right bank):

1. Shanti Sagar

2. Haridra and Syagalihalla
3. Upper Chikka Hagari.

B. The Vedavati basin:

4. Upper Chenna Hagari
5. Lower Chenna Hagari
6. Garani Halla
7. Ranikere
8. Upper Vedavati
9. Middle Vedavati I
10. Middle Vedavati II.

The watersheds so delineated at the district level help to identify the lead sector for development and decide the macro-land-use for the area.

For detailed watershed management at the *taluk*/block level, watersheds may be delineated on a topographic map of scale 1 : 63,360 or 1 : 50,000. Figure 13.2 has been prepared to identify watersheds in Hosadurga *taluk*. It will be seen that the *taluk* has been divided into 18 watersheds on the basis of the terrain characteristics, existing tanks and other infrastructure facilities.

It hardly needs emphasis that a rational division of watersheds for a district in isolation is difficult. It should be attempted only in the larger regional framework. Similarly, it will be seen that the *taluk* boundaries cut across many watersheds. So that demarcation of watersheds at the *taluk*-level also should be attempted in the broader regional framework of the stream systems.

Watersheds as Planning Units

Watersheds so delineated should provide the ecological framework for land and water development activities. The principles of land utilization have been discussed earlier. It is, however, useful to note here that in a topographic situation, like that of Chitradurga district, the upper reaches of the streams should be under forest/trees. Agriculture (crop farming) should be encouraged only in that land which is not too slopy and which has adequate soil moisture either through irrigation or rainfall. Hilly areas should be under trees. The remaining land should be left under grasses.

Figure 13.2

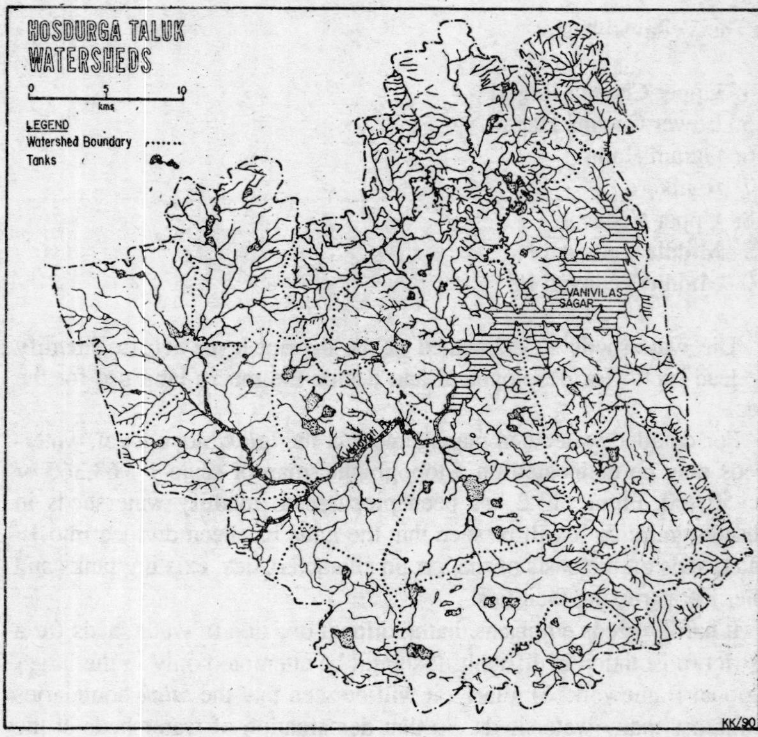

It would be ideal, if all planning and development activities are organized within the framework of these physical divisions. Under the existing conditions at least the land and water development programmes should conform to watershed systems. Gradually, all rural area development programmes should be integrated and implemented in conformity with the principles outlined in watershed planning.

Spatial Planning

Watersheds offer ecological and areal framework for the development of land and water resources. The service centres provide the spatial frame for social and economic planning. The concept of service centres and the method of identifying them has already beeh explained elsewhere. This chapter deals with the hierarchy of service centres identified in Chitradurga district.

As stated earlier, special planning, among others, implies an optimum location of roads, schools, factories, hospitals, etc., with respect to human settlements so that people can use them with ease. In the absence of such an effort, sectoral investments would be made haphazard in terms of space and may not converge in their desirable combinations at the most appropriate locations to give optimum results. The bunching of various activities has the merit of optimizing the development efforts in space. In the unguided planning, it may happen that an agricultural marketing and an agricultural processing function may get located in different places; one need not emphasize the point that there will be great advantages in bringing them together in a single location so that the farmer, who comes to sell his produce in the market place, can also get his goods processed at the same place. Similarly, two localities, not too far away from each other, may set up middle schools which may compete with each other for pupils and keep both the schools below the optimum strength. Thus, it is necessary to rationalize the locations of various investment programmes.

In the context of district or block level planning, there are three types of activities which impinge on location:

1. The key projects and support projects that are identified in the area in the productive sectors of the economy and high level services like hospitals, colleges, etc.
2. The provision of infrastructures which will include physical structures like buildings, roads, electricity, economic infrastructure, like provision of marketing, ware-housing processing facilities, and agricultural servicing of various kinds and social infrastructure which is really the provision of the basic minimum needs to the population like schools and dispensaries.
3. The setting up of institutions which will include the social organizations of human groups, co-operatives or agencies.

The group activities above mentioned have a generative role and will be concentrated in a few specific locations which may be called growth centres or growth points. The activities mentioned in 2 and 3 above will have a servicing role and will be dispersed in as many locations as possible, so that they are accessible to the local population within a reasonable distance. These will be "service centres". Thus, the planning for rural growth centres and service centres constitutes an essential part of area planning.

TABLE 13.1: Typical Standards for Spatial Distribution of Facilities

Facilities/Activities	*Max. travel distance (km)*	*Other Standards*
Regulated Market	10—15	Quantity
Godown	10—15	of produce marketed
Cold Storage	10—15	
Technical College	10—15	
Hospital	5—10	
Hardware	5—10	
Tractor & Pump Repair	5—10	
Primary Health Centre	5—10	One per 25,000 population
Bank	5—10	Minimum population or money flow
Technical School	5—10	
Collection Yard	5—10	Quantity of produce marketed
Doctor	3—05	
High School	3—06	
Secondary Health Centre	3—06	
Veterinary Dispensary	3—06	One per 4,000 to 5,000 population
Fertilizer and Seeds	3—04	
Middle School	2—03	
Post Office	2—03	
Daily Shopping	1	
Cycle Repair	1	
Primary School	1	

Note: Distance will vary depending upon population density and settlement pattern.

We may now elaborate on the method of going about the tasks of planning for infrastructures. The planning of locations for infrastructures in the rural areas will have three basic constraints: Service population, maximum travel distance and finance. Systematic planning would involve firstly discovering the existing norms for population and distance on the basis of the availability of existing facilities and, then, setting-up appropriate distance and population standards, taking into account constraints of topography and settlement pattern. The National Minimum Needs Programme implemented during the Fifth Plan spelt out some population and distance standards for some services. The pilot projects on rural growth centres which were attempted during the Fourth Plan in 20 blocks experimented on these problems. The lessons of these pilot projects will be useful in this context. As an indication of the kind of standards that could be thought of, we give below Table 13.1, which is purely meant as a frame of reference and which is only illustrative and not prescriptive.

While making the inventory of resources, the inventory of all infrastructures/facilities/institutions/services should also be made. Both the quantum and the qualities of such services available should be collected. They should be mapped and their spatial reach (catchment areas) to the village communities should be identified. On the basis of realistic norms, the spatial and functional gaps must be identified and a suitable programme should be drawn up on the basis of such analysis.

Before launching the kind of service centre planning discussed above, it is necessary to decide and determine, first, what should be the package of basic services/minimum needs in a given rural area or cluster of villages. Second, what should be the minimum population threshold and distance standard at which these services should be available?

Service Centres of Chitradurga

The district consists of 1,268 villages and 12 towns. The size-categories of villages are as follows:

Population size	*Number*
More than 5,000	3
2,000–4,999	97
1,000–1,999	291
500–999	431
Less than 500	446
All Villages	1,268

The towns of the district with their respective population in 1971 are listed below:

Towns	*Population*
Davangere	1,21,100
Chitradurga	50,254
Harihar	33,883
Hiriyur	17,368
Challakere	16,913
Hosadurga	8,753
Holalkere	7,776
Jagalur	7,573
Molkalmuru	6,347
Turuvanur	5,316
Mayakonda	3,897
Nayakanhatti	3,757

The following service centres have been identified in the district:

Growth centres	2
Growth points	7

The location and name of each of these places are given in Figure 13.3. Service centres and central villages have also been identified. For example, in Jagalpur *taluk* (Fig 13.4) the number of these are :

Growth point	1
Service Centres	9
Central villages	21

The growth points, service centres and central villages identified are to be developed during the first five years of the perspective plan. Once a comprehensive development plan is accepted for implementation, they should be reviewed and new pattern evolved to meet the needs of future development.

Basic Minimum Needs Approach

Meeting the basic minimum needs of the people is the first and the most basic objective of a rural planning exercise. There are four types of needs which come under the basic category. These are:

1. Needs which, pertain directly to three basic necessities of life and have to be provided to each individual or household – food, clothing and shelter. They include water, fuel and other related items;
2. Needs which enhance the general welfare of the people and improve individual's capacities to produce more and which have to be provided only to groups – medical care, education, transportation and communication, power, marketing, political and social institutions, etc.;

Figure 13.3

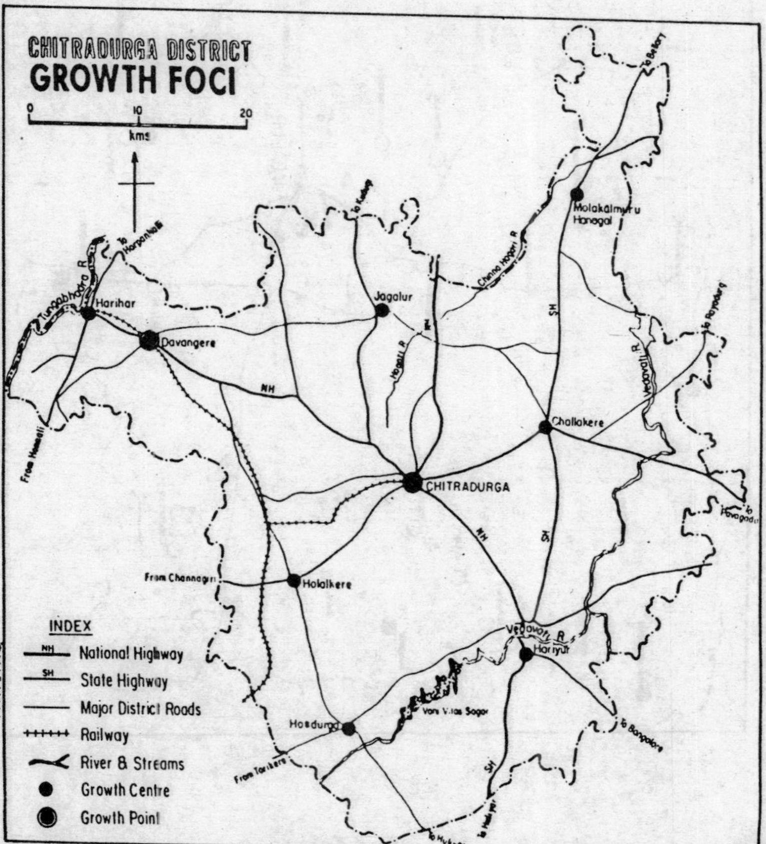

Figure 13.4

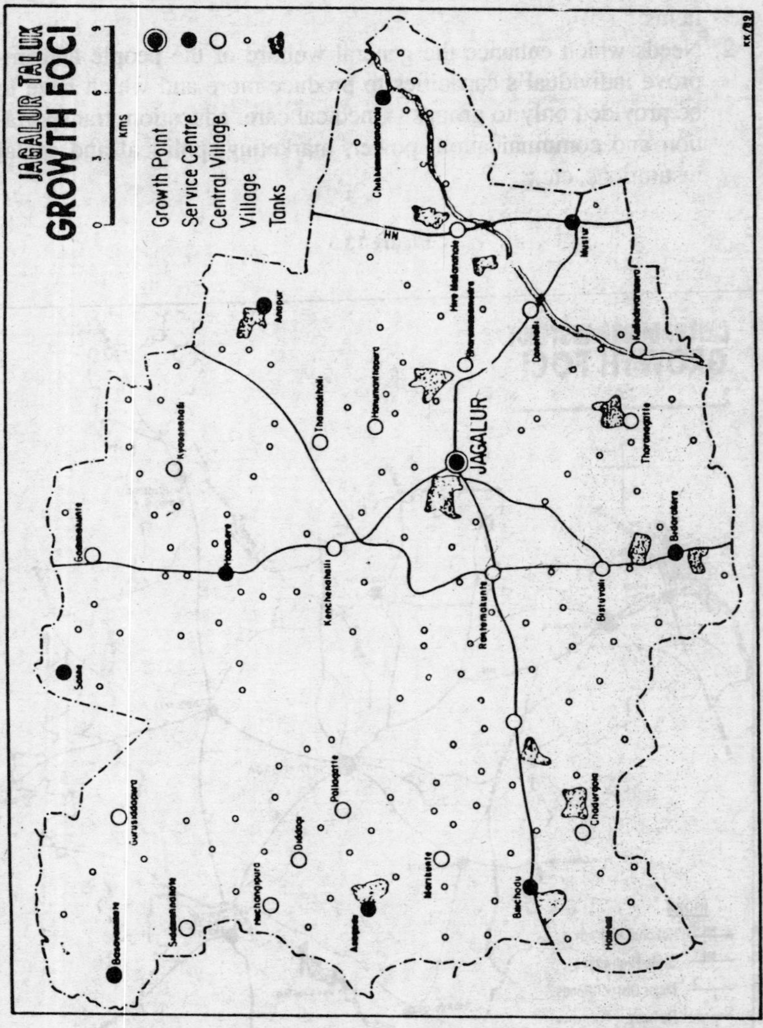
JAGALUR TALUK
GROWTH FOCI
0 3 6 9
Kms
Growth Point
Service Centre
Central Village
Village
Tanks
JAGALUR

3. Needs which improve the access to the means of production and economic opportunities (such as natural resources, capital, employment and income); such needs can be satisfied by structural reforms in society, as much as by economic growth with social justice; and
4. Needs which give a sense of security and freedom of decision-making such as human right, social security, social defence and the rule of law. Such needs are met through a national policy and are applicable to all citizens, but more so to the weaker sections of the society.

The quantity and quality of the Basic Minimum Needs (BMN) that should be planned for any community depends on the community's own perception of the situation and other related forces. The creation of an integrated and egalitarian system of social consumption is a challenging task for policy-makers. The problem implies a reduced and minimized state of conflict among social and personal goals. A state of minimized conflict, or if possible, a simultaneous realization of as many targets as possible would certainly be desirable. The question is how to identify the BMN for action.

The adoption of a purely clinical approach to development isolating the minimum needs problem from the over-all problem of development is not desirable. Improving the quality of life of the people must constitute an integral part of the programme of employment, economic growth, etc.

The steps in the identification of BMN can be stated as follows:

Step 1. Identification of the level and accessibility of the present social services.

Step 2. Comparison of the above levels with national/State average using indicators.

Step 3. Distribution of population and services in the planning area and identification of sub-areas with the least accessability to services.

Step 4. Estimate of the magnitude of provision desired to reach national/State average in respect of each service on the basis of the population growth rate and the national/State average standards.

Step 5. Comparison of the total requirements and the available resources. The determination of the extent to which the existing gaps can be reduced. Formulation of a realistic plan of minimum programme package.

Step 6. Working out the spatial optimization of the proposed services using growth centre framework.

Using the above steps the basic minimum needs of Chitradurga have been worked out. It is estimated that by the turn of this century, all the basic individual and social needs can be adequately met given the political will and people's readiness to fight for and work towards this goal.

The individual needs are:

1. Nutritious food for all.
2. Twenty metres of cloth per head per year.
3. A tiled house with two bed-rooms, kitchen and other facilities including safe drinking water.

The social needs are:

1. Primary school with facilities found in urban areas within a distance of two km. and High School within 10 km.
2. Health centre with doctors within four km. and small hospital within a distance of 15 km. and large hospital within a distance of 30 km.
3. Road network with public transport to all central villages.
4. Full employment.

Lead Sector Approach

The approach is designed to get maximum returns from the scarce resources. Instead of investing these resources in too many projects, it is better to identify the sector(s) which is/are likely to give optimum results and build other sectoral projects around the lead sector(s) so identified.

This approach is not intended to minimize the importance of the sectors which are of less importance. Nor is it meant to evolve a non-integrated development strategy. The lead sector approach is meant to evolve an integrated development strategy with a major and most productive sector/project forming the core project/sector.

For Chitradurga district the lead sectors identified for integrated development are:

1. Hybrid jowar and maize production.
2. Livestock enterprise.
3. Forestry and horticulture.
4. Agro-industries.

Target Group Approach

It is often seen that economic growth is rarely accompanied by fair distribution of the fruits of development. Those who are poor are left out in the race and their socio-economic status deteriorates further. It is, therefore, essential that in a society where poor constitute an important segment of population, special attention is paid to them. This is the only way to ensure their progress in the process of over-all economic development.

The BMN programme can partly take care of the problems of the poor, but that is not all. They must have access to productive resources. Therefore, special projects of structural reforms and production have to be devised for the poor. This alone can enable them to catch up with the better-off people.

In Chitradurga district, the target groups for which special programmes have to be evolved are:

1. Scheduled castes and scheduled tribes.
2. Landless labourers.
3. Farmers with two hectares or less of dry land and with no other source of income.
4. Artisans residing in rural areas without land and without any other source of income except their traditional occupations.

The programmes to be evolved for them have to be of two types:

1. Those which give them access to income in the immediate run, but not necessarily on an enduring basis.
2. Those which give access to income on enduring basis.

The first category of programmes and projects are meant to give immediate relief while the second ones offer permanent relief and enable them to stand on their own feet. Construction activities of various types fall in the first category. Provision of permanent employment or productive resources for self-employment fall in the second category.

There is no doubt that the solution of the problem of poverty lies in the programmes of second category. Nevertheless, it has to be appreciated that it is not so easy to accomplish it without adequate socio-economic structural changes. Moreover, at least 40 per cent of the population of the district is steeped in abject poverty. It needs immediate relief which may be even a costly proposition from a purely economic efficiency point of view. It cannot wait for the long-term solutions. Here lies the significance of programmes of the first category.

14

LAND RESOURCE DEVELOPMENT

DEVELOPMENT PROGRAMMES in the drought prone areas should necessarily aim at the rational utilization of the basic resources like land and water. It is a known fact that the present utilization of these resources is not the optimum one. Rapid growth of human and animal population in the past few decades has created great pressure on the available resources. Indiscriminate destruction of forests and grassland for cultivation and other purposes has resulted in ecological imbalance. It is necessary that such an imbalance is corrected through judicious use of the basic resources, particularly the land.

New Classification of Land

Rational utilization of land resources implies allocation of each piece of land to the use to which it is most suited. Such an allocation requires a thorough study of the suitability of land for different uses. Pending a comprehensive land capability survey, which is a time consuming exercise, it should be possible to assess the suitability of land for the broad land-use categories with the help of aerial photo-interpretation and/or study of topographic maps. Satellite imageries have now become available for the planner.

An attempt has been made to identify broad classes of land in the district on the basis of the information available from the one inch to one mile scale topographic sheets of the Survey of India. While identifying the areas under different land-use classes the ecological principles of land-use have been the guiding criteria. Nature of terrain, availability of moisture and vegetative characteristics of the area have been considered. The land-use classes are only broad and generalized ones and should help in identification of the lead sector and formulation of the development strategy.

Category A : Forest Land

Areas suggested for development of forests include rugged terrain and land with slope generally exceeding 10 per cent. This category includes all hilly areas where run-off is usually very rapid and where soil erosion is a serious problem. In view of the necessity to check run-off and to reduce the hazards of soil erosion, all such areas should be covered by thick vegetative growth.

This class of land includes much of the areas under the existing State forests as well as areas which are presently under the control of individual or the Village Panchayat. Usually such areas are devoid of population. In some cases, a few hamlets may come under the forest area. In such cases, the villagers should be allowed to retain the land, but they should be instructed to grow tree crops only. This will, of course, entail tremendous extension work, persuasion and, may be, legal force also.

Care has to been taken to keep the forest area as compact blocks mainly with a view to reduce the expenditure on fencing. One of the serious impediments in the development of forest in this part of the State is the depredation by the stray cattle. As these areas receive only scanty rain-fall, the trees once destroyed by cattle rarely grow again. The safeguard against cattle by fencing is usually a costly proposition. Hence, while identifying the areas for forests development, contiguity and compactness have been taken into account to keep the fencing expenditure at the minimum.

Such areas which may presently be under the jurisdiction of the forest department, but which are almost level and are fit for pasture development or even grain-farming under irrigation have been left out of the forest area. Such areas may be allotted, after necessary land development, and, if possible, irrigation facilities should be provided to the villages lying in the proposed forest area. Given proper attention and incentives, farmers should be encouraged to shift to these new areas.

Much of the existing forests in the district are devoid of trees. They are forests only in the sense that the ownership of the land rests with the forest department. This situation is undesirable. It does not help to bring about the desired restoration of ecological balance. It does not check the heavy run-off and washing away of the fertile soil mantle. It hardly needs emphasis that all the areas delineated for forest growth should genuinely be covered by forests. This will demand concerted efforts and heavy expenditure. It is possible that the expenditure on development of forests may not be economical in the short-run in view of the cost benefit analysis, but it will certainly be rewarding in the long-run.

Along with development of forests by the State Department of Forests, the local bodies, like the Village Panchayats and the Municipal bodies, should also be encouraged to develop and maintain trees. Social forestry for fuel, farm implements and furniture should be developed to the maximum. It may be desirable to bring a legislation obligatory on large farmers, say with more than five hectares each, to put a part of their holdings, say about 20 per cent, under tree crops. Land under tree crops may be declared tax free until the trees start yielding income.

The development of forestry in the district will not only help in reducing the run-off, checking soil erosion and restoring ecological balance, it will also provide gainful employment to the large number of landless labourers. It may also wean away a part of the marginal farmers from the undependable subsistence grain farming. Unlike soil conservation (contour bunding) and road formation works, afforestation will generate employment largely of continuing nature.

It need not be reiterated that land-use in this category should be enforced with rigidity. These areas are quite vulnerable ones because of the steep slopes and rugged terrain and any laxity will frustrate the very purpose of ecological land-use planning.

Category B : Pasture Land

These areas cover lands where slope is usually between five to ten per cent. Over greater part of this area rainfall is scanty and, more than that, highly variable and unreliable. Crop cultivation, dependent as it is on uncertain rainfall, is highly risky. The farming is invariably of subsistence level.

In such areas, crop farming should be practised only under protection of irrigation. Thus, areas under the ayacuts of tanks, or areas in the vicinity of streams where sub-soil water could be harnessed profitably, should be retained under agriculture. The rest of the land should go to pastures. Grass species with greater tolerance of droughts should be popularized. The Animal husbandry should be the lead sector in these areas. It should aim at dairy products as well as meat and wool. In certain parts of the district (particularly in Challakere and Hiriyur *taluks*) sheep are already very popular. In these areas sheep rearing should be organized on scientific lines. The strategy should stress, among other things, on development of pastures, improvement of breeds, sound management practices, proper health care and efficient marketing of the produce.

Marketing of animal products is a serious problem in rural areas. Though milk and other animal products have become rare commodities these days in rural India, the capacity of our village population to consume dairy and other animal products is only nominal. Almost entire animal products from the villages are consumed by the large industrial or metropolitan centres. No such large centre lies close to the producing areas in Chitradurga district. The only two large centres of consumption are Davangere and Bangalore which are already quite well-served by the nearby areas. Thus, chilling plants and cold storages become essential for development of animal husbandry in this district. It may be worthwhile to look for fresh avenues for utilization of animal products. The traditional household industry of preparing ghee, with necessary modernization, holds great promise in this respect.

Possibilities of organizing producers' co-operatives should be fully explored and harnessed. Every care should be taken to ensure fair return to the farmer who is rearing the animals.

Category C : Arable Land

There are four main areas in the district where farming should be practised as the major occupation:

(a) Eastern parts of the district in Harihar and Davangere *taluks* under the command of the Bhadra irrigation system,
(b) Parts of Hiriyur *taluk* under the command of the Vanivilas Sagar canal system,
(c) The south-eastern part of the district in Holalkere taluk where soil moisture availability is largely sufficient for crop growth, and
(d) The valleys of the larger streams like the Vedavati, the Chenna Hagari and the Chikka Hagari, where sub-soil moisture can be tapped for crop growth.

Apart from these major areas, cultivation of field crops should be permissible in *atchkats* of tanks where availability of irrigation could be fairly assured.

As irrigation water in these areas is scarce, it should be allowed only for semi-dry crops. This would result in coverage of a larger area and the protection against the vagaries of monsoon could be provided to a much larger section of the community.

It has been observed that even though water is scarce in these drought prone areas, its utilization is very often wasteful. In case of the Bhadra irrigation system, though the regulations allow cultivation of only semi-dry crops in the winter months, it is common knowledge that the contravention of the regulations is a rule rather than exception. Even for the second winter crop the farmers go for paddy which demands heavy irrigation. This does not result only in denial of the benefit of irrigation to the tail-end farmers, but also in wasteful use of water. In many areas considerable land has become water-logged and has gone out of cultivation because of salinity and alkalinity. In Harihar *taluk* alone about 1/15th of the cultivable land has been affected and rendered uncultivable in the short spans of 12 years of irrigation. It is high time that steps are taken to ensure optimum use of the scarce irrigation facilities for the maximum benefit of the community.

Figures 14.1 and 14.2 show the existing and the proposed land-use patterns. *Taluk*-wise details of the approximate area under the three land-use categories appear in Table 14.1.

As noted earlier, there are certain ecological principles on the basis of which the above land-use pattern has been suggested. The slope of the land and the soil moisture determine the land-use. Here the objective is to protect the land from further deterioration without adversely affecting the present and future agricultural productivity and production.

It is apparent from that all those areas which constitute the upper reaches of the rivers and form waterparting and are slopy have been earmarked for forestry. Those areas which form water-parting, but are not so steeply sloping are earmarked for pastures. Only those parts of the district which are irrigated or which have adequate soil moisture for at least one secure crop are earmarked for crop production purpose.

The land-use pattern suggested in is highly generalized. When we study the topography, soil moisture, rainfall, drainage, soil texture, etc., in greater detail, say, for example, using a map on a scale of 1 : 25,000 or air photographs and satellite imageries, we get a more detailed pattern. In fact, there is need for detailed maps to be prepared for each village. Then alone it would be possible to evolve an ecologically balanced land-use system.

TABLE 14.1: Approximate Figures for the three Categories of Land for each of the Taluks

(*Area in km²*)

Sl. No.	*Taluk Name*	*Forest land*	*Pasture land*	*Arabile land*	*Total*
1.	Harihar	50	40	400	490
2.	Davangere	150	280	530	960
3.	Holalkere	450	540	110	1100
4.	Chitradurga	400	780	180	1360
5.	Jagalur	350	440	170	960
6.	Molkalmuru	370	210	160	740
7.	Challakere	200	1430	430	2060
8.	Hiriyur	410	900	390	1700
9.	Hosadurga	420	880	130	1430
	Total	2800	5500	2500	10800

The classification of land into three broad categories for future development does not mean that the land earmarked for a specific purpose cannot be used for any other purpose. What it really means is that the land, earmarked for forests, should be predominantly used for that purpose. The following is the rough share of forestry, pasture and crop farming within the three categories of land (Tables 14.2, 14.3 and 14.4)

Of the 10,800 square km. of total land area of Chitradurga district, the area allocated for different purposes from each category of land has been presented in Table 14.3.

The above land-use system is to be evolved by 2001 A.D. In the meantime certain measures have to be taken which would lead to the emergence of the above pattern of land-use.

TABLE 14.2: Appropriate share of land for different purposes in each category of land

Category of Land	*Percentage devoted to*			
	Forestry	*Pastures*	*Crops*	*Other uses*
A. Forest land	80	10	5	5
B. Pasture land	10	40	40	10
C. Arable land	5	5	80	10

Figure 14.1

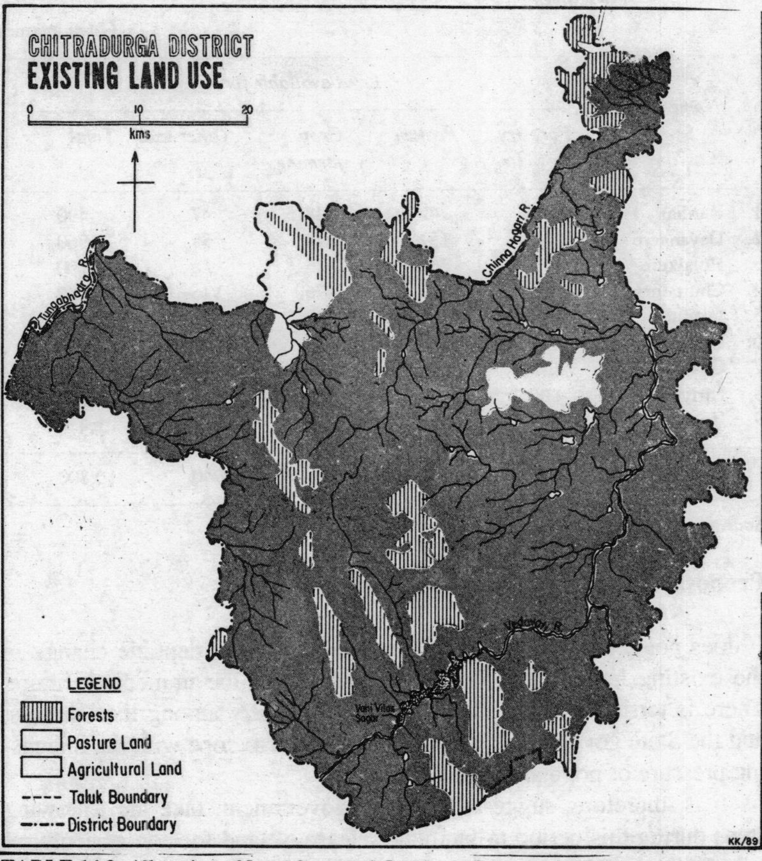

TABLE 14.3: Allocation of Land from each Land-use Category for Different Purposes

Catagory of land	*Area allocated for various uses in km²*				*Total area (Sq. km²)*
	Forestry	*Pasture*	*Crop*	*Others*	
A. Forest land	2,240	280	140	140	2,800
B. Pasture land	550	2,200	2,200	550	5,500
C. Arable land	125	125	2,000	250	2,500
All lands	2,915	2,605	4,340	940	10,800
Percentage	27.0	24.1	40.2	8.7	100.0

TABLE 14.4: Allocation of Land for Different Uses according to the Suggested Lad-use Pattern

(Area in km^2)

Sl. No.	Name of Taluk	Land available for: Forestry	Pasture	Crop farming	Other uses	Total
1.	Harihar	64	41	338	47	490
2.	Davangere	174	154	544	88	960
3.	Holalkere	420	266	326	88	1,100
4.	Chitradurga	407	361	476	116	1,360
5.	Jagalur	333	219	330	78	960
6.	Molkalmuru	325	129	230	56	740
7.	Challakere	324	614	926	196	2,060
8.	Hiriyur	438	420	693	149	1,700
9.	Hosadurga	430	401	477	122	1,430
	District Total	2,915	2,605	4,340	940	10,800

Source: Computed by the authors.

Proposal for the Next Ten years

It does not seem possible that there would be a perceptible change in the existing land-use pattern in Chitradurga in the immediate future There is terrific amount of land hunger specially among the landless, and the State government is finding it difficult to cope with the increasing pressure of population on land.

It is, therefore, suggested that the government, take the following steps during this period to facilitate release of land for non-agricultural uses later:

1. A comprehensive land survey should be conducted to classify different categories of land according to the land capability.
2. Detailed inventorization of land resources up to the farm level and preparation of land-use plans for each village using the watershed principle.
3. Detailed land development plan for each village giving the nature of soil conservation and water management measures.

Figure 14.2

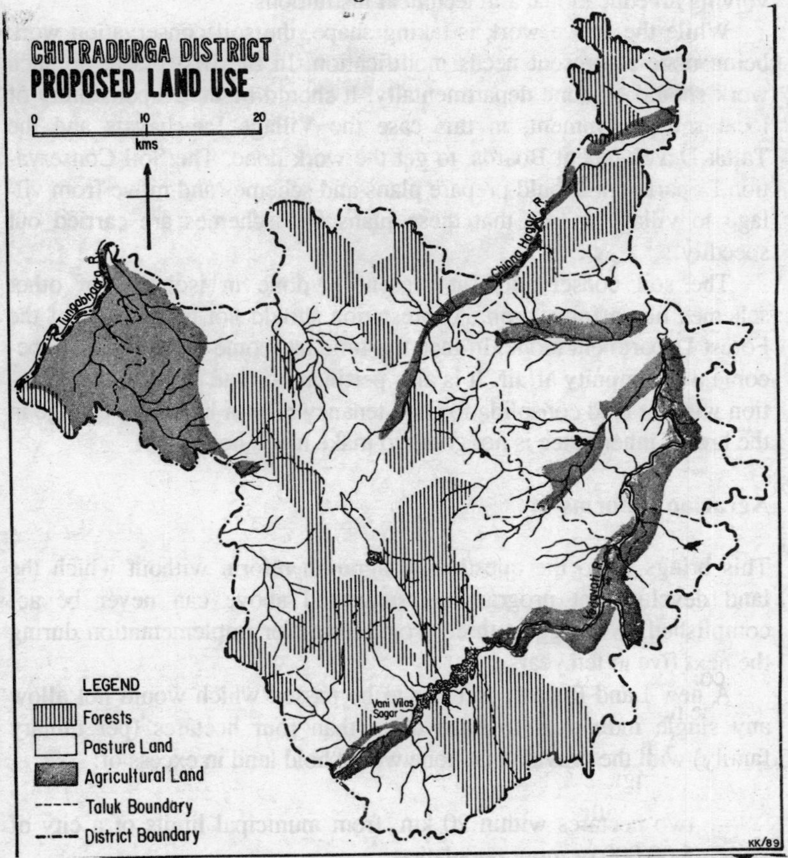

It is expected that as the cost of production increases, the marginal land without irrigation will become uneconomical for farmers to hold on to it. Hence, if development of the agro-industrial and tertiary sector activities are speeded as envisaged in this plan, many farmers would change over to these activities. That would be the time when a Rural Land-Use Control Act should be passed prescribing the use of land for designated purposes only. This is, however, possible only if master plans are ready for each village.

The existing machinery for land-use survey, soil testing and soil survey is so inadequate and ineffective, that it may take about 100 years before it produces detailed land development and soil maps. There is a great need for carrying out this work on a war footing involving all educational and technical institutions.

While the above work is taking shape, the soil conservation work being done at present needs modification. In the first place, no such work should be done departmentally. It should be the responsibility of local self-government, in this case the Village Panchayats and the Taluk Development Boards, to get the work done. The Soil Conservation Department should prepare plans and schemes and move from village to village to see that these plans and schemes are carried out speedily.

The soil conservation at present is done in isolation of other schemes like afforestation. Afforestation should not be the task of the Forest Department alone. In fact, the time has come when it should become a community affair. It is also pertinent to note that soil conservation without land consolidation and tenancy reform including change in the law of inheritance is not going to make much headway.

Agrarian Reforms

This brings us to the question of agrarian reform without which the land development programmes suggested above can never be accomplished. We suggest three programmes for implementation during the next five to ten years.

A new Land Reform Act has to be passed which would not allow any single individual to have more than four hectares (per unitary family) with the proviso that none would hold land in excess of:

- two hectares within 20 km. from municipal limits of a city of 5,00,000 or more population.
- three hectares within 10 km. from the municipal limits of a city of one lakh or more population.
- two hectares within the municipal or corporation limits of any city provided the land is used for agricultural purposes.

A standard hectare should be equivalent to any land which can produce two crops either rain-fed or canal irrigated. Dry land producing only one crop a year should be equivalent to half the value of standard land. The maximum limit of even dry-land one can hold should not exceed eight hectares.

At present, quite a large number of agriculturists have more than eight hectares of dry land. The excess should vest with the government.

In lieu of compensation, the government should start minor irrigation schemes and see that within five years of the start of the scheme, the four hectares of land left with the farmer is fully irrigated. This will serve a number of purposes. First, some more land would become available to landless. Secondly, irrigation facilities would improve; and thirdly, agricultural production would go up. Whenever it is not feasible to provide irrigation, the farmer affected should be assisted to start a supplementary agricultural or agro-industrial activity with the help of the funds which he ought to have got as compensation.

Along with these measures, another reform should be taken up. No one should be allowed to hold land who does not stay at the land. Suitcase farming should be abolished. Further, anyone whose income from non-agricultural sources is 10 times the per capita income of the State should not be allowed to own land. The land so released should be distributed among the landless.

Law should also be passed prescribing at least five per cent of the land to be kept in forest or orchards. This is one of the important ways of promoting social forestry. The land reform law could also have a provision under which a person can have additional one hectare of dry land above the ceiling of four hectares provided he would grow trees in the additional one hectare and would not use it for cultivation of crops. This Act should also prohibit sub-division of holding beyond two hectares and should also prescribe consolidation of holdings.

The measures suggested above do not fall within the jurisdiction of district administration. It has, however, been discussed here because one of the objectives of district planning in a drought prone area is to bring the land back to ecological stability. It is necessary that the State government takes step to enable the district to meet these objectives effectively. If the State level administration fails to do all this, the funds being spent in the DPAP would not be of much avail.

[illegible] and [illegible] government [illegible] such transfer [illegible] [illegible] [illegible] [illegible] [illegible] and [illegible] [illegible] a Block Development [illegible] [illegible] [illegible] [illegible] [illegible] [illegible] [illegible] [illegible] [illegible] [illegible] [illegible] [illegible] [illegible] order [illegible] [illegible] and [illegible] tenancy [illegible] would [illegible] [illegible] [illegible] [illegible] [illegible] [illegible] [illegible] [illegible] [illegible] [illegible] [illegible] [illegible] [illegible] [illegible] or [illegible] [illegible] [illegible] [illegible] [illegible] [illegible] [illegible] [illegible] [illegible] [illegible] [illegible] [illegible] [illegible] or [illegible] [illegible] [illegible] [illegible] [illegible] [illegible] [illegible] [illegible] [illegible] [illegible] [illegible] [illegible] [illegible] [illegible] [illegible] [illegible] [illegible]

[illegible] [illegible] [illegible] [illegible] [illegible] [illegible] [illegible] [illegible] [illegible] [illegible] [illegible] [illegible] should be allowed [illegible] [illegible] [illegible] [illegible] [illegible] [illegible] [illegible] [illegible] [illegible] [illegible] should be [illegible] [illegible] [illegible] [illegible] [illegible] [illegible] [illegible] agricultural [illegible] the [illegible]

[illegible] [illegible]

15

WATER RESOURCE DEVELOPMENT

IN VIEW of the fact that water is the most crucial factor in the economy of drought-prone areas, development of water resources should receive the top priority in the development strategy of the district. Development programmes should broadly aim at the twin objectives of restoration of ecological balance and provision of assured water supply to ensure agricultural production. It has already been pointed out in (chapter 13) why the different parts of a watershed from the valley bottom to the hill top should be managed in such a way as to promote harmonious balance in the eco-system. It may be noted again, even at the cost of repetition, that the upper reaches of the streams with steep slopes, should invariably be brought under permanent vegetative cover. Areas with gentle slopes could be allowed for controlled cattle grazing and development of pastures and forests. Only such land which is level and has fertile soil and adequate soil moisture should be allowed for cultivation.

Proper management of the catchment area with adequate vegetative cover by way of forests and pastures will serve a variety of purposes. The vegetative cover will not only protect the soil from erosion, it will also check the speed of rain water and hold it on the surface for a longer time. There is, thus, greater possibility of the water percolating underground to recharge the groundwater storage. Underground storage of water keeps the valuable water safe from evaporation losses and also saves fertile land of the river valley from submergence in case of surface storage. Also, the utilization of underground water is always much more efficient than that of the surface water.

Water Potential

Chitradurga district is an area of scanty and erratic rainfall. There can be no two opinions about the fact that the district has limited potential for irrigation. Still, with proper management of the watershed, the surface flow of streams will certainly gain greater stability in flow because of sub-surface seepage. It is well-known that our rainfall is torrential in nature and many times the rain water flows away unused. Overflowing of tanks and reservoirs is not uncommon. Even a big reservoir like the Bhadra Reservoir, adjoining the district to the south-west, is reported to have surplussed in six out of 13 years between 1963 and 1975. According to a survey conducted in Jagalur *taluk*, it was found that the potential of surface storage could be increased by about 50 per cent even under the existing ecological conditions.[1] Given the environmental conditions resulting from the master-plan for land-use suggested in the earlier chapter (chapter 13), there is every possibility of greater underground percolation and larger sub-surface seepage in the stream channels.

On the basis of the case study of Jagalur *taluk* and the investigations of the Irrigation Department of the Government of Karnataka, conducted from time to time for the various normal and special development programmes, it is possible to obtain reliable estimates of the potential of surface water resources that are still available for future development. A conservative estimate would put such potential at 20,200 hectares (Table 15.1) for the district as a whole. There are already a few medium and minor irrigation projects under execution, the prominent among them being the Deverbelkere project in Harihar *taluk* and the Rangayanadurga project in Molakalmuru *taluk*. There are also a large number of irrigation pick-ups under construction in Harihar and Davangere *taluks* to utilize the waste water of the Bhadra canals. Similarly, numerous lift irrigation schemes are being taken up throughout the district to utilize the available surface water flow.

Apart from these medium and minor irrigation projects, there is a major irrigation project being investigated by the Irrigation Department to divert part of the Bhadra river flow to support development of the drought-prone areas of this district. The scheme can provide irrigation to about 75,000 hectares in Holalkere, Hosadurga, Chitradurga, Jagalur, Challakere and Molkalmuru *taluks*. The people of these areas are waiting for the project with great expectations. The scheme, if taken up, will transform the whole economy of these dry areas.

The situation is much more promising in case of underground water resources. The surveys conducted by the State Department of Geology, Government of Karnataka, reveal that the underground water potential is about three times greater than the resources presently harnessed.

TABLE 15.1: Surface Water Potential in Chitradurga District (Taluk-wise)

Sl. No.	Name of taluk	Estimated surface water potential available for development
1.	Harihar	5,500 *
2.	Davangere	2,000
3.	Holalkere	2,000
4.	Chitradurga	2,000
5.	Jagalur	1,200
6.	Molkalmuru	1,500 +
7.	Challakere	2,000
8.	Hiriyur	2,000
9.	Hosadurga	2,000
	District Total	20,200

* Includes 4,918 hectares under the Davarabelkere project.

\+ Includes 1,052 hectares under Rangayandurga project.

Source: Estimated by the authors on the basis of medium and minor irrigation projects listed in Integrated Development Plan of Chitradurga district and schemes under investigation by the Irrigation Department, Government of Karnataka, for various development programmes.

It is well-known that the underground water body is recharged through infiltration of rain water, seepage from tanks, canals and rivers, lateral flow of groundwater and through return recharge from irrigation. The recharge is largely dependent on the topography, rock structure, its porosity and permeability, and vegetative cover of the ground. As all these factors are highly variable and their relationships highly complex, the estimates of underground recharge exhibit wide variations. The contribution of rain-fall to the groundwater storage in this area has been found to vary from three to ten per cent of the total rainfall.[2] Return recharge from irrigation has been found to range from 20 to 30 per cent of the water flow in case of canal and tank irrigation, and 10 to 20 per cent in case of well irrigation.

In the absence of actual figures relating to run-off and evaporation losses, it is generally assumed that infiltration of rainfall to recharge the groundwater will be three per cent in rocky areas, 20 per cent in alluvial areas and 10 per cent in other areas of the district. For an estimate of underground resources for this study, it is considered desirable to take the low value of five per cent for all areas of the district. In case of return recharge from irrigation, the lower values of 20 per cent of water flow in canal and tank irrigation and 10 per cent in well irrigation has been adopted. A crude, but fairly reliable, estimate of the groundwater potential in the district has been worked out in Table 15.2. These are essentially conservative estimates as is always better to err on the saferside.

The total recharge of groundwater, according to present estimates (Table 15.2), works out to 432 million cubic metres (MM^3). Of this, only 150 MM^3 is presently being utilized. Thus, two-thirds of the groundwater potential remains unutilized.

Programmes for Development of Water Resources

The programmes of development of water resources in the district should aim at:

(i) Desilting of tank beds and repairs to bunds, sluice-gates, waste-weirs and channels;
(ii) construction of new tanks; and
(iii) harnessing of underground water.

It is well-known that most of the older tanks in the district have silted-up and their storage capacity is greatly reduced. Not only these tanks can store lesser water, the spread of water is now much larger, resulting in heavy losses by way of evaporation. The desilting of tank beds has been engaging the attention of the irrigation engineers for quite some-time. But the heavy cost of desilting (Rs. 10,000 per hectare) has stood in the way. Economic viability of tank irrigation in this part of the country allows an investment of Rs. 4,000 to Rs. 6,000 per hectare of irrigated area. The argument of economic viability should, however, be considered in the light of the chronic poverty of this area and the need to provide these people with the basic minimum needs. Taking up construction of the Rangayanadurga project in Molakalmuru *taluk* at an estimated cost of Rs. 11,000 per hectare is a welcome sign. The desilting of tank beds should be undertaken as a relief measure to provide employment to the farmers in the off-season. The fertile soil of the tank bed, which is particularly rich in organic matter, should be used as manure in the fields. In fact, such practice has been in vogue in many parts of the country. Thus, desilting of tanks will enhance the

Table 15.2: Underground Water Potential in Chitradurga district (**Taluk**-wise), 1974-75

Sl. No.	*Name of Taluk*	*Total Geographical area (ha)*	*Annual rainfall (cm)*	*Area irrigated by surface water flow (ha)*	*Amount of water allowed for irrigation @ 10,000 M^3[1] hectare (MM^3)*	*Number of irrigation wells*	*Total discharge from wells @ 10,000 M^3 per irrigation well (MM^3*	*Recharge from rainfall @ five per cent infiltration (MM^3)*
1	2	3	4	5	6	7	8	9
1.	Harihar	48,445	55	11,165	111.65	177	1.77	13.32
2.	Davangere	95,660	64	23,361	233.61	749	7.49	30.61
3.	Holalkere	1,09,711	66	597	5.97	1,452	14.52	36.20
4.	Chitradurga	1,36,158	64	3,679	36.79	2,505	25.05	43.57
5.	Jagalur	95,520	54	2,463	24.63	749	7.49	25.79
6.	Molkalmuru	73,859	59	1,937	19.37	1,926	19.26	21.79
7.	Challakere	2,06,219	45	4,872	48.72	4,653	46.53	46.40
8.	Hiriyur	1,70,093	53	5,601	56.01	1,945	19.45	45.07
9.	Hosadurga	1,42,870	60	2,154	21.54	823	8.23	42.86
	District Total	10,78,535	58	55,829	558.29	14,979	149.79	

Table 15.2 *(Contd.)*

Sl. No.	*Name of Taluk*	*Return recharge from irrigation water*		*Total Recharge (Cols.9+10+11) (MM³)*	*Total present draft (MM³)*	*Balance under-ground water available for development (Cols. 12—13) (MM³)*	*Additional number of wells possible @ (10,000 M² water per well)*	*dditional area to be brought under well irrigation @ two hectares per well*
		Surface flow @ 20 per cent infiltration	*Wells @10 per cent infiltration*					
1	2	10	11	12	13	14	15	16
1.	Harihar	22.33	0.18	35.83	1.77	34.06	3,406	6,812
2.	Davangere	46.72	0.75	78.08	7.49	70.59	7.059	14,118
3.	Holalkere	1.19	1.45	38.84	14.52	24.32	2,432	4,864
4.	Chitradurga	7.36	2.51	53.44	25.05	28.39	2,839	5,678
5.	Jagalur	4.93	0.75	31.47	7.49	23.98	2,398	4,796
6.	Molkalmuru	3.87	1.93	27.59	19.26	8.33	833	1,666
7.	Challakere	9.74	4.65	60.79	46.53	14.26	1,426	2,852
8.	Hiriyur	11.20	1.94	58.21	19.45	38.76	3,876	7,752
9.	Hosadurga	4.31	0.82	47.99	8.23	39.76	3,976	7,952
	District Total	111.65	14.98	432.24	149.79	282.45	28,245	56,490

Source: Computed by the authors on the basis of data available from the Revenue Department and the Groundwater studies of the Department of Mines and Geology, Government of Karnataka, 1976.

storage capacity of tanks, will generate gainful employment to the people in the off-season and add to the fertility of the fields. These efforts to desilt the tank beds should primarily be initiated by the farmers of the *atchkat* who are the beneficiaries of the increased storage capacity of the tanks.

It is also known that most of the tanks suffer from lack of proper maintenance and repairs. The profile of the bunds, sluice-gates and the channels need repairs in most cases. Such repairs will substantially increase the irrigation potential of the tanks.

Notwithstanding the general impression that there is precious little possibility to construct new tanks in view of the scanty rainfall, it is worthwhile to investigate the possibilities. A study of Jagalur *taluk* reveals the possibility of 12 new tanks to generate irrigation for over 700 hectares. Similar studies should be taken up in other *taluks* also.

A programme to develop surface-water resources through renovation of existing irrigation works and construction of new ones has been worked out for Jagalur *taluk* to demonstrate and emphasize the possibility of substantial increase in irrigation potential.

The investigation reveals that repairs to the existing tanks in the *taluk* will stabilize assured supply of water to the existing *atchkat* of about 3,000 hectares, and extend irrigation to another 648 hectares. Construction of 12 new tanks will create irrigation potential to cover another 728 hectares. Jagalur is one of the drier *taluks* of the district. If such improvement in irrigation potential is possible in Jagalur, there is no reason why a similar or even greater improvement could not be effected in other taluks of the district.

It is strongly recommended that investigations on the pattern of the Jagalur should be undertaken for all the *taluks* and all efforts should be made to develop the available surface-water resources.

The possibilities of development of underground water resources are greater than that of surface resources (Table 15.2). A conservative estimate of the total recharge of underground water potential and the present draft reveals a balance of about 282 million cubic metres (MM^3) which can be developed for irrigation and for other purposes. At an average draft of 10,000 M^3 per well, it should be possible to have about 28,000 additional wells. Taking two hectares as the average land irrigated by each well, an additional area of about 56,000 hectares can be brought under irrigation. The possibilities are particularly significant in the areas of canal and tank irrigation in Harihar, Davangere and Hiriyur *taluks*.

Groundwater studies of the Department of Mines and Geology, Government of Karnataka, indicate that irrigation wells in the district are mostly shallow, ranging in depth from eight to ten metres. Their diameter is usually large, five to ten metres. The depth of water-table varies from five to ten metres depending upon the rock formations and the season. In the rainy season, water is available at shallow depths; it gets lowered by four to six metres in the dry season. The shallow wells seldom pass through the full extent of the saturated zone. Consequently, they are dry or contain only little water during the dry season. To maintain supply of water even in the dry season, it is necessary that the wells are deep enough to tap the aquifers adequately. The groundwater experts recommend a depth of about 40 to 50 metros for the purpose. The cost of a bore-well to about 50 metres depth works out to about Rs. 20,000 on an average. The credit institutions should come forward in a big way to finance construction of such bore-wells and installation of irrigation pump-sets.

Conservation of Water Resources

It would not be enough to attempt to develop the water resources for the present use. It is equally necessary to conserve the resources for use of future generations that will follow us. With the ever-increasing population, human and animal, the demand for water resources is going to be much more than what it is today.

Conservation of water resources could be attempted in various ways. Management of watersheds in consonance with the ecological requirements will certainly go a long way in augmenting the reserves, both surface and under-ground. Afforestation of slopes and development of pastures (with controlled grazing) will lead to stabilization of the water supply from streams, tanks and wells.

Optimal utilization of the available water is just another way of its conservation. Nobody will dispute the fact that the present utilization of this precious resource is far from the optimum. It is not uncommon to see wastage of water in fields, gardens and homes. One can find areas of water scarcity and plenty in close vicinity. One has only to go to the Harihar and Davangere *taluks* to witness scenes of excessive irrigation and misuse of water. This happens at the cost of the farmers at the tail-end of the canal where crops wither for want of water. Substantial farm land in these two taluks has been rendered unsuitable for cultivation because of water-logging and salinity. Already the problem has assumed great proportion and many farmers have lost their livelihood and have been reduced to the state of abject poverty and starvation.

Unfortunately, the government finds it difficult to retrieve the situation. The Irrigation Department rules allow cultivation of a 'wet' crop (rice) in the Kharif season and semi-dry crops during the rest of the year. But these rules are observed only in their breach. The rich and influential farmers manage to get irrigation water for as many as three crops of rice in a year. If rice is grown in the higher level fields, it has to be grown at lower levels also because seepage of water makes it difficult to grow different crops in the lower level fields. This results in excessive moisture and waterlogging at the lowest level and ultimately the fields are rendered unsuitable for farming.

As discussed earlier, irrigation by canals and tanks also helps in recharging the underground water storage which remains largely untapped because of supply of canal water throughout the year in this area. In such a dubious situation wherein the government finds it difficult to enforce the cropping pattern regulations excessive irrigation results in waterlogging and salinity, underground water remains untapped and farmers at the tail-end are starved or irrigation water, the short-run solution to all these problems lies in restricting the supply of canal and tank water to only one season. This will result not only in assured supply of water at the tail-end *atchkat*, but also in extension of irrigation to a larger area. Thus, farmers over a larger area will be able to get assured supply of water at least for one crop. They may utilize the underground water for second and third crops, if needed. This will also take care of the problem of waterlogging and salinity and in due course of time all the affected areas could be reclaimed.

Better management of water also implies change in the irrigation technology. The present practice of flow irrigation is much less efficient as compared to other techniques. Sprinkler or drip irrigation, for example, can save a substantial amount of precious irrigation water for use by a larger section of the community. Though it involves heavy initial investment, it should not be out of reach of the rich farmers of the irrigated areas. The government could arrange supply of the equipment (or course, without subsidy) at reasonable prices.

Conservation of water resources also demands a rational selection of crops to utilize the precious irrigation water. Though heavy investments have been made by the government to provide irrigation water, precious little has been done to educate the farmers on selection of crops. The important consideration in selection of crops by the farmers today is the yield of crops per unit area. If water is a more precious element in agricultural production as compared to land, the profitability of the crops should be measured in yield of per unit of water Unfortunately, this precious resource is not sold in measured quantities. It is either available in plenty or not at all.

It is worthwhile to devise ways and means to regulate flow of water and supply water in measured quantities. It may not be possible at the present to supply measured water to the individual farmers, but it should not be difficult to do so for groups of farmer who get water from the same opening in the irrigation channel.

The farm extension agencies should be activated to educate the farmers in judicious use of water. An important area of agricultural extension is the amount of water needed for a good crop of rice. The majority of farmers carry the impression that rice field should be flooded with as much water as possible. it is for the extension workers to dispel this, and similar false notions of the farming community and to educate it in scientific management of irrigation water.

The Over-all View

The development and conservation programmes, discussed above, will increase the irrigation potential by more than 100 per cent. The irrigation facilities covered 72,500 hectares in 1974-75. If all the development programmes are implemented in additional area of about 20,200 hectares can be covered by improvements to the existing tanks and by developing the available surface flow and another 56,500 hectares can be brought under irrigation by fully harnessing the underground water potential. Thus, benefits of assured irrigation could cover about 1,49,000 hectares, i.e., more than one-third of the total farm land, by 1991 or so (Table 15.3).

In 1974-75, an area of about 25,000 hectares received irrigation for more than one crop in case we aim to build an egalitarian society and extend the fruits of development (irrigation facilities in the present case) to a larger segment of the rural poor, the State government could decide to limit irrigation from government sources to only one crop. Thus, an additional area of 25,000 hectares could have the benefit or irrigation, bringing the total irrigated area of about 1,74,000 hectares or about 40 per cent of the total farm land.

TABLE 15.3: Total Irrigation Potential in Chitradurga District (Taluk-wise) 1974-75

Sl. No.	Name of Taluk	Existing net irrigated area	Additional irrigation potential (hectares)			Total irrigation potential (Cols. 3+6)	Total cultivated area according to the suggested land-use pattern	Percentage of cultivated area that can be irrigated
			Surface	Underground	Total			
1	2	3	4	5	6	7	8	9
1.	Harihar	11,300	5,500	6,800	12,300	23,600	33,800	70
2.	Davangere	24,800	2,000	14,100	16,100	40,900	54,400	75
3.	Holalkere	1,700	2,000	4,900	6,900	8,600	32,600	26
4.	Chitradurga	5,800	2,000	5,700	7,700	13,500	47,600	28
5.	Jagalur	3,300	1,200	4,800	6,000	9,300	33,000	28
6.	Molkalmuru	3,100	1,500	1,700	3,200	6,300	23,000	27
7.	Challakere	11,800	2,000	2,900	4,900	16,700	92,600	18
8.	Hiriyur	7,500	2,000	7,700	9,700	17,200	69,300	25
9.	Hosadurga	3,200	2,000	7,900	9,000	13,100	47,700	27
	District Total	72,500	20,200	56,500	76,700	1,49,200	4,34,000	34

Source: Columns 4 and 5 drawn from Tables 14.1 and 14.2 respectively; Col. 8 derived from Table 13.4.

As discussed earlier, there is considerable scope to effect economy in the utilization of the irrigation water by adopting better irrigation technology and appropriate cropping pattern. At a conservative estimate, such economy may save enough water to irrigate an additional area of about 50,000 hectares. It should, thus, be possible to cover about 2,24,000 hectares or about 50 per cent of the farm land with assured irrigation facilities at least for one crop in the year.

NOTES

1. Based on a survey conducted by Mr. R. Rajappa, Assistant Engineer, P.W.D. (Minor Irrigation), Jagalpur, Chitradurga district, 1975.
2. B.P. Radhakrishna and S. Kumar, (1972) "Estimated Annual Recharge, Taluk-wise, Master Plan for Development of Underground Water Resources in Mysore State, Ground Water Studies, No. 74, Government of Karnataka.

16

AGRICULTURAL PRODUCTION PROGRAMME

IT IS customary to suggest further increase in cultivated land as one of the means to increase agricultural production. The Fifth Five-Year Plan of the district laments that only 47 per cent of the land fit for cultivation is actually under cultivation. It is rarely realized that use of marginal land for crop production is not really the answer to the problem of a drought-prone area.

In the previous chapter, it was pointed out that by the end of this century, only about 40.2 per cent of the total land of the district should be under plough. This does not mean that the rest of the land is to be left unproductive. What it really means is that apart from the forest land, the remaining uncultivated land should be used for pasture which can sustain a vigorous dairy farming and other animal-based activities or for forests, etc. We will examine below the feasibilities of these.

Food Requirements

The population of Chitradurga district in the year 2001 is expected to be of the order of 24 lakh (Table 16.1). It is assumed that growth of population on an average will be two per cent per annum. It is realistic in the sense that even if by 2001 A.D. growth rate comes down to 1.5 per cent, it was more than 2.5 per cent at least up to 1985. Nevertheless, two per cent increase has been used for all the years for the sake of simplicity and it may hold good for most of the *taluks* except Harihar and Davangere.

Given the above population, the requirements of cereals at the rate of 500 gramms per head per day would amount to 2.63, 3.14 and 3.79

lakh tonnes by 1981, 1991 and 2001 A.D. Taluk-wise requirements of cereals are given in Table 16.2. The requirements of other foods for a balanced diet are given in Tables 16.3, 16.4, 16.5, 16.6, 16.7 and 16.8. The production and requirement of various agricultural commodities are given in Table 16.9.

TABLE 16.1: Projected Population of Chitradurga District

		Actual		*Projected*	
Sl. No.	*Taluks*	*1971*	*1981*	*1991*	*2001*
1.	Harihar	1,24,112	1,48,934	1,78,720	2,14,464
2.	Davangere	2,76,747	3,32,096	3,98,515	4,78,218
3.	Jagalur	97,340	1,16,808	1,40,169	1,68,203
4.	Chitradurga	2,09,915	2,51,898	3,02,277	3,62,733
5.	Holalkere	1,34,863	1,61,836	1,94,203	2,33,044
6.	Molakalmuru	73,272	86,926	1,05,511	1,26,613
7.	Challakere	1,82,632	2,19,158	2,62,990	3,15,588
8.	Hiriyur	1,58,776	1,90,539	2,28,637	2,74,365
9.	Hosadurga	1,39,799	1,67,758	2,01,311	2,41,573
District Total		13,97,456	16,75,953	20,12,333	24,14,801

Source: Compiled by the authors on the basis of 1971 data obtained from Census of India Series 14, Chitradurga district, Part X.

TABLE 16.2: Requirements of Cereals, 1981 — 2001 A.D.

(*in Tonnes*)

Sl.No.	*Taluks*	*1981*	*1991*	*2001*
1.	Harihar	23,383	28,059	33,671
2.	Davangere	52,139	62,567	75,080
3.	Jagalur	18,339	20,007	26,408
4.	Chitradurga	39,548	47,458	56,949
5.	Holalkere	25,408	30,490	36,588
6.	Molkalmuru	13,647	16,565	19,878
7.	Challakere	34,408	41,290	49,547
8.	Hiriyur	29,915	35,896	43,075
9.	Hosadurga	26,338	31,606	37,927
	District Total	2,63,125	3,13,938	3,79,123

Note: 86 adultunits are equivalent to 100 persons.
Source: Compilted by the authors.

TABLE 16.3: Requirement of Pulses in Chitradurga District at 70 Gramms Per Head Per Day

(*in Tonnes*)

Sl. No.	*Taluks*	*1971*	*1981*	*1991*	*2001*
1.	Harihar	2,732	3,280	3,937	4,724
2.	Davangere	6,093	7,315	8,778	10,533
3.	Jagalur	4,125	2,573	3,087	3,705
4.	Chitradurga	4,623	5,548	6,658	7,990
5.	Holalkere	2,970	3,565	4,278	5,133
6.	Molkalmuru	1,614	1,915	2,324	2,789
7.	Challakere	4,023	4,827	5,793	6,951
8.	Hiriyur	3,497	4,197	5,036	6,043
9.	Hosadurga	3,079	3,695	4,434	5,321
	District Total	32,756	36,915	44,325	53,189

Source: Compiled by the authors.

TABLE 16.4: Requirement of Groundnut at 10 Gramms Per Head Per Day

(*in Tonnes*)

Sl. No.	*Taluks*	*1971*	*1981*	*1991*	*2001*
1.	Harihar	390.3	468.6	562.4	674.9
2.	Davangere	870.4	1,045.0	1,254.0	1,504.7
3.	Jagalur	306.4	367.6	441.0	529.3
4.	Chitradurga	660.4	792.6	951.1	1,141.4
5.	Holalkere	424.3	509.3	611.1	733.3
6.	Molkalmuru	230.6	273.6	332.0	398.4
7.	Challakere	574.7	689.6	827.6	993.0
8.	Hiriyur	499.6	599.6	719.4	863.3
9.	Hosadurga	439.9	527.9	633.4	760.1
	District Total	4,396.6	5,273.8	6,332.0	7,598.4

Source: Compiled by the authors.

TABLE 16.5: Requirement of Vegetables at 232 Gramms Per Head Per Day

(in Tonnes)

Sl. No.	*Taluks*	*1971*	*1981*	*1991*	*2001*
1.	Harihar	9,015.0	10,758.2	12,992.1	15,589.0
2.	Davangere	20,106.9	21,139.5	28,967.4	34,758.9
3.	Jagalur	7,078.5	8,490.9	10,187.1	12,226.5
4.	Chitradurga	15,255.9	18,308.4	21,971.4	26,367.0
5.	Holalkere	9,801.0	11,764.5	14,117.4	16,938.9
6.	Molkalmuru	9,326.2	6,319.5	7,669.2	9,203.2
7.	Challakere	13,275.9	15,929.1	19,119.9	22,938.3
8.	Hiriyur	11,540.1	13,850.1	16,618 8	19,941.9
9.	Hosadurga	10,160.7	12,193.5	14,632.2	17,559.3
	District Total	1,05,560.2	7,18,753.5	14,6,172.5	1,75,523.0

Source: Compiled by the authors.

TABLE 16.6: Requirement of Milk at 200 Gramms Per Head Per Day

(in Tonnes)

Sl. No.	*Taluks*	*1971*	*1981*	*1991*	*2001*
1.	Harihar	7,806	9,372	11,248	13,498
2.	Davangere	17,408	20,000	25,080	30,094
3.	Jagalur	6,128	7,352	8,820	10,586
4.	Chitradurga	13,208	15,852	19,022	22,828
5.	Holalkere	8,486	10,186	12,222	14,666
6.	Molkalmuru	4,612	5,472	6,640	7,968
7.	Challakere	11,494	13,792	16,552	19,860
8.	Hiriyur	9,992	11,992	14,388	17,266
9.	Hosadurga	8,798	10,558	12,668	15,202
	District Total	87,932	1,04,686	1,26,640	1,51,968

Source: Compiled by the authors.

TABLE 16.7: Requirement of Fruits at 25 Gramms Per Head Per Day

(*in Tonnes*)

Sl. No.	*Taluks*	*1971*	*1981*	*1991*	*2001*
1.	Harihar	1,444.11	1,733.82	2,080.88	2,497.13
2.	Davangere	3,220.48	3,866.50	4,639.80	5,567.39
3.	Jagalur	1,133.68	1,360.12	1,631.70	1,958.41
4.	Chitradurga	2,443.48	2,932.62	3,519.07	4,223.18
5.	Holalkere	1,569.91	1,884.41	2,261.07	2,713.21
6.	Molkalmuru	853.22	1,012.32	1,228.40	1,474.08
7.	Challakere	2,126.39	2,551.52	3,062.12	3,675.58
8.	Hiriyur	1,848.52	2,218.52	2,661.78	3,194.21
9.	Hosadurga	1,627.63	1,953.23	2,343.58	2,812.37
	District Total	16,267.42	19,513.06	23,428.04	28,115.56

Source: Compiled by the authors.
Note: Same are the figures for fats, oils and flesh food.

TABLE 16.8: Requirement of Sugar/Jaggery at 40 Gramms Per Head Per Day

(*in Tonnes*)

Sl. No.	*Taluks*	*1971*	*1981*	*1991*	*2001*
1.	Harihar	1,361	1,874	2,249	2,700
2.	Davangere	3,481	4,180	5,016	6,018
3.	Jagalur	1,225	1,470	1,764	2,116
4.	Chitradurga	2,541	3,170	3,804	4,564
5.	Holalkere	1,697	2,037	2,444	2,932
6.	Molkalmuru	942	1,094	1,328	1,593
7.	Challakere	2,298	2,758	3,310	3,972
8.	Hiriyur	1,998	2,398	2,877	3,452
9.	Hosadurga	1,757	2,111	2,533	3,040
	District Total	17,300	21,092	25,325	30,387

Source: Compiled by the authors.

TABLE 16.9: Production and Requirement of Various Agricultural Commodities in Chitradurga District

	Items of food								
	Cereals	*Pulses*	*Groundnut*	*Vegetables*	*Fruits*	*Milk*	*Fats and oils*	*Flesh Food*	*Sugar/gur*
1	2	3	4	5	6	7	8	9	10
Requirements according to nutritional standards—1978 (Tonnes)	2,65,000	37,000	5,300	1,20,000	20,000	95,000	20,000	20,000	21,000
Estimated production average (1972–75)—(Tonnes)	2,00,000	30,000	30,000	60,000	6,000	90,000	—	10,000	15,000
Production available for consumption (Tonnes)	2,00,000	30,000	6,000	60,000	6,000	90,000	—	10,000	10,000
Production consumed by the urban sector:									
Prorata (Tonnes)	40,000	6,000	1,200	12,000	1,200	18,000	—	2,000	2,000
Actual (Tonnes)	40,000	7,200	1,500	15,600	1,560	24,3000	—	2,700	2,700
Production consumed by the rural sector:									
Prorata (Tonnes)	1,60,000	24,000	4,800	48,000	4,800	72,000	—	8.000	8,000
Actual (Tonnes)	1,60,000	22,800	4,500	44,400	4,440	65,700	—	7,3000	12,300
Per capita availability (Gramms)	332	47	9	92	9	136	—	15	25
Per capita required (Rural) (Gramms)	400	70	10	232	37	241	38	35	40
Deficit per capita (Rural) (Gramms)	77	23	1	140	28	105	—	20	15

Source: Compiled by the authors.

The foregoing tables show that the district is almost self-sufficient in cereals. It has shortage of pulses – the only major source of protein in vegetarian food. It produces adequate amount of groundnut to meet the needs of the district. Milk is in short supply and so is flesh food. There is also shortage of vegetables.

The per capita income of the district from agriculture and animal husbandry is about Rs. 625 (1974-75). Given the disparities in income, it is apparent that half of the population of the district does not benefit from the availability of various food items. Added to this is the seasonality in the availability of such items like fruits. During the season, mango, for example, is too plentiful, but for the rest of the year fruit supply is marginal. Same is the case with vegetables too. In order to maintain supply all through the year, there is need to promote cultivation of fruit crops which are not seasonal. Similarly, vegetables productions has to increased.

In this connection, it has to be noted that Chitradurga district is a subsistence agriculture district. Of the total food crop output, on an average 40 per cent is sold. All of this is not sold in the district. In fact, much of the sale of rice from two *taluks* of Davangere and Harihar goes outside the district. Since the rest of the *taluks* are drought-prone and poor, the consumption of cereals is less than required. The problem acquires more serious dimensions during the drought periods.

Thus, the problem of this district is not only deficient production of food items like pulses, fruits, vegetables, milk and flesh foods, but also unequal distribution of the agricultural resources. The irrigated areas of the districts in Harihar, Davangere and Hiriyur *taluks* are fairly prosperous. The agricultural productivity in these areas is quite high and marketable surplus is substantial. But rest of the district suffers from the vagaries of rainfall, low agricultural production and mass rural poverty. The strategy of agricultural production in the district should not only aim at increased production. It should also strive to narrow the gap between the affluent farmers of the irrigated areas and the poor ones of the unirrigated areas. In sum, the agricultural development programmes should be geared in such a way that each rural family becomes economically viable and generates enough to meet the basic minimum needs.

The amelioration of the living conditions of people in the dry areas, which constitute almost 80 per cent of the district, could be achieved by three important measures:

(i) Increased crop production by provision of irrigation, improved seeds, fertilizers and plant protection measures;
(ii) diversification of rural economy by introduction of dairying, sheep and goat rearing, and agro-industries based on local raw materials and local skills; and
(iii) more equitable land ownership.

TABLE 16.10: Yield of Major Crops in Chitradurga District, 1974-75

Sl. No.	*Crops*	*Irrigated or unirrigated*	*Area ('000 ha)*	*Yield (Q/ha)*
1.	Jowar:			
	Hybrid	Irrigated	18	27
		Unirrigated	60	10
	Local		40	5
2.	Ragi	Irrigated	16	20
		Unirrigated	64	10
3.	Navane	Unirrigated	51	8
4.	Rice	Irrigated:		
		Winter/Summer	9	22
		Kharif	24	15
		Unirrigated	1	—
5.	Bajra	Unirrigated	27	7
6.	Save	Unirrigated	10	4
7.	Horsegram	Unirrigated	49	4
8.	Tur	Unirrigated	17	7
9.	Groundnut	Irrigated	16	20
		Unirrigated	13	5

Source: Area obtained from Revenue Department and yield from Bureau of Economics and Statistics and Department of Agriculture, Government of Karnataka.

Crop Production Programme

Crop production programme should aim to maintain the self-sufficiency in foodgrains despite the growth of population at the rate of about two per cent per year. The only way to reach the target of food production to meet the growing demand is to raise the productivity of the crop land. Fortunately, there is tremendous scope to improve the productivity as the present levels are terribly low. The present yield of the major crops of the district has been given in Table 16.10. It will be seen that the yield of jowar, which is the most important crop and accounts for almost one-fourth of the crop area of the district, is as low as five quintals/hectare in case of local varieties and 10 quintals/hectare in case of hybrid varieties under rainfed conditions. The yield of hybrid jowar goes up almost three-fold under irrigation. Same is true of other crops also. Substitution of local varieties with high yielding varieties results in about 50 to 100 per cent increase and provision of irrigation results in about 100 to 150 per cent improvement in the yield. Apart from irrigation and improved seed, the other factors which contribute to better yield are plant protection measures and improved farming practices.

Assured supply of moisture is undoubtedly the most important element in improvement of crop yield. Despite the fact that Chitradurga is a drought-prone area, there is considerable scope to augment irrigation facilities. The major thrust of crop production programme in the district has to be on development of irrigation facilites. As detailed in Chapter 15, irrigation facilities can be developed to cover about 2,25,000 hectares of crop land by 1991. Thus, half of the crop land can be protected from the vagaries of monsoon and the farmers can have at least one assured crop.

Supply of good quality seed should receive priority next only to irrigation. It is common experience that quality seed is usually not available in the market, and if available, it is sold at exorbitant price and its quality is often doubtful. These factors – unavailability, high price and doubtful quality – explain the low adoption of HYV seeds despite three decades of extension work by the State government. It is, therefore, necessary that institutional arrangements should be evolved to supply good quality seeds as well as fertilizers and pesticides to the farmers at reasonable price. It is also important that quality seed should be produced locally. The government farms and agrilcultural land under local bodies could be utilized for the purpose. Seed production could also be entrusted to individual farmer unders strict supervision of the appropriate authority.

Cropping Pattern

The subsistence agriculture of Chitradurga district is characterized by dominance of low value and low yielding foodgrains. These foodgrains, mostly millets, occupy about three-fourths of the crop land. The yield of most of these crops is terribly low. Local jowar, navane, bajra, save and other minor millets, which together occupy about

TABLE 16.11: Suggested Use of Crop Land in Chitradurga District

('000 ha)

	Crops	*Area 1974-75*	*Desired area by 2,000 A.D.*
	1	2	3
1.	*Cereals*:		
	Jowar - Hybrid	78	100
	Local	40	—
	Ragi	80	60
	Navane	51	20
	Rice	34	40
	Bajra	27	30
	Others	12	10
	Total cereals:	322	260
2.	*Pulses*:		
	Horsegram	49	40
	Tur	17	30
	Others	10	30
		76	100
	Total foodgrains	398	360
3.	Sugarcane	3	10
4.	Fruits, Vegetables and spices	22	40
5.	*Oil crops*:		
	Groundnut	29	40
	Coconut	14	15
	Sesamum	12	15
	Others	6	5
	Total Oil Crops	61	75
6.	Cotton	44	50
7.	Miscellaneous Crops	15	
	Total cropped area	529	540

Source: Compiled by the Authors.

1,40,000 hectares (more than one-fifth of the cropped area), yield as low as eight quintals/hectare or even less. There is obvious need to change the existing cropping pattern. In view of the marginally reduced crop land as envisaged in the suggested land-use plan (Chapter 14), the allocation of crop land could be changed as outlined in Table 16.11. Such allocation has been worked out in view of the long nutritional requirements of the people (Tables 16.2 to 16.8). It will be seen from Table 16.12 that the area under cereals has been substantially reduced and that under pulses and fruits and vegetables increased. This slant in favour of pulses and fruits and vegetables is necessary in view of the general protein deficiency of the diet of the people. The area under cereals should progressively decrease from the present level of 3,22,000 hectares to about 2,60,000 hectares by the turn of this century.

TABLE 16.12: Estimated foodgrains production in Chitradurga District by 2000 A.D.

	Food Production		
Crops	*Area ('000 ha)*	*Yield (Q/ha)*	*Production ('000 tonnes)*
1	2	3	4
Cereals:			
Jowar	100	20	200
Ragi	60	20	120
Rice	40	40	160
Bajra	30	15	45
Navane	20	15	30
Others	10	15	15
Total Cereals	260		570
Pulses:			
Horsegram	40	10	40
Tur	30	15	45
Others	30	10	30
Total Pulses	100		115
Total foodgrains	360		685

Source: Estimated by the authors.

There is need to reduce considerably the area under low yielding crops like local jowar, navane, save and other small millets. The area under pulse crops should gradually be increased to have greater production of protein-rich grains. This is particularly important in view of the dietary habits of the rural population. The majority of people in the district being Lingayats and vegetarians, flesh foods are not important. The allocation of area for pulse crops should, therefore, be increased gradually from the present level of 76,000 hectares to about 100,000 hectares by 2000 A.D. Area under commercial crops should also be increased to boost up income from the agricultural sector.

Area under rice has shown an upward trend in recent years in the irrigated aress of the district. Increasing production of rice in such areas has already started showing signs of deterioration of crop land due to waterlogging and salinity. In the Bhadra canal area in Harihar taluk just 12 years of canal irrigation has rendered about 1/15th of the crop land unsuitable for cultivation. This happens mainly because of the exessive irrigation which in turn results from the tariff policy of the Irrigation Department and ineffective agricultural extension education. It is, therefore, necessary to control excessive irrigation for rice cultivation and save water for the starving crops at the tail-ends.

A similar upward trend in crop area has been noticed in case of sugarcane, particulary with the establishment of the sugar factories. Though sugar cultivation is commercially profitable, its benefits accrue to just a handful of farmers. The crop requires large amount of water. It is estimated that irrigation water needed for one hectare of sugarcane can support about three to four hectares of semi-dry crops like jowar, bajra and ragi. If our development strategy has an egalitarian slant and aims at benefit to the largest number of people, it would be appropriate to restrict area under sugarcane cultivation.

It need not be emphasized that the solution to the problem of growing demand for food does not lie in extending the crop area, but in intensification of the agricultural activities. The agricultural land is stipulated to shrink marginally under the revised land-use plan (Chapter 14) from the present level of 650 thousand hectares (493,734 hectares net cultivated area and 111,106 hectares current fallow) to about 434 thousand hectares by 2000 A.D. Much of the agricultural land is presently used for growing just one crop in a year because of the constraint of water supply. Wherever water supply is adequate, as many as three crops are being grown. The intensity of cropping (total cropped area expressed as per cent of net shown area) is only 106 at present. In view of the possibility of increased irrigation facilities to covered about one-half the total cultivated land, it is safe to assume that the intensity of cropping will go up to about 125 per cent by 1990 and to about 150 per cent by the end of this century. If this could be done, the total cropped area could be maintained at the present level even after reduction in the cultivated area. A moderate increase in crop yield by about 50 per cent should be enough to meet the total food requirements of the population in 2001 A.D. Given assured irrigation over about 50 per cent of the crop land, use of HYV seed for all crops (irrigated and unirrigated) adequate plant protection measures and scientific methods of cultivation, it should not be difficult to raise the yield of crops by 50 per cent by 1990 and by 100 per cent by 2000 A.D. Crop-wise details of food production at the end of this century has been outlined in Table 15.12. It will be seen that foodgrain production will increase from an estimated average of 2.30 lakh tonnes – 1972-75 to about 6.85 tonnes by 2000 A.D., thus, achieving the 200 per cent growth.

17

HORTICULTURE, ANIMAL HUSBANDRY AND ALLIED PROGRAMMES

IT IS now widely accepted that diversification of economy is as necessary as improvement of crop farming in the drought-prone areas. Despite all efforts to develop irrigation potential and to utilize the irrigation water, most rationally and economically, it would not be possible to protect more than half the cultivated land against the vagaries of monsoon. The other half of crop land will always be exposed to failures and uncertainty of rainfall. Crop production in these drought-prone areas will always remain risky.

For a long time, it was held that development of drought resistant crop varieties and appropriate agronomic practices could sustain crop production in the drought-prone areas. Two decades of dry farming experience in the country has amply demonstrated how risky it is to depend on grain farming even with improvement of strains and farming practices. It is now being realized, with greater conviction, that tree crops can resist the droughts better than the grain crops. It is in this context that development of horticulture, social forestry and animal husbandry assumes great importance in development of drought-prone areas.

Diversified economy was an important weapon which our ancestors used to fight droughts. Even in times when persistent droughts damaged grain crops, fruit trees and other trees could survive. The leaves of trees, like bamboo, *shisham*, could provide sustenance to the livestock population for quite some time. Animal products like milk and meat, and fruits could sustain the people during drought periods. Unfortunately, rapid increase in human population and craze for crop land to produce foodgrains have resulted in destruction of forests and pastures and depletion of animal wealth. Overemphasis on grain farming in recent years coupled with unimaginative programmes like mechanization and tractorization have contributed to the neglect of livestock population. It is now high time that we learn from the wisdom of our ancestors and take programmes to diversify the rural economy.

Horticultural Programmes

Different tree crops and groves occupy about 15,000 hectares in the district. Another 14,000 hectares are devoted to cultivation of fruits and vegetables. Together tree crops and fruits and vegetables occupy about three per cent of the land area. Though opportunities for horticultural development are immense, the development efforts in the successive Five-Year Plans have been only lukewarm. The Fifth Five-Year Plan document of the district recognizes the importance of horticultural programmes, and stresses the need to supply seed and seedlings of good quality and laments that 'since there is not sufficient control over the trade of seeds and planting material, cultivators are facing great difficulty in securing the better varieties of seeds and planting material'. This sums up the approach of the horticultural department. Like any other programme, horticultural development has suffered from the malady of sectoral isolation. It is of prime concern to the development planners to revitalize and strengthen the programme in a co-ordinated manner.

The Horticulture Department of the State Government maintains as many as 19 farms/nurseries in different parts of the district. The size of these farms/nurseries varies from one hectare to 42 hectares. In all, they cover 225 hectares. These orchards grow guava, sapota, papaya, mango, banana, grapes, coconut, cherries, citrus fruits, jack and such other fruit trees/vines. Most of these farms supply seedlings to the farmers. Apart form these farms the department maintains five dry orchards under the Drought-prone Area Programme and conducts many other programmes including training of gardeners and demonstrations.

Despite all these efforts horticultural programmes have had only limited impact on the over-all agricultural development .

The Horticulture Department is also involved in programmes like development of arecanut and cashewnut plantations. As these crops are capital intensive and risky, only affluent farmers can afford to go for these crops. It will, therefore, be more purposeful and profitable to concentrate on schemes of larger appeal and application.

The horticultural development efforts should be grouped in four categories:

(i) Provision of quality planting material;
(ii) plant protection measures;
(iii) transport and marketing arrangements; and
(iv) sustenance for the gestation period.

The horticulture department should have nurseries for the popular and locally adapted plants at block and *mandal* levels. As tree crops go a long way in improving the environmental quality by checking run-off and helping re-charge of groundwater storage, checking soil erosion and moderating temperature, the supply of the planting materials should be taken up as a welfare measure and should be made available to the people free of cost or at nominal price. Similarly, pesticides and plant protection equipment should be supplied at subsidized rates. It is sometimes argued that development of horticultural farms is uneconomic if cost-benefit ratio is worked out. It would be appropriate to take into account the ecological benefits accruing from the horticultural farms while attempting economic evaluation of such projects. If this is done, horticultural programmes will never be uneconomic.

Extension education should be geared not only to successful production of fruit crops, but also at proper utilization of the product. Efforts should be made to absorb much of the produce locally. Organizational set-up should be evolved to manage the marketable surplus.

In fact, transport and marketing are the most crucial factors in deveolpment of horticulture on commercial lines. It is common experience that peripheries of cities and metropolitan centres have flourishing horticultural activities mainly because transport and marketing channels are well developed. It is, therefore, necessary to organize marketing of surplus horticultural produce. The Agricultural Marketing Board should come forward to create the necessary facilities in this regard.

Tree crops usually take a long time before they start bearing fruits. It is difficult for the small farmers to sustain themselves during the intervening period. Co-operative societies and credit institutions should come forward to lend support. In fact, the same institutional set-up should manage nursery, plant protection measures, credit and marketing of the surplus. Such horticultural development should invariably form part of the larger integrated agricultural development programme and should be organized at different spatial levels.

Social Forestry

Indiscriminate destruction of trees in the wake of rapid population growth in the last few decades has resulted in shortage of wood for fuel, furniture, house construction and variety of other uses. It also had its telling effects on ecological balance. Denudation of slopes has led to accelerated run-off and floods, reduced percolation of water underground and increased hazards of soil erosion and associated problems. The Forest Department has, in fact, an area of about 85,000 hectares under its jurisdiction and this area is for afforestation. But, in reality, hardly one-third of this area is forested. The department has made efforts towards afforestation and some eucalyptus plantations have come up in the past few years.

Apart from the normal development programmes of the Forest Department, efforts have been made from time to time to improve forests under the special programmes like the Pilot Intensive Rural Employment Project (PIREP) and the Drought-Prone Area Programmes (DPAP). Some afforestation work was taken up in Harihar block under PIREP as an employment programme. Afforestation has been an important programme under the DPAP. Some 4,000 hectares were taken up in the Fourth Five-Year Plan and another 4,000 hectares in the Fifth Plan. This includes social forestry.

The impact of these efforts has, however, been limited partly because afforestation has never been taken up as part of an integrated development programme and partly because of the general dryness of the area. Protection of growing plants against the deprecations of the stray cattle has posed a real problem. The area being extremely dry, a plant once damaged by cattle has rare chances of survival. Protection of forests has suffered because of lack of community interest. Afforestation has always been taken up as a government programme and the people have been left uninvolved, unconcerned and indifferent. Thus, a major break-through in afforestation programme could be achieved if people are involved and they take up plantation and protection of new forest stands. The following specific programmes should be taken up to promote quick growth of forests:

1. Under the revised land-use plan (Chapter 14), an area of about 2,91,500 hectares (or 27 per cent of the total area) has to be brought under forests by the end of this century. 2,24,000 hectares of this area lies in the forest zone covering the upper reaches of streams (Fig. 14.2) where afforestation should be undertaken as an ecological measure. Suitable statutory provisions should be enacted to enable the land-owners to plant their holdings with forests. Exemption from land revenue for the area planted with trees, provision of planting material, plant protection service and technical expertise free of cost, long-term loans on easy terms for sustenance till the forests start yielding fruits/wood and creation of marketing system for purchase of forest produce at reasonable price are some of the measures which should be taken up to promote quick afforestation of the upper reaches of the streams.
2. In the pasture and arable land zones, 55,000 and 12,500 hectares, respectively, have to be brought under forests. It is well-known that almost every farmer has some marginal land which is not quite suitable for crop farming. All such marginal lands should be brought under social forestry. It should be made obligatory for all farmers to put at least five per cent of their holdings under social forests. Incentives suggested above could also be provided to the farmers of these zones.
3. *Panchayat Raj* Institutions, State and Central governments, public and private sector undertakings, banks, co-operative societies, schools, etc., be required to plant vacant lands under their control with trees. Planting matertial, plant protection service and technical expertise should be arranged by the Forest Department at low cost. The marketing of the forest produce should also be managed adequately.
4. Forest land with inadequate stand of trees should be leased out to unemployed landless people for plantation of trees. Planting material, plant protection service and technical supervision should be made available by the Forest Department. Maintenance allowance, preferably in the form of foodgrains, could be provided to such planters in the initial stages. The right to land should vest with the Forest Department and that to forest produce with the people when the forests start yielding produce.
5. Cutting of trees should be controlled and regulated. No individual/organization should be allowed to fell trees without requisite permission, while making rules in this regard, one should

keep in view that controls often breed corruption.

6. As suggested earlier (chapter 14), land reform law should allow one hectare of dry land in addition to the ceiling of four hectares, provided this additional land is used for plantation of trees and not for cultivation of crops.
7. Afforestation programme should be linked with rural employment programme and the local production system. In some instance, the Forest Department has opted for use of mechanized ripper using a bulldozer of 110 hp. to form furrows for planting seedlings. It is argued that mechanical ripping is cheaper and speedier as compared to manual trenching. On close scrutiny of the cost of afforestation, it is found that the economics of mechanical ripping are not real. Apart from heavy investment in purchase and maintenance of the machinery, mechanical ripping restricts the employment opportunities which will otherwise be available in case of manual trenching. Manual trenching should, therefore, be preferred to mechanical ripping in all afforestation programmes.

Animal Husbandry Programme

In olden days, the rural economy was diversified in order to provide a safety valve against the havoc wrought by droughts. Every family in the rural areas would invariably rear a few heads of cattle and buffaloes for milk and milk products. In the past few decades, however, rapid growth in human population has resulted in greater demand for agricultural land. The pasture areas have progressively shrunk in size. Overemphasis on grain farming has resulted in neglect of animal wealth. Consequently, the animal population has shown little growth in the past few years. The number of cattle, which account for two-fifths of the total livestock population, actually decreased from 5.2 lakh in 1961 to 5.0 lakh in 1972. Nevertheless, the livestock population of the district remains high (14.73 lakh) and on an average there is one head of livestock available for every person. If developed properly, such large livestock wealth can go a long way to meet the growing demand for food.

Under the revised land-use plan, a large chunk of land (one-fourth of the total) has been earmarked for pastures. The pasture area is the most extensive in Challakere, Hiriyur and Hosadurga *taluks*. These also the *taluks* which have the higest density of livestock population (607, 501 and 408 heads per km², respectively) and the lowest density of human population (89, 93 and 97 per km^2, respectively). These *taluks* together account for one-half of the total pasture area as well as one-half of the livestock population. Animal husbandry should be the lead sector of development in all these areas.

Cattle population is higher in Harihar and Davangere *taluks* than in other *taluks* primarily becasue of the high moisture availability consequent on canal irrigation. Cattle and buffalo rearing could be equally successful in all the *taluks* in areas where irrigation water or sub-soil moisture is available for production of adequate fodder. Sheep rearing has ideal environmental conditions in the dry *taluks* of the districts, particularly Challakere and Hiriyur. These two *taluks* together account for a little over 50 per cent of the total sheep population of the district. Goat rearing is equally popular throughout the district and so is poultry farming.

Despite the great potentials, the present level of livestock development in the district is quite low. The yield of milk and meat per animal is depressingly low. A cow, for example, yields about half a litre of milk per day during the milking period on an average. The bane of animal husbandry development in the district, as also elsewhere in the State, has been the highly sectoralized approach with absolutely no co-ordination within the department or with other allied departments like agriculture. The Fifth Five-Year Plan of the district states that the cattle development programmes "have yet to grow into a properly co-ordinated multipronged scheme that pays equal attention to breeding, feedings and marketing". The efforts to improve bread, fodder and veterinary health care are run in complete isolation of one another. It is not infrequent to find ignorance of and indifference to the development programmes and facilities in the other sub-sectors. About marketing, the less said the better. So far, no organizational set up has been thought of for the processing and marketing of the surplus produce.

It is, therefore, of prime importance that livestock and poultry development should be taken up as an integrated programme in co-ordination with other development sectors like agriculture, horticulture, forestry, agro-industries and co-operation. The organizational set-up provides a good spatial framework for such co-ordinated effort.

One point which needs special emphasis is the participation of the people in these programmes. The initiative for development should come from the people. Producers co-operatives may be on the Anand pattern, with a membership of about 200 should be organized at the Village Panchayat level for management of breeding facilities, provision of credit and disposal of the marketable surplus. The government agencies should provide breeding material, veterinary medical services and technical expertise in adequate measure and at low cost.

Fishery Development

Chitradurga district has two large reservoirs and about 400 major and minor tanks which are suited for fishery development. There are also the fishing communities who have special skills. Still, fishery development is only in the embryonic stage.

The fishery development programme too suffers from isolated approach. The skeletal staff available for the purpose finds itself unequal to the large area reponsibility. It is, therefore, necessary that this programme should be linked with livestock and poultry development progammes in particular and agricultural development programmes in general. A large number of tanks in the district have silted up, resulting in larger waterspread and consequently greater evaporation loss as well as in reduced storage capacity and drying up of tanks in the dry season. Desilting of these tanks should be linked with pisciculture and employment programmes of the area. The fertile silt excavated from the bottom of the tank should provide fertile soil to the fields. The increased storage of tanks should result in more irrigation and larger fishery activities. It is, therefore, suggested that pisciculture, minor irrigatioin desilting of tanks and employment should all be taken up as one integrated programme. The government should come forward to provide fingerlings, improved nets, technical expertise and marketing facilities. As fish are perishable products, efficient transport and marketing play the key-role in development of pisciculture.

Agro-industrial Development

Industrial development in Chitradurga district is at a low ebb. The industrial production accounts for hardly eight per cent of the district income. In the past few years, however, some small-scale industrial units have come up and industrial development is slowly picking up. The district has a large fleet of rural artisans and this local skills should be harnessed in full measure.

The district possesses some mineral resources and industrial units are being established to process the same. But the real potential for industrial development lies in processing of agricultural and silvicultural products. Already some units have started processing products like cotton, sugarcane, oilseeds, tobacco, wood products and leather. In view of the vast potential lying untapped so far and the large skilled labour force available to work, development of agro-industries presents great scope for employment and production.

The suggested pattern of the use of basic resources like land and water envisages large scale afforestation and plantation of fruit crops and other trees. Proper utilization of the products of these tree crops is an important element in the success of these programmes. The Khadi and Village Industries Board has worked out the utilization of some of these crops. The indigenous use itself offers clues to more efficient and rational utilization of many trees which have adapted to the drought-prone environment of these areas. Tamarind and *neem* are good examples. The following account of the utilization of *neem* tree and its products will show how locally adapted trees could be put to industrial uses to improve the local economy. Similar possibilities exist in case of a large number of agricultural and silvicultural products. Apart from the fact that these trees are drought resistant, their utilization is labour-intensive and can generate rural employment.

Utilization of Neem (Azadirachta indica juss) and its Bye-products

Neem tree is an ever-green tree widely adapted to drought-prone dry areas. It bears valuable oilseeds and refreshes the air as all its parts are highly medicinal and it gives profuse shade, pesticides and manures for agriculture. It is mostly grown as avenue tree or as groves. The plant is versatile and every part is utilized in some form or the other. The bark, roots, sap water, leaves, flowers, seed, oil – all have medicinal value. The timber seasons well and is used for house-building, furniture and agricultural implements. It is not attacked by white ants and is valued in making statues for workshop. Leaves are used as cattle fodder, for protecting books, clothes and grains from insects, white ants, etc.

It is a fast growing sturdy tree which can be established without irrigation in many semi-arid regions. It grows well on poor, shallow, stony or sandy soils where agricultural crops give poor yields despite application of fertilizers or fail altogether. The powerful and extensive roots of neem give it an unique physiological capacity to extract nutrient elements which are subsequently restored to the top soil in the litter of fallen leaves and twigs. In this way the nutrients become available to shallow-rooted agricultural crops subsequently. A *neem* plantation provides shelter and could protect adjacent crop land from wind and water erosion. The tree matures in 10 to 15 years. It yields fruits which contain one or two kernels enclosed in a tough shell. Each tree yields about 50 kg per year. The crops mature in May – June. The fresh fruit is usually hand-picked from the ground and de-pulped. De-pulped seed is then dried and supplied to the seed collecting centres at the rate of about one rupee/kg. The pulp water and waste matter are allowed to the compost pit to get a better compost manure. The fruit purchased is thoroughly dried in sun, foreign matter is separated by using slanting sieves of different sizes before storing it in gunny bags. The seed/fruit is decorticated in stone-*chakki* or decorticator, the husk is separated with winnowing fan or *supa*. The kernels crushed in *ghani*/expeller give 30 to 40 per cent oil. *Ghani* gives about five per cent less oil. The *neem* oil sells for about Rs. 6 to 8 per kg. and *neem* cake sells for about Rs. 4 to 6 per kg. By-products like shell and husk are used as fuel or in briquettes or hardboard making. Shells are also used for manufacture of activated carbon or tooth-powder. Damaged fruit and shell are used as manures.

Neem oil is mainly used in soap manufacture. The bitters separated from *neem* oil are used in pharmaceutical industry and also for pesticidal and fertilizing purposes. *Neem* cake used with other manures and fertilizers protects the crops from white ants. Citrus fruit crop can be protected from its pest by spraying the solution of *neem* cake or *neem* oil.

Neem cake is used as cattle and poultry feed. The feed-mix fortified with three per cent *neem* cake is found to be nutritious, appetizing and germicidal for cows and buffaloes. The economics of raising neem trees is provided in Table 17.1. The different uses of neem fruit can be summarized as below:

The above description of the plantation of *neem* tree and processing of its products is illustrative. There are hundreds of such other plants and projects which can be thought of. There may not be immediate local demand for the processed goods, but as the living conditions of the people improve, the local demand will increase. The rational utilization of the resources as discussed earlier and the employment guarantee scheme detailed in a subsequent chapters will generate greater purchasing power for a larger section of the rural population. The increased purchasing power will, in turn, create more demand for consumer goods like soap, oil, toothpaste, etc. Programmes should be conceived in advance to meet the local demand for many such consumer goods.

Figure 17.1

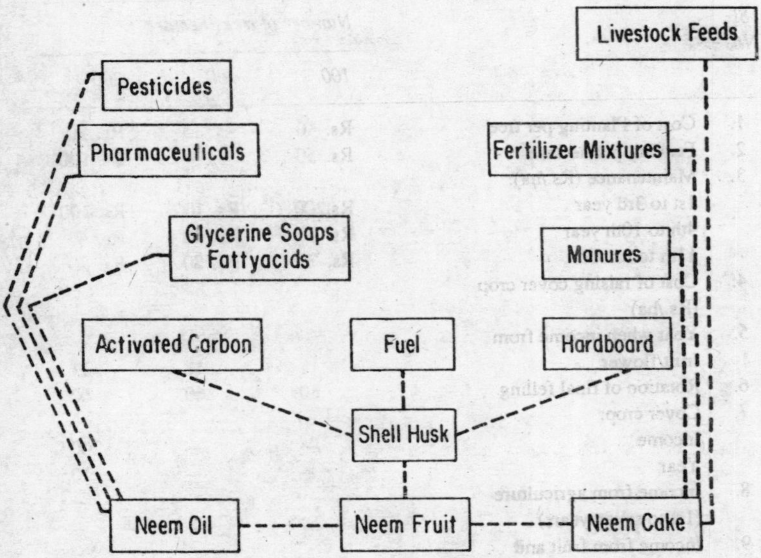

It needs no emphasis that all the programmes discussed in this chapter and in chapter 18 should form part of one integrated employment-cum-production programme and should be organized at the *Panchayat*, *Mandal*, *taluk* and district levels as suggested in Chapter 16.

TABLE 17.1: Economics of Raising Neem Trees

Sl. No.		*Number of trees/hectare*		
		100	*150*	*200*
1.	Cost of Planting per tree	Rs. 10	Rs. 15	Rs. 20
2.	Fencing per hectare	Rs. 50	—	Rs 100
3.	Maintenance (Rs./ha):			
	1st to 3rd year	Rs.200	Rs. 100	Rs. 100
	4th to 10th year	Rs. 50	Rs. 40	Rs. 40
	11th to rotation	Rs. 20	Rs. 20	Rs. 20
4.	Cost of raising cover crop (Rs./ha)	—	—	—
5.	Year when income from fruit/flower	11	11	11
6.	Rotation of final felling	60	60	60
7.	Cover crop:			
	Income	—	—	200
	Year	—	—	10
8.	Income from agriculture (1st to seven years)	—	—	—
9.	Income from fruit and flowers to seven years rotation (Rs./ha)	1,000	1,000	1,000
10.	Income at final felling (Rs./ha)	20,000	20,000	20,000
11.	Internal rate of return (Percentage)	14.0	10.0	12.0

Source: C.M. Kelkar, *Utilization of Neem and its By-products, Non-edible oils* and *soap industry*, Khadi and Village Industries Commission, Poona.

18

INFRASTRUCTURE AND SOCIAL SERVICES

Infrastructure

INFRASTRUCTURE is that set of facilities without which optimum production and human development goals cannot be achieved. Most of these facilities are of multi-purpose nature, e.g., transport and communication network, power, social services, etc. They are needed irrespective of the activity being generated. It is, therefore, an essential dimension of development and attracts inputs irrespective of the nature and focus of the plan.

While looking into the infrastructural needs of an area, one often sees it from the point of view of what the area needs in order to develop its economic and social potentials. This naturally leads one to think of all those infrastructural facilities which can be developed provided the resources are available. But looking at it from the point of view of a planner, one gets a different perspective. In a multi-level planning situation, we plan only for those elements which fall within the scope of the planning authority. For example, while planning for a district, we do not include rail-road development project. We can only indicate the need for a railway line. Railways are planned at the national level. Not even the State governments include railway projects in their plans. The question of their inclusion in still lower level plans, therefore, does not arise.

Infrastructural development schemes at the district and block levels, therefore, are of two types. The first type is the indicative one without detailed schemes. They indicate the needs as perceived by the local population. To what extent such needs can be met on a priority basis has to be determined at the higher territorial levels – State and nation. The second type of schemes are those which have to be planned and developed at the district or block levels and for which adequate resources and technical know-how has to be found at those levels. Only the second type of schemes should find place in detailed plans. Thus, for each territorial level, there are certain functions and activities which have to be worked out in detail while there are certain others which have only to be referred to.

The infrastructural development, to give optimum results at the minimum cost, must have a spatial framework. By spatial framework we mean the system of nodes and networks which integrate the whole area and provide the needed linkages with the surrounding regions. Unfortunately, this is rarely done by infrastructural planners. This happens because even the infrastructure is seen as a sectoral phenomenon, even though it is essentially a spatial one.

The concept of nodes and the procedure for their selection has already been explained earlier in this volume. In this chapter, only the use of the nodes so selected as growth centres, growth points, service centres and central villages in infrastructural development is given. There are two types of infrastructural locations – linear and punctified. Among the first category are transport networks, communication lines, etc. In the second category fall various social services and other institutions.

For efficient functioning of the various infrastructural elements, it is necessary that they should be developed within a given spatial framework. The suggested nodes and the transport (road) networks connecting them is given in Fig. 13.3. Similar exercises should be done for all linear infrastructures.

For punctified infrastructures, we can take the case of educational facilities. While it is good that every village in Chitradurga district has a primary school, it is too bad that there is not a single school which can be classified as a standard one. It is, therefore, suggested that the school locations, barring exceptional cases, could be tied to the focal points forming part of the spatial framework as given below:

Growth centre	:	College
Growth point	:	High school
Service centre	:	Middle school
Central village	:	Standard primary school
Revenue village	:	Lower primary school

By standard primary school, we mean a school which has the same facilities which India could afford to provide in major cities like Bombay and Bangalore. There should be special programmes for enrollment of the children of the weaker sections among the people. The educational institutions should become the community centres around which variety of other cultural activities should be generated.

It would not be possible to give detailed plans for each of the linear or punctified elements of the infrastructure. Suffice to say that all these elements should be so located that they create a cluster of activities and generate interdependencies among them. These activities should include administrative infrastructure too.

Social Services

It is not enough to develop adequate infrastructure for the socio-economic development of the rural areas. The linear and punctified institutions must be run much differently than they are being run at present. The case of education is given below as an illustration of how the social services can become important forces in promoting rural development.

The goals of the educational development programme could be set as follows:

1. To make aware every individual household in the project area with a package of information on:
   (a) natural environment
   (b) productive activity
   (c) social situation and institutions, and
   (d) rural technology.
2. To carry the above to the people through their own representatives, leaders and sons and daughters.

To achieve the above, the following objectives could be set before us:

1. To restructure and improve the formal education programme at all levels – college, high, primary and nursery schools.
2. To see that every child of school-going age attends the scnool, in order that illiteracy does not remain a scourge of the coming generation.

3. To convert the schools into community centres and develop strong ties between the students, parents and teachers with a view to use these ties as vehicles for improving formal education and introducing informal educational processes through a variety of social, cultural and production-oriented activities.
4. Link up formal and informal educational processes with rural technological development programmes through a series of fabrication and production centres, and to train the youth of the village to secure self-employment.

Action Programme

To achieve the above objectives the following action programmes are to be started in the project area at an early date.

Restructuring of Formal Education

There are three basic human elements in the formal education system. They together constitute a triangle.

Figure 18.1

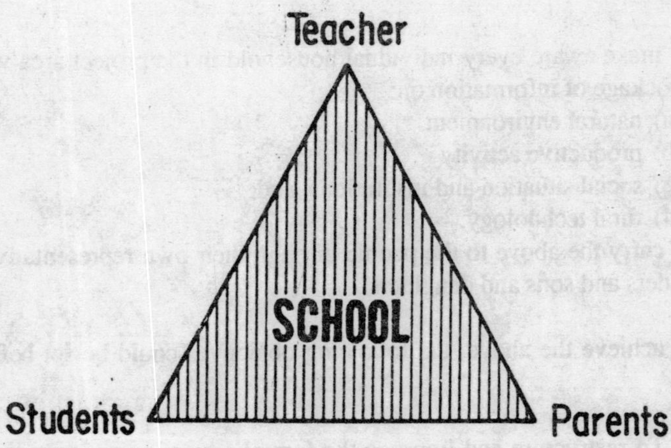

The quality and relevance of education imparted depends upon degree of co-ordination and co-operation among the three. Any educational development programme, must consider these three elements as the target elements.

Apart from the human triad, there is a material triad which is a significant determinent of quality of education. This consists of quality of education, physical environment of the school, the equipments and teaching aids and reading materials. All of these have to be taken care of in educational development programme.

Figure 18.2

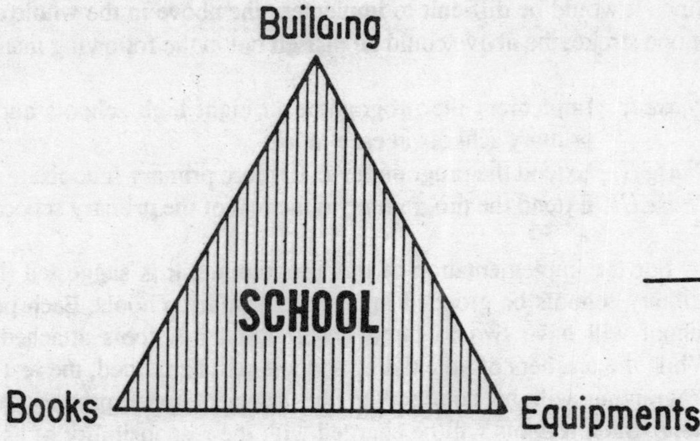

Restructuring of formal education system would involve rethinking on each of the above six elements. Some proposals in this regard are given below:

Teachers: A training programme for teachers of the project area should be organized to acquaint them with the latest methods of teaching.

Parents: Parents should be brought closer to school either through Village Panchayat system or through parents' organization using local leadership.

Building: Immediate efforts should be made to determine minimum space requirements for primary schools keeping in view the capacity of State and local community to bear the cost of construction and maintenance, and additional space would be made available.

Books: Immediate steps be taken to develop suitable books for children together with handbooks for teachers on how to teach. Libraries should be opened in each school.

Equipment: Each school should be provided with minimum furniture and equipment to teach various subjects. Some extra funds should be made available for outdoor activities.

Implementation

Since it would be difficult to implement the above in the whole district at one stroke, the above could be phased out in the following manner:

Phase I: Implement the programme in eight high schools and eight primary schools in each *taluk*.
Phase II: Extend the programme to 10 more primary schools.
Phase III: Extend the programme to the rest of the primary schools.

For the implementation of this programme, it is suggested that the primary schools be grouped into upper primary schools. Each primary school will have two to three lower primary schools attached to it. While the teachers of all existing schools will be trained, the rest of the programme will be confined to the selected upper primary schools alone. Such schools will be charged with the responsibility of assisting the lower primary schools in implementing the instructional improvement programme.

In order to make the school as a community institution, responsive to local needs and aspirations, the changes in work schedule would be effected.

1. Schools will be closed for two weeks or more during the sowing and harvesting times.
2. Schools would open at 9 a.m. and close at 3 p.m. to accommodate two requirements:

   (a) Children should be available for household work for at least three hours daily.
   (b) The school building should be available for non-formal educational programmes after 3 p.m.

Before we close this section, it would be worthwhile to reiterate that creation of healthy environment for children to learn is a *sine qua non* for any educational development programme. To do this, it is not enough that we train teachers, organize the parents and local resources, but we must think of some major actions too, such as shifting the schools to a better and more open place, opening children's library in conjunction with rural public library, etc. A thorough study of the facilities in existing schools is needed, before we launch the project.

To Attract Every Child to School

The purpose of this programme is to eliminate adult illiteracy after this generation of illiterates fades out. Instead of attempting to literate hundreds and thousands of people who have no or little motivation for literacy, we should attempt to secure the future, not so much because we are more interested in the future than in the present, but mainly because we cannot handle the present as effectively as we should and also because our tomorrow would be our children's today.

To achieve this objective there is need for door to door campaign with local leaders, teachers and parents to spot out the children of school going age and help their parents to send them to school. This would involve the study of reasons the parents advance for not sending the children to school.

Rural educational processes can be relevant only when they respond to rural ethos and needs, the rural culture, speed of life, the rural sociology and economy, and to the rural environment and style of life. Not that the rural boy or girl must be taught to acquire only those traits which are essentially rural, but rather he should be prepared to acquire abilities to discriminate between what is good and what is bad. All this means a drastic change in school curricula, method and content of teaching and above all, the philosophy of teaching.

To make the school environment more attractive, extra curricular programmes through non-formal educational programmes and parents' participation would have to be linked with formal education. Children must learn through doing and participation in line with the principles laid down by Mahatma Gandhi.

Non-formal Education

Linked with the first two objectives is the non-formal education. Hence, even at the cost of repetition, it should be stressed that non-formal education is not the same thing as adult education, which in turn is not the same thing as adult literacy. Non-formal education is not discriminatory against any age-group, nor is it a programme of teaching three R's (reading, writing and arithmetic).

One of the major points of departure in non-formal education is that teaching and education become responsibility of all citizens, young and old, and "the enormous energy and resources of the people is brought to bear on problems that they are willing and able to solve", and much of it is outside the four walls of schools and colleges.

None has so far evolved a method of non-formal education which can be said to be ideally suited to Indian conditions. Yet the non-formal education continues. Even the most illiterate man knows more about his environment today than his counterpart a decade ago knew. Through a variety of participatory activities–election, travel, social interaction, etc., people learn a lot even though their learning may remain unsystematized.

The proposals in this regard are:

1. The local school building, as stated earlier, would be converted into a community centre after 3 p.m. on working days and on holidays. The community centres would be used for:

   (a) discussion on current topics of interest to rural people;
   (b) film and slide shows on rural activities specially animals, plants, soils, seeds and agricultural operations in India and abroad;
   (c) music and drama performance, by local artists;
   (d) sports meet and games on Sundays; and
   (e) meeting of village *panchayat* and parents to discuss problems of rural education.

2. Helping the people to follow the advice given by the scientists and others for improving their productive capacity. At the time of sowing, advice should be rendered on how to plough, what to sow, what seeds to use, what fertilizers to use, etc. In the same way advice on animal rearing should be available. This would enable people to learn scientific ways while doing the work.
3. Special programmes for women's education would have to be chalked out covering such vital areas as nutrition, child health, family planning, cooking, sanitation, etc.
4. At a later stage, programme of adult literacy could be started depending upon the interest and demand of the people.

Self-Employment of the people could be achieved only through training in those productive activities which are relevant to the project area. The local youths must be trained in constructing low-cost houses, in repairing bicycles, motor-cycles, irrigation pumps, electrical goods, etc., to mention a few. Some training centres would have to be opened to train people not so much through a structured curricula leading to a diploma or degree, but through a process of learn-while-you-earn.

19

RURAL EMPLOYMENT

The Problem

ALONG WITH increased agricultural production through ecologically sound land and water management techniques, generating adequate employment opportunities to the unemployed is a major objective of the drought-prone area programme. In fact, this is the focal point of all development plans and programmes in the country. It, however, acquires greater significance in the drought-prone areas because undependable agriculture is the main producing sector of the economy of these areas.

Apart from the fact that there is a vast population which is un- or under-employed in rural areas, the periodic failure of rains renders a majority of people in the drought-prone areas destitute. It is, therefore, essential that drought-prone area planning should have programmes and projects which not only provide employment to the landless, and small and marginal farmers in normal years, but also during the periods of droughts.

It is important to note here that employment can be of two types – wage employment and self-employment. In the present context of rural situation in India, these two types serve two different purposes. The first one is useful in providing immediate employment on short-term basis, while the latter is meant to solve the problem on a long-term basis.

In an inequitous society like ours , where the access to the means of production are limited to a few, a fairly large number of people have either no or very poor economic base. It is especially so in the rural areas, where about 40 per cent of the land holdings are too small to provide enough income for the householdings to meet their basic needs

(Table 19.1).

To improve the living conditions of the small holders, it is necessary that their economic base is widened. Since the opportunity for part-time employment in non-agricultural sectors is limited or almost non-existent, the only solution is to engage themselves in dairying, horticulture, forestry and agro-processing activities on a regular basis. All these, however, take some time to develop. In the intervening period *ad hoc* employment in construction, soil conservation, forestry, etc. could be provided.

TABLE 19.1: Size of Land Holdings in Chitradurga District

	Chitradurga district		*D.P.A.D.Taluks*	
Size of holdings (ha)	*Per cent number*	*Per cent area*	*Per cent number*	*Per cent area*
Marginal				
Less than 1	17.8	2.6	16.8	
	41.7	11.5	40.3	20.8
Small 1 - 2	23.9	8.9	23.5	
Medium 2 - 5	35.0	27.5	35.5	26.6
Large 5 -10	15.0	26.o	15.0	25.1
Very large				
More than 10	8.3	35.0	9.2	27.5
Total	100.0	100.0	100.0	100.0

Source: World Agricultural Census, 1970, Karnataka State, Chitradurga district.

In brief, the strategy for full employment in the drought-prone areas should aim at self-employment through agricultural diversification. But to provide relief to the un- or under-employed immediately and during the severe drought conditions, civil works to desilt the tanks, to construct village roads, to conserve the soil and water, and to develop assets to provide the basic needs and social services, should be taken up.

Before we go into further details of the schemes which could be fruitfully taken up in the drought-prone areas, it is important to discuss the approach. As suggested earlier, no rural development scheme would work unless the *Panchayati Raj* Institutions are revived and the district administration is de-bureaucratized substantially and reorganized as a rural development administration. The approach to rural employment should be two-fold:

1. Co-operative
2. Household

Co-operative approach means that the local popular organizations like the *Panchayati Raj* Institutions should establish labour banks or co-operatives which should take up civil works of various types eliminating the contract system. In fact, these banks or co-operatives should become the contracting agencies.

The household approach means that the family should be the basic unit in any empolyement generating scheme. Effort should be made to see that each household stands on its own feet. There is no point in taking the averages. If a family has, let us say, only one hectare of dry land, it needs subsidiary activities like dairying, etc., to be economically viable. Such families could be brought together for joint efforts, but they should be considered as separate units while evaluating the progress of the schemes.

Several exercises have been carried out both in the field of organization and the execution of Rural Employment-oriented projects. PIREP was one of those recent endeavours and the preparation of block plans for full employment is the latest amongst the attempts to evaluate and organize the rural employment. Thus, adequate expertise is already available in this field. And this could be made use of in providing employment in DPA. In fact, PIREP was in operation in Harihar block of Chitradurga district.

Project Identification Criteria

The first important step in employment guarantee scheme is the indentification of the projects to be executed. It is important that the projects are well conceived and form integral part of a total scheme to better manage the land and water resources of the drought-prone areas. This calls for detailed land-use planning which is not done at present. We think this is one of the major weaknesses of the DPAP. The thrust of the employment guarantee programme has to be on these plus on those infrastructures and permanent assets which the rural areas need.

This calls for detailed physical planning on watershed basis. There is no organization at the State, district and local levels to do this work. Nor this aspect is considered important by the administrators. Much of our planning is geared to financial allocations for various projects which stand apart without much linkages. This, is thus a need to resort to physical planning of the land and water resources. The over-all development plan should be within the framework of the physical plan.

We suggest that the government initiate physical planning for each watershed in the drought-prone areas without further delay. These plans would provide the guidelines for the long- as well as short-term projects to be selected by the district administration for implementation year after year.

Employment Guarantee Scheme of Maharashtra[1]

Before we go into the details of the scheme that we propose to commend for the DPAP, let us review a similar scheme being implemented in Maharashtra for a long time.

Main Features of the Scheme are:

1. The beneficiaries of the guarantee have no choice as to the type of work on which they will be employed or where they will be employed.
2. The guarantee is given at the district level. In order to avoid undue hardships for the labourers, the operational limit of the guarantee is as far as possible the *Panchayat Samiti* or the block. If productive employment is not available within the *Panchayat Samiti* area, steps are taken to provide work in the adjoining block. Instructions issued require that work should be provided within a radius of five km of the village where the labourer has registered. If employment is provided beyond five km, then arrangements for camping including huts, potable water, sanitary arrangements, first-aid medical facilities and a fair price shop have to be made.
3. Work has to be provided within 15 days of its being demanded.
4. Work has to be provided for 15 to 30 days at one stretch.
5. Productive works of a labour intensive nature suited to the implementation of the guarantee include minor irrigation (percolation and storage tanks), water and soil conservation, *nala* bunding, canal excavation, land development, command area development, afforestation, flood control.
6. Works are undertaken departmentally and not through contractors. At least 60 per cent of the expenditure must be for wages to the labourers.

7. Wages are determined by piece rates calculated to ensure that as far as possible a labourer working seven hours a day gets Rs. three. Wages are paid on a weekly basis on measurement of output of work done. Necessary implements are provided by the government.
8. Works are chosen according to the following priorities:

   (a) the completion of works started for drought relief in 1972-74;
   (b) productive works which have a direct or indirect effect on stimulating or expanding agricultural production, such as minor irrigation, soil conservation, command area development works, land development; and
   (c) in areas where no such works are available, or possible, the construction of roads and the metalling of roads are allowed. This applies especially to backward hilly and inaccessible areas to enable implementation of the guarantee.

The District Collector, who manages the scheme, has the responsibility to see that the normal labour requirements of farm and allied operations are met before the Employment Guarantee Scheme (EGS) becomes active in any locale. At the same time, the Collector must ensure that those who are employed in agricultural operations receive the minimum wage in agriculture prescribed by the State. The several regulations that apply to the provision of employment are designed to help the Collector maintain the balance between existing demand, wage rates and employment provided under the EGS.

Under the regulation, the provision of employment should be ordered as follows:

(i) employment must first be provided under existing plan or non-plan works;
(ii) the employment potential on existing works or on incomplete productive works must be exhausted; and
(iii) if (i) and (ii) above fail to satisfy the demand for employment, and if 50 or more persons require employment, only then can a new work be started.

To ensure efficient completion of works and the control of overhead costs, the regulations require that:

(i) the size of the work, as far as possible, should be such that it can be completed within one or two work seasons (i.e., the dry season of October to June);

(ii) works which can be approved locally have to cost at least Rs. 20,000 (equivalent to a norm of 4,000 man-days or 200 persons for 20 days). For any work that costs above Rs. 500,000 (equivalent to 100,000 man-days or 500 persons for 200 days in a year) prior permission of the State government is required.

The District Administrations have been asked to prepare 'blue-prints' of productive works under the normal plan and non-plan budgets as well as a contingency list of works which can be financed under the EGS. The aim is to have blue-prints which cover a two-year period. The blue-print for each work must show how it is phased over the period according to each of the two work-seasons covered. At the same time, a 'manpower budget' of labour demand and supply is to be prepared at the block level. Together, the blue-prints of works and the manpower budgets comprise the format according to which the planning of works and the provision of the employment guarantee is made.

The Village *Panchayats* are required to maintain a register of work-seekers to forward to the block level. At the block and at the district levels there are co-ordination committees which include elected members from Parliament and the State Assembly, local office-holders and officials concerned with the major development departments. The District Collector is in over-all charge of the EGS. He authorizes works, allocates them to the respective agencies which normally execute such works and is charged with the responsibility of ensuring that the guarantee is fulfilled within the prescribed rules.

Over half the EGS programme falls within the purview of the *Zilla Parishad* and is executed by that agency departmentally. In Maharashtra much of the capacity to undertake development work remains in the State sector under the State level technical directorates and under the Collector as the District Co-ordinator. The Collector has, therefore, been authorized to allocate works to the corresponding State sector departments wherever necessary. The decision to place the collector in over-all charge of the EGS is primarily because the guarantee is given by the State government. Hence, it must be fulfilled by the higest representative of the Government at District level. It also reflects a mouldering dissatisfaction with the dominance of patronage systems in the working of local government. Moreover, during periods of drought when the EGS would stand suspended, it is the Collector who takes charge of relief works and is, therefore, in a position to shift the EGS works machinery to the relief works programme.

Initial preparatory work on the EGS suggested a need to provide Rs. 50 crores per year for the scheme once it was established.[2] An early decision was taken that half the amount should come out of the regular plan budget of the State and the other half was to be raised by special taxation. The EGS budget represents about 10 per cent of the annual State plan outlays. If outlays on power, largely for generation and, therefore, controlled at the State level, are excluded, Maharashtra devolves over half the plan budget to the district level. Allocations at the district level for employment type activities – agriculture, irrigation, transport and the EGS – amount to just under half the total, and the EGS itself to 14 per cent.

The EGS administration enjoys wide discretionary powers, especially at the district level and, to a lesser extent, at the block level. Each district is allotted a quarterly budget provision with which to operate. The quarterly arrangement is intended to provide flexibility to the management of the scheme. The EGS fund retained at the State level is designed to meet district disparities as they arise.

By the end of the financial year, the scheme will be running at almost full capacity as originally planned. The demand for employment was calculated mainly from a national sample survey. The EGS, it was calculated, would have to provide 143 million man-days per year.

The average cost of providing a day's work was settled at a little over Rs. three. The norms that govern the piece rates are designed to provide a daily wage of Rs. three. Moreover, up to 40 per cent of the total expenditure in the EGS can be charged to 'overheads' – mainly supervision and materials. The average figures suggest that (i) the over-heads have been kept low and (ii) the average wages paid are somewhat below Rs. three. The lower than planned average daily wage appears to be due to women completing less work within a day than the norm provides for, some labourers preferring shorter days than applies in the norms used to set the piece rates, and by overcrowding at work sites. The latter has arisen from a failure of the registration system, and the man-power budgets, to be properly utilized. Labour seeking work tends, rather than to register, to join existing public works. The number employed on a work can thus grow beyond at which labour can work and can be supervised efficiently. The result is that daily work output and, therefore, wages fall. The relative paucity of supervisory staff and of prepared alternative works in the locality hampers the start of new works to ease the position. The occasional inability of supervisors to meet the requirement that wages be paid weekly is a symptom of the same phenomenon.

A Modified Employment Guarantee Scheme

One of the chief drawbacks of the Maharashtra scheme is its disintegrated nature. Each project is thought of independently of the other. For example, soil conservation is not linked with forestry, better cropping, etc. This drawback can be partly remedied if physical planning as suggested earlier is resorted to.

The Maharashtra scheme suffers from another drawback. It fails to create institutions at the base level which can organize the rural poor. The Village *Panchayats* are entrusted with the responsibility of maintaining a register of work-seekers. It is, however, suggested labour banks/co-operatives should be created for a group of five to ten villages forming a watershed. All works should be entrusted to these institutions. Part of the wages should be pooled to develop resources which could be deployed in projects to provide self-employment to the members. In Maharashtra scheme 10 per cent of the wages earned under the EGS go to individual savings accounts. Pooling of part of the wages will be an improvement over it.

If our suggestion to reduce land under cultivation is accepted and also that at least five per cent of the land-holdings with four hectares or more be under forests or tree crops is accepted, then there could be more than enough work for all those who seek employment in DPAP. Similarly, if our suggestion to diversify the agriculture of small holders is also accepted, then most of the small and marginal farmers can also shift to forestry, horticulture, dairying, etc. All this would involve lot of additional work which can be speedily completed under the Employment Guarantee Scheme.

For the success of this scheme, it is not enough that the government set aside a given amount annually. The financial institutions like banks, etc., have to be brought into the picture.

Extent of Employment Generation and Cost

In the five DPAP taluks of Chitradurga district, there are about 80,000 agricultural labourers and about 18,000 small and marginal farmers.

The number of these three categories in the whole of the Chitradurga DPAP is given in Table 19.2

TABLE 19.2: Number of Small, Marginal Farmers and Agricultural Labourers

Sl. No	*Name of the District and taluk*	*Small farmers*	*Marginal farmers*	*Agricultural labourers*
I.	*Chitradurga district:*			
	1. Chitradurga	5,600	4,134	22,682
	2. Hosadurga	2,804	2,463	7,641
	3. Jagalur	3,351	1,792	12,894
	4. Molkalmuru	1,840	855	11,412
	5. Challakere	4,133	1,712	26,058
	Total	17,728	10,956	80,687
II.	*Chikmagalur district:*			
	6. Kadur	6,632	5,415	6,652
III.	*Tumkur district:*			
	7. Sira	—	10,123	12,231
	8. Koratagere	—	7,420	7,613
	9. Madhugiri	—	20,073	19,322
	10. Pavagada	—	4,507	22,836
	Total	—	42,123	62,002

Source: DPAP Reports.

If we take only the agricultural labourers, there are about 80,000 in Chitradurga D.P.A. taluks and about 1,50,000 in the whole D.P.A. area. If each one needs employment for, let us say, 120 days a year, in Chitradurga alone 80,000 x 120 = 96,00,000 man-days work has to be provided. For the whole D.P.A. about double of this, i.e., 1.80 million man-days work is needed.

Considering the vast scope for work in the area of land and water developments, this should not be a difficult task. The cost of such a programme will amount to Rs. nine million or, let us say, about a crore per year. If the cost of most of the projects is shared by the beneficiaries and the financial institutions come forward to lean money, the pressure on the government exchequer would be no more than Rs. 50,00,000 per year. If the small and marginal farmers are brought into the scheme and provided employment for 60 and 90 days per year, respectively, the share may go up to a crore.

It should be noted here that the benefits of such a scheme would be very many apart from the obvious ones. More money in the hands of the poor would improve their intake of food and create market for a variety of industrial goods which have a very limited market. This should boost industrial production.

Lastly, we would add that the Karnataka Government can impose an Employment Guarantee Tax on all those who are employed. This tax should fetch about Rs. 10 crores annually. If another sum of Rs. 10 crores are added by savings made elsewhere, there would be no dearth of funds to extend this scheme to the whole State.

Phasing the Programme

Naturally, the immediate concern should be to provide wage employment with continuation of the plan and non-plan projects. This would take care of the immediate requirements.

However, within a year's time, the extent of un- and under-employment should be identified geographically and also quantified. Based on this information appropriate projects should be worked out.

In phase II, within five years at least 50 per cent of identified un- and under-employed should have been provided with self-employment bases.

In phase III, the remaining 50 per cent should be provided with such employment.

Thus, over a period of 10 years, a full-employment situation should be created in the district. After that wage employment projects should, as much as possible, cease to exist.

REFERENCES

1. Norman Reynolds and Pushpa Sundar, *Maharashtra's Employment Guarantee Scheme: A Programme to Emulate*? (Mimeographed), Ford Foundation, New Delhi.
2. The figure, Rs. 50 crores, was calculated as follows: 143 million man-days of employment would be demanded at Rs. 2.50 per day = Rs.. 35.75 crores. The wage component of the EGS would be 60 per cent (a conservative figure), hence the total annual cost would be Rs. 59.60 crores.

20

DEVELOPMENT ADMINISTRATION

THE CRITICAL role development administration plays in planned development is obvious. It is now an often repeated assertion that the failure of Indian Planning could largely be attributed to the failure of development administration. This view may not find favour in all quarters for the reason that it is too simplistic. Nevertheless, one cannot deny that snags in implementation are some of the major causes of failure.

The question now is, what should be done? Is there a model of good development administration which we can adopt? One can indeed think of a wall structured model – scientific and rational, and geared to the task of planning and development. Good to look at, such a model would, however, serve no useful purpose. Development administration cannot be conceived out of the socio-economic context in which it has to function. The search for a general model is, therefore, fruitless. What we need is a model which is adapted to the local situation and context although derived from something which is logical. rational and scientific.

A number of scholars have suggested models of development administration for different territorial levels. The Administrative Reforms Commission has given one model. The National Commission on Agriculture has suggested another. The present development administration has evolved through time incorporating some of the suggestions and recommendations made by various commissions and committees. The problem underlying the recommendations of each of these bodies is the narrow angle from which they view development administration. The ARC report may be considered to be most broad-based one, but even here the commission could not appreciate fully the needs of a society which is essentially rural, non-egalitarian and poor.

It had considered the problem keeping the existing structure of bureaucracy intact. According to it, continuity is the golden path of development.

In this chapter an attempt is made to give a model of development administration we need at the district and lower levels which can plan and implement rural development programmes efficiently and effectively. This model has to be fitted in the State and lower level sub-systems.

Functions of Development Administration

There are three types of functions which administration at the district level performs:

1. Regulatory functions,
2. Maintenance functions, and
3. Development functions

The following chart gives a generalized picture of the situation.

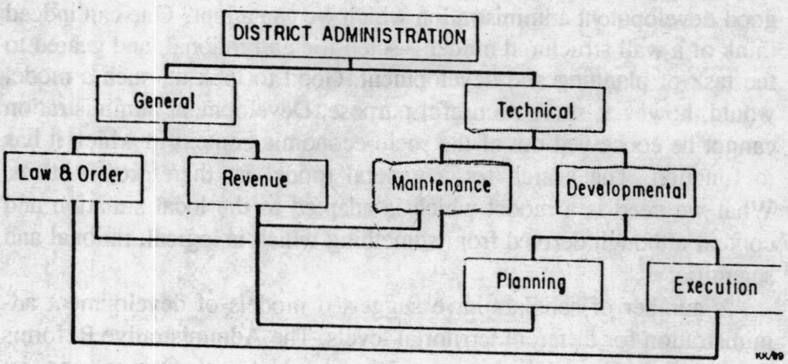

The various sectoral departments of the district administration and their linkages with State, division, *taluk* and village level administrations and the comparative characteristics of the above functions of district administration are given in Table 20.1.

The law and order, and revenue functions are carried out under the strict observance of the rules and regulations. They may be called regulatory functions.[1] The authority and procedure for these functions are well established and deviation from them is infrequent, if not rare. The maintenance functions are essentially technical, but have the full backing of the general administration. The maintenance of the assets created is borne on the budgets of the technical departments. The rules regarding the periodicity, cost, etc., of the maintenance are well laid down. Who plays various process roles is also well-established.

TABLE 20.1: Comparative Characteristics of the Functions of District Administration

Sl. No.	*Characteristics*	*Regulatory*	*Development*	*Maintenance*	*Remarks*
1	2	3	4	5	6
1.	Over-all Policies and Plans	1. Objectives and rules precisely laid down	2. Only objectives broadly defined and given	1. Objectives broadly defined and rules clearly laid down	
		2. Highly deterministic	2. Highly probabilistic	2. Slightly probabilistic	
2.	Patterns of leadership	1. Authoritative	1. Participative	1. A mix of both	
3.	Organization structure appropriate:				
	Departmentation	1. Departmental function	1. Integrated geographically or processwise with sequencing	1. Functional	
		2. Pure hierarchy	2. Impure hierarchy with super subordinate relationships and parallel groups on area bases functions.	2. Pure hierarchy with decentralized tasks and individual functions	
4.	Authority relationship	1. Super Authority	1. Overlapping Authority	1. Superior authority	
		2. Limited staff Authority	2. Staff and line authorities highly delineated	2. Line authority	
			3. Managerial function important	3. Technical functions	
			4. Subordinate acceptance vital		

(Contd.)

TABLE 20.1: *(Contd.)*

Sl. No.	*Characteristics*	*Regulatory*	*Development*	*Maintenance*	*Remarks*
1	2	3	4	5	6
5.	Delegation	1. Unity of command	1. A mix of formal and informal authority relationships		
		2. Absolute accountability of the formal authority	2. Group accountability	2. Individual responsibility and accountability of formal authority	
6.	Control	1. Objectives defined and measurable in units in the short term	1. Objectives partly in quantitative term only in the short run	1. Standards defined and measurable	

It is only the development functions where problems are serious; where the procedures cannot be so easily laid down; and where the line of authority has to be achievement-oriented and diffused. "The development function is conceptually an antithesis of the regulatory function with the maintenance function falling somewhere midway along the line between the two. Here, objectives are given and broadly defined, and it is for the group to devise the day-to-day working in a highly probabilistic situation governed by the local socio-technical responses. The pattern of leadership is more participative and is essentially a group function with different functionaries depending on the same set of data generated from a homogeneous resource area. Thus, the organizational structure necessitates a geographically integrated approach wherein the technical functions seek to realise targets and objectives laid down. This necessarily gives rise to super-subordinate relationships in an impure hierarchy situation and group function on an area basis".[2]

The developmental functions at the district level can be divided into four groups:

(i) Functions carried out by the District Planning Officer.
(ii) Functions carried out by various technical departments.
(iii) Functions carried out by the B.D.O. and his colleagues.

(iv) Functions carried out by special agencies created for specific programmes and projects.

In all the cases, the Deputy Commissioner is the co-ordinating agency. The District Planning Officer prepares the annual and five-year plans, revises them and submits them to the Deputy Commissioner and State authorities. He is also a liaison between the Deputy Commissioner and various technical departments in matters of planned schemes. His powers and responsibilities in matters of plan implementation are, however, practically nil.

As regards the technical departments at the district level, they are under the direct technical control of their respective superiors at the divisional or State level. Only for administrative purposes they come under the control of the Deputy Commissioner. Each department has its own budget and evolves programmes within the framework of the budgeted funds.

The BDO is the Chief Executive Officer of the Taluk Development Board (TDB). Most of the Assistant Development Officers working under the BDO are under the technical control of their district officers. The delegation of powers both administrative and technical is nominal, if at all. It is in no case commensurate with their responsibilities as field Officers whose credibility in the eyes of the public depends on the ease, spontaneity and timeliness with which they can provide 'relief' and solve the problems. In effect the implementation of the plan projects is squarely in the hands of the taluk level Development officers – BDO, ADO and VLWs. The other officers at the district, divisional and State levels, are only to supervise and oversee their work.

The TDB's role in development has progressively dwindled. They are now more concerned with the maintenance of schools, construction of feeder roads, minor irrigation works, etc., using the share of the revenue the State government allots to them annually.

The special development programmes like DPAP, SFDA, etc., have further added to the confusion prevailing at the district and *taluk* levels. Each of these special projects has a director with some supporting staff. The development activities coming under its purview are carried out by the director through the normal district department agencies.

In case of the DPAP, there is a DPAP authority at the district level which is headed by the Deputy Commissioner or the Divisional Commissioner – the latter being the case where more than one district area come under the jurisdiction of the authority such as the Chitradurga DPAP. The Project Director is only a co-ordinator of the programme. He is not adequately vested with powers for the allocation of funds for various projects nor can he execute even minor projects without technical clearance from higher ups in the sectoral departments.

To add to the confusion, the State government set-up in July 1975, a special plan formulation and evaluation unit for DPAP at the State level for preparation of master plans and annual plans for the DPAP, and for periodic review of progress and evaluation studies. The Director of this unit has the over-all responsibilities of planning, implementation and evaluation of DPAP – a role which rarely rest with one department. In any case, this leaves the Project Director, DPAP, with no other function, but of co-ordination and field supervision. He is none better than a District Development Assistant, except where, because of his personal qualities, he has been able to impose his will and acquire a status which the rules deny him. It is so with the Director, DPAP, Chitradurga – a highly successful development officer.

Need for Decentralized System

There is a great need to reform the existing pattern of administration from a revenue-based authoritarian organization structure to a development-based participative and supporting agency at the district level and below. The ARC Report on Machinery for Planning (1967) had identified three reasons for the ineffectiveness of the district planning and they were:

- (i) Lack of adequate efforts to work out an appropriate methodology for planning from below;
- (ii) ambiguity as regards the scope of district planning; and
- (iii) the absence of proper personnel to undertake the responsibility.

It had recommended that "apart from insisting on a minimum effort for the development of social services, the district planning agencies should be given greater degree of freedom to decide their own programmes of development. The scope of the district plans should be mainly confined to programmes which have to be evolved in view of the nature and magnitude of local resources. A district plan should be an integrated one for the rural as well as urban areas". However, since

1967, many changes have taken place in the political and economic scene in the country, and it would not be wrong to state that in such changed context the recommendation of the ARC, useful as they were in 1967, have to be looked into afresh.

For the success of development planning at the district level, the administration has to be evolved at four spatial levels:

1. District,
2. Block,
3. Sub-block (*Anchal* or *Mandal*) consisting of 10 to 15 Village Panchayats, and
4. Village Panchayat.

At each of these four levels administrative machinery appropriate to the task of development has to be created. But that alone would not make any significant change in the planning and development processes. In fact, it may further bureaucratize the development administration and bring into being a host of officials whose main task would be to exploit the people.

A careful analysis of data pertaining to personnel working at various levels and in various departments in a district shows that each *taluk* has no less than 1,000 to 1,500 government officials. Quite a few of these are over-worked, but most others do not have adequate work or they do not do the work entrusted to them. They in fact are the stumbling blocks in rural development. Micro-studies of rural situation in Karnataka point to the fact that a sizable amount of resources of the rural people passes on to the officials through a variety of dubious channels. This alone is enough to suggest that any further increase in the strength of the bureaucracy should be carefully weighed against the development functions it may perform.

What appears to be needed is the re-allocation of tasks and responsibilities to the officials already in position and their deployment at the field level rather than supervisory level. The present situation is that there are more supervisors, inspectors and directors than workers. Whom do they supervise? – themselves, their lower level colleagues or the people; what this country needs today is the workers, rather than supervisors. It needs officials who can be close to the people, work with them and help the people perform their activities more scientifically and efficiently; the officials can help people get the inputs they need and sell the products they produce. Such people are so much in demand that there could be half a dozen of them in each Village Panchayat. It is this type of development administration that we need.

But that is not enough. It is important that the growth of development administration is matched by the growth of popular institutions. Unfortunately, the *Panchayati Raj* Institutions have almost been debilitated, if not killed, during the past one-and-half decades. They exist only in name. The government machinery functions independent of the popular institutions and we have now come to a situation where the *Panchayati Raj* Institutions are almost taken off the development processes. This is an unfortunate development. Development without popular participation is just not possible.

The future administrative set-up for rural development has, therefore, to be re-cast only in relation to the future set up of the popular institutions. The following are the tentative suggestions in this regard.

Popular Institutions

We suggest a four-tier popular institutional set-up. These are:

1. District level	..	District Development Board (DDB)/ Zilla Parishad.
2. Block level	..	Block Development Board (BDB)/ *Taluk* Development Board
3. Sub-Block level	..	*Panchayat Samiti/Mandal Samity*
4. Village level	..	*Gram Panchayat.*

Functions of the DDB/Zilla Parishad

1. To prepare master plans for development of the whole district.
2. To raise and allocate funds to BDBs/TDBs.
3. To implement the projects spread over to the whole district.
4. To oversee and co-ordinate development activities generated by the lower level units.

Functions of the BDBs/TDBs

The Block Development Boards would have the same functions as the DDBs pertaining to their respective areas. Additionally, most of the development projects of the districts would be operated by the BDBs in co-operation with the *Panchayat Samitis* and *Gram Panchayats.*

Functions of Mandal or Panchayat Samitis

The *Panchayat Samitis* would be the most pivotal unit in rural development. It would develop a *Gramodaya* centre which would provide all facilities for people to interact and meet their needs. It would be backed by the sub-block level government organization which would work with the people. All developmental activities falling within the areal jurisdiction of the *Samiti* would be carried out by it. Governmental organization would provide the necessary technical support.

Functions of the Gram Panchayats

The functions of the *Gram Panchayats* would be the same as at present. But they would be reorganized to play their roles effectively. They would also be backed by resources and official support matching their responsibilities.

We do not propose to go into the mechanics of the constitution of each of the above bodies. It requires a separate detailed study. It may be emphasized here that the *Mandal/Panchayat Samiti*, in this four-tier set-up, would be the pivotal one serving from 15,000 to 25,000 rural population. This tier would have adequate resources generated internally as well as externally and would function through its representatives in each Village *Panchayat*. *Mandal/Panchayat Samiti* would be the main institution for implementation of programmes and projects. The *Zilla Parishad* and TDBs would be planning-cum-executing bodies, but only for those programmes and projects which extend to more than one *taluk* or *mandal*.

Administration

The plethora of officers posted at various levels would have to be decentralized so that more of them would be available at the *Mandal* level. The departmental line of hierarchy would have to be cut at the district level and all the staff irrespective of the department would have to be designated as *Zilla Parishad* staff. The staff would work directly under the Deputy Commissioner, who for some time to come would continue to be the Chairman of the *Zilla Parishad*. They would be responsible to their technical superiors above the district levels only in respect of those technical issues which need their approval.

The district officials should be re-grouped into five divisions –

agriculture, industry, engineering, social services and planning.

At the Block/*Taluk* level, the status of the block level officials would have to be raised. An Assistant Commissioner should be in over-all charge of the *taluk*/block. He should be assisted by eight BDOs. to look after development works. These are:

1. BDO (Planning)
2. BDO (Resource Development/Watershed Management)
3. BDO (Agriculture)
4. BDO (Animal husbandry)
5. BDO (Industry)
6. BDO (Engineering)
7. BDO (Social services)
8. BDO (*Panchayat Raj* and Co-operation).

Sub-Block Level

The sub-block should be headed by Rural Development Officer (RDO) of the rank of a BDO. The RDO should be assisted by the following officers:

1. ADO (Planning)
2. ADO (Agriculture)
3. ADO (Agro-industries)
4. ADO (Animal husbandry)
5. ADO (*Panchayat Raj*, Co-operation and Social Services).

Village Panchayat Level

Each Village *Panchayat* should have a Village Development Officer (VDO), who should be of the rank of an ADO. The VDO should be assisted by:

1. Village Accountant
2. Village Level Worker
3. School Headmaster
4. Secretary, Co-operative
5. Health Worker
6. Other personnel working at the village level.

Special Programmes like DPAP

In the reorganized administrative frame for district development, special programmes like DPAP would not have any special place at all. In fact, instead of attempting to develop a new set up to match the task, the whole district development administration has to be reorganized to meet the new challenges.

At each level of the administration within a district, emphasis would have to be laid on the most crucial problem. If it is a drought-prone area, special emphasis would have to be laid on ecological balance and employment generating projects. If it is a tribal area, emphasis would rest with tribal welfare and development. Depending upon the urgency and need, there would be special grants for certain specific purposes. But all such activities would be conceived and implemented within the over-all framework of the district development.

Planning and Implementation

The *Zilla Parishad* should have elected representatives such as members of Legislative Assembly and the Legislative Councils, representatives from *Taluk* Development Boards, representatives of credit and research institutions, representatives of voluntary agencies and most importantly of the weaker sections of the society. These representatives in *Zilla Parishad* should guide the activities of the Chairman in the over-all developmental efforts of the district. The chairman should be directly elected by the people.

At the Block level, the Assistant Commissioner working directly under the executive control of the Deputy Commissioner should be guided by the elected representatives and the representatives of *Panchayat* and Credit Institutions. Functional specialization should be broad-based at this level as between sectoral agencies. However, the Assistant Commissioner should be in over-all charge of all such sectoral agencies. The chairman of the block *Samiti* should be elected by the *Panchas* of Village *Panchayats*.

A change is necessary in the functional jurisdiction of development officials. At present, the Assistant Development Officers are sectoral officials looking after agriculture, animal husbandry, industry, etc., and are stationed at the Block headquarters. In the new set-up, while maintaining the present sectoral specialization, the Assistant Development

Officers should be dispersed from the Block headquarters. Each ADO should be put in charge of a *Mandal* or a group of villages wherein he will supervise all sectoral agencies. However, he will continue to control his own sector at the Block level.

The idea behind the proposed decentralized set up is to enable the decision-making process to be realistic and quick and to have personnel at the grass-roots level, where the need is the greatest, rather than get concentrated at the block headquarters. The supervisory function, which has become the hallmark of the present suspicion-oriented revenue-based administration, should be lesser at block level and below, and more at the district level. The purpose is to have more field workers who are actively involved in the rural developmental process at the village level.

In the decentralized administrative machinery as suggested above the development efforts would be operated in two ways, viz., (i) Plan formulation; and (ii) Plan implementation.

Plan formulation

It is suggested that watersheds should be the spatial framework for overall planning. Plan formulation cannot be done within the confines of block boundaries as watershed boundaries may stretch beyond the block boundaries. It is, therefore, desirable to do land-use planning at the district level. Technical expertise could also be more economically provided at district level. Necessary co-ordination and control as between various blocks will also be possible.

However, this does not mean that the plan formulation is centralized at the district level. Necessary resource, evaluation problem identification and project details have to be worked out at the respective block level. The role of *Panchayati Raj* Institutions like Taluk Development Boards and the *Panchayat Samitis* has to be quite dominant in these activities, for they know their requirements better. Thus, in the plan formulation, the data (regarding needs and resources) are collected at the lower levels and overall planning based on the watershed is to be carried out at the higher level.

This would help the peparation of development plans which would reflect the real needs of the people at grass-roots level. The initial exaggerated claims of various villages would only help in the preparation of long-term, medium-term and short-term plans keeping in mind the overall resource constraints.

Plan Implementation

With the district level administration being purely planning and co-ordination agency, the plan implementation is to be carried out vigorously at block-level and *mandal*-levels.

The field workers from the respective sectoral agencies such as, education, health, veterinary, small-scale industry, fisheries, social welfare, etc., will be the final links in the whole administrative set-up.

Every effort should be made to strengthen the participation of the weaker sections of the society. The entire planning exercise should be oriented to them so that they are not bystanders in the endeavour. For this, the weaker sections of the society should be encouraged to organize themselves into effective groups. The representative of such groups should be associated at the Village, *Mandal*, Block and District levels.

The main objective of the decentralized development administration is to bring down the developmental efforts to the lowest levels of hierarchy for the optimum benefits to the people. It is, therefore, suggested that Rural Secretariats be created for each *Mandal*. All officials at the *Mandal* level should be accessible to the people in these Secretariats daily. The Revenue Inspectors, *Panchayat* Secretaries, officials of the Electricity Board, Co-operative Banks, *Shanbhogs* and *Gramsevaks* would be attending their offices in the Secretariat and try to solve the problems of the villagers. The elected representatives of the people should also be located there.

People's Participation

People's participation has not been considered prominently in this chapter, as it calls for State level action for any change in the current situation. Suffice it to repeat here, that development administration even in its transformed state should not try to take over the work of the people. It should back the efforts of the people, help them articulate their needs and ideas and translate them into plans and actions.

In a real democratic set-up the heads of the *Zilla Parishads*, Block *Samitis*, *Mandal Samitis* and *Village Panchayats* would be directly elected by the people with the exception of *Village Panchayat* where choice should be by concensus and elections should be held only where concensus is not possible and that too as a last resort. Indirect elections will breed electoral corruption and likelihood of rich and unscrupulous people getting elected through money or muscle power would increase.

APPENDIX

Proposals for Utilization of Surface Water Resources in Jagalur Taluk *

Jagalur *taluk* has the following major tributaries that drain the *taluk* to the Krishna river:

Name of the series and sub-series	Total catchment area of the series (km^2)	Estimated supply of catchment (Units)	Estimated supply taken up by tanks (Units)	Surplus (Units)
I. *Tungabhadra Right Bank Series*				
1. Sokkehalla sub-series	222	1,156	558	598
2. Hagari sub-series	747	3,604	1,717	1,887
II. *Chinnahagari Series*				
1. Jagalur sub-series	521	4,261	1,994	2,267
Total	1,490	9,021	4,269	4,752

Based on a survey conducted by Mr. R. Rajappa, Assistant Engineer, P.W.D. (Minor Irrigation), Jagalur, Chtradurga district, for the Institute of Development Studies, University of Mysore, 1975.

There is scope for doubling the irrigation potential in the *taluk*. Even though all the existing valleys have been harnessed, there is possibility of having a few more tanks. The existing irrigation works (33 tanks) with an *atchkat* of 2,987 hectares can be better maintained and improved to assure water supply to the existing *atchkat* as well as to cover some new *atchkat*.

On varifying the conditions of old tanks and channels it is observed that the bunds and channels have not been improved for a long time except for the normal repairs and maintenance. To feed assured *atchkat*, it is found very difficult to draw water from the channels. Most of the tank channels are silted-up and some of the channels in embankment area have been eroded. In such a condition, the ryots draw water to their fields by providing temporary protections on such eroded places and thereby full *atchkat* cannot be fed with water. Consequently, nearly 75 per cent of water goes waste. To protect this major wastage, the improvement of channels and tank bunds could be taken up.

Already efforts have been made to provide protection to the channels by constructing concrete lining and side revetments and C.D. works wherever required. Specially in medium tanks like Gadimakunte, Thuppadahally and Sangenahally, great improvements have been done to provide water to the tail-end where the tail-end *atchkat* was not at all fed with water right from the inception of the tanks. Improvements taken up under these tanks by constructing pipe crossings to some of the *Kattes* which were acting as balancing reservoirs in its length. In some places, the alignment of the channel has been changed by opening out the channel in the upper margin of the *Kattes*. By making all these improvments the water will reach the tail-end *atchkat* within a short time.

By providing this pipe crossings through these *kattes* the advantage that has been effected are:

(i) Reclaiming the water spread land and completely saving the land below the *kattes* from the effect of seepage; and
(ii) Good lot of time has been saved in making the flow of water in pipes to reach the tail-end at an early period.

Previously, the time that was taken to reach the ninth sluice of Gadimakunte tank channel was 15 days. Now the water is being fed to the tail-end within three days. This reduction in time has stood to be most advantageous to the *atchkatdars* who could utilize the water within the same period from first sluice to the tail-end sluice. Further, wastage of water has been avoided by providing pipe outlets with the valve arrangements as is provided in the town water supply system for regularizing the full control under each sluice. This has really worked out to be very advantageous to feed the *atchkat* without wasting water.

In spite of so much of improvements having been done, the channels have been tackled only in part. Balance length of the channels have to be provided with cement concrete lining and masonry walls to avoid seepage and some other difficulties to assure irrigation to the entire *atchkat*.

Some proposals for improvements are being listed herewith to utilize the surplus water of the series by taking up of 12 new tanks to irrigate 728 hectares afresh at an estimated cost of Rs. 47.5 lakhs and by improving the existing tanks and channels to irrigate another 648 hectares afresh at an estimated cost of Rs. 44.5 lakhs. Alongwith creation of an extra potential to the extent of 1,376 hectares, these projects will also stabilize the existing *atchkat* of 2,987 hectares by making improvements to the existing tanks and channels and strengthening the tank bunds.

The projects have been drafted, making all the provisions to upkeep the existing tanks and channels and construction of new tanks, lift irrigation schemes and opening feeder channels to create the irrigation potential in the *taluk*. The details of these proposals are given in following pages.

Schemes for utilization of Irrigation Potential of Jagalur Taluk in Chitradurga District

Sl. No.	*Name of the work*	*Atchkat Benefited (ha)*		*Estimated cost (Rs. in lakhs)*
		Old	*New*	
1	2	3	4	5
I.	*Repairs to the Existing Minor Irrigation Works :**			
1.	Sangenahalli tank	648	60	45.00
2.	Thuppadahally tank	566	80	30.00
3.	Gadimakunte tank	408	80	25.00
4.	Magadi tank	227	–	14.00
5.	Gurusiddapura tank	129	20	6.00
6.	Jagalur tank	112	16	12.00
7.	Bharamsamudra tank	102	32	12.00
8.	Jammapura tank	86	–	11.00
9.	Hosakere tank	76	–	5.00
10.	Lakkampura tank	72	–	6.00
11.	Malemachikere tank	66	–	3.00
12.	Anabur tank	54	12	4.00
13.	Hiremallanahole tank	47	8	8.00
14.	Nibagur tank	46	8	6.00
15.	Billichodu tank	33	12	5.00
16.	Asagodu tank	30	8	4.00

(Contd.)

1	2	3	4	5
17.	Chadragola tank	37	12	3.00
18.	Agasanahalli tank	28	—	3.00
19.	Hire Arkere tank	30	12	4.00
20.	Helavadandi tank	25	8	4.00
21.	Musthagarahalli Doddakere	22	8	
22.	Halekal tank	21	—	2.00
23.	Kyasanahalli tank	8	—	2.00
24.	Bidarakere tank	14	4	1.50
25.	Mustagarahalli Chikkakere	12	—	1.50
26.	Chennapura tank	12	8	1.50
27.	Rasthemachikere tank	11	8	1.00
28.	Kelagote tank	7	—	1.00
29.	Gode tank	6	12	1.00
30.	Siddammanahalli tank	6	—	1.00
31.	Mudlamachikere tank	6	12	1.00
32.	Madanahalli tank	4	8	1.00
33.	Byranaikanahalli tank	4	4	1.00
			Total:	227.50

Schemes for Utilization of Irrigation Potential of Jagalpur Taluk in Chtradurga District

Sl. No.	*Name of the work*	*Nature of repairs*	*Estimated cost (Rs. in lakhs)*
1	2	3	4
II.	*Repairs to Existing L.I. Scheme:*		
1.	L.I. Scheme near Chikkamallanahole	Channel is to be excavated and some protective works to pump house and repairs to machineries and inlet well.	0.50
III.	*Repairs to Existing Feeder Channels:*		
1.	Halekal tank	Requires the protection works, removing the silt and opening out and repairs to the scoured portions of both the channels.	1.00
2.	Bharamasamudra tank	Channel being very small is to be widened and CD to be widened and further excavation to be done and protection to be made.	1.00
3.	Bidarkere tank	Channel is silted up. Requires to be improved and protections to be done. Widening is also to be done.	1.00
4.	Jammapura tank	Since the channel is completely silted up, it has to be opened out a fresh with necessary CD works and protections.	2.00
5.	Hiremallanahole tank	Improvements to be made by protection works and channel to be widened by removal of silt.	0.50
6.	Jagalur tank	Improvement to be made by protection works and channel to be widened by removal of slit.	0.50

(Contd.)

1	2	3	4
7.	Madanahalli tank	-do-	0.50
8.	Agasanahalli tank	-do-	0.50
9.	Mudalamachikere tank	-do-	0.50
10.	Rasthemachikere tank	-do-	0.50
11.	Nibagur tank	-do-	1.00
12.	Hire Arakere tank	-do-	1.00
			10.00
IV.	*Raising the Waste-weir of Tanks:*		
1.	Hire Arakere tank (Old *atchkat* 28 hectares and new *atchkat* 12 hectares)	The tank is having good catchment and one feeder channel is also there. So restoration is required to feed water to an extent of 30 acres afresh.	3.00
2.	Thuppadahalli tank (Old *atchkat* 567 hectares and new *atchkat* 80 hectares)	The tank is constructed across Chikkahagari which is having good catchment. As such, necessary restoration is required.	4.00
3.	Gode tank (Old *atchkat* 6 hectares and new *atchkat* 12 hectares)	The tank is having good catchment. As such, by restoration of the tank, water will be available for further *atchkat* of 30 acres of land.	3.00
			10.00

Sl. No.	*Name of the work*	*Atchkat*		*Nature of repairs*	*Estimated cost (Rs. in lakhs)*
		Old	*New*		
V.	*Opening out New Feeder Channels:*				
1.	Bilichodu tank	33	20	Diverting the halla near Mukhnur to a catchment of 0.5 sq. miles.	5.00
2.	Kyasarahalli tank	18	4	Diverting the halla near Thamadihalli with a catchment of	1.50

				0.7 sq. miles.	
3.	Asagodu tank	30	16	Diverting the halla near Marikunte with a catchment of 0.5 sq. miles.	1.50
4.	Chadamgola tank	37	12	Diverting the halla near Chatidurga with a catchment of 0.5 sq. miles.	1.00
5.	Sanganahalli tank	648	80	Diverting the halla near Gowrammanahalli with a catchment of 4.5 sq. miles.	5.00
					14.00

Sl. No.	*Name of the tank*	*Atchkat benefited (ha)*	*Estimated cost (Rs. in lakhs)*
VI.	*New Tanks:*	288	15.00
1.	Construction of a new tank at Guddadanaikanahalli near Ujjappanadarahalli		
2.	-do- Raingainadurga	28	2.50
3.	-do- across tekakahalla near Gurusiddapura	12	1.00
4.	Construction of a new tank near Diddigi	48	4.00
5.	Construction of new tank near Gowramannahalli	56	4.00
6.	Construction of a new tank near Arasinagundi	24	2.00
7.	Construction of a new tank near Kananakatte	68	5.00
8.	Construction of a new tank across Yerehalla near Bommagatte	12	1.00
		80	5.00
9.	Construction of a new tank near Marikunte	60	4.00
10.	Construction of a new tank near Marikatte		

11.	Construction of a new tank near Medaginkere	40	3.00
12.	Construction of a new tank near Vyasagondana-halli	12	1.00
		728	47.50

RECERENCES

1. N.V. Ratnam and P. Das, Management of Rural Development, Indian Institute of Management, Bangalore (Mimeographed) pp. 213-15.
2. *Ibid.*, pp. 215-16.

Dr. K.V. SUNDARAM
A Profile

KAVASSERY VANCHI SUNDARAM was born on 30th November 1929 in a family of modest means at Calicut in Kerala State in India. His father, Mr. K.A. Vanchi Iyer, migrated to Tamil Nadu in 1930 and was, for long years, Headmaster of the N.S.M.V.P.S. High School at Devakottai, a small town in Ramnad District. Sundaram had his high school education at Devakottai and his undergraduate Collegiate education at the M.D.T. Hindu College, Tirunelvelli, and Madura College, Madurai. In 1948, he joined the Madras University for his Master's Degree in Geography which he completed in 1951. The same year, he was appointed as Lecturer in Geography in Alagappa Chettiar College at Karaikudi, which has now become Alagappa University.

Sundaram has been a research-oriented scholar from the very beginning of his career. After seven years of teaching, he moved over to New Delhi in 1958, and joined the Town Planning Organisation, Government of India, as a Research Associate. He worked with a multi-disciplinary team of Physical, Economic and Social Planners engaged in rural and urban studies, leading to the preparation of a Regional Master Plan for metropolitan Delhi, which was the first of its kind in India. He worked closely with Mr. Albert Mayer, the well-known American planner of Etawah Community Development Planning fame, in drawing up a Development Plan for rural Delhi based on the principles of service centre planning, called by Albert Mayer as "Village Cluster Planning". This was one of the earliest works done in India on spatial planning, applying the Christaller's theory of Central Places to the Indian context. Working in a Master Plan team dominated by physical planners was not an easy task and this experience equipped Sundaram with some of the essential qualities required of a researcher and government servant, e.g., tolerance for the opinions of others, ability to get on with other members of the team, ability to communicate and skills in negotiation. These qualities stood him in good stead, as he rose up in government and occupied some key positions later as Member of Project/Study Teams, Project (Team) Leader, Chief Co-ordinator, Adviser, or Member of Consultative Groups, Committees and Review Missions, or as Resource Person in International Seminars, Expert Group Meetings, etc. He has partly recorded his experience as member of an interdisciplinary team in his paper "Some Problems of Interdisciplinary Team Work and Research in Urban and Regional Planning", which originally appeared in the journal *Interdiscipline* and was later included in his work on *Urban and Regional Planning in India*.

After the Delhi Master Plan work was completed, Sundaram was seconded to the Central Regional and Urban Planning Organisation (CRUPO), which later on merged with the Town Planning Organisation to become the Central Town and Country Planning Organisation under the Ministry of Works and Housing. Here he worked on a number of major regional planning projects in the country. This included the planning for the Rajasthan Canal Region, the Dandakaranya Development Region, the South-east Resource Region and the dacoity infested districts of Morena, Bundelkhand and Bharatpur. This wide on-the-job regional planning experience stimulated his thinking on inter-state regionalisation for planning and led to the preparation of a paper on "Planning Regions of India", which was discussed in a special session of the International Geographical Congress held at New Delhi in 1968. On the basis of this paper, the Town and Country Planning Organisation vigorously advocated the cause of inter-state regional planning to be undertaken on a country-wide scale.

Another important contribution made by Sundaram while in the Town and Country Planning Organisation relates to a critical evaluation of the Town Group concept adopted in the Indian census upto 1961 and suggestions for a more rational approach to the de-limitation of urban area boundaries. Following this study, the Indian Census of 1971 adopted the Standard Urban Area (SUA) concept.

In 1965, Government of India appointed a high level committee on Rural-Urban Relations under the Chairmanship of Mr. A.P. Jain, a former Central Minister for Food and Sundaram was appointed as Senior Research Officer of this committee. This afforded him opportunities to visit a number of States, conduct a number of case studies and study the emerging issues in rural-urban linkages in the country. In

1969 Sundaram participated in a training programme on "Physical Planning in Development Countries" organised by the German Foundation for Developing Countries at Berlin. This helped him compare the processes of development in developed and developing countries.

This account of Sundaram's major research activities in the Town and Country Planning Organisation will be incomplete without a reference to his study on the spatial planning for the Bastar District, a tribal region. This was done as part of a research study which I directed for a project on "The Role of Growth Poles and Growth Centres in Regional Development and Planning in India" undertaken for the United Nations Research Institute for Social Development, Geneva, during 1969-70. Later, this was included in the joint book which myself, Sundaram and Prakasa Rao wrote titled *Regional Development Planning in India: A New Strategy* (Vikas, 1974), a widely quoted book on Regional Planning.

In 1972, Sundaram participated in the first Indo-British Geographical Seminar held in Delhi, in which he presented his paper on "Kotla Mubarakpur, an Urban Village", which marked a new frontier in geographical research, as it was bearing on a theme which had not been researched upon before. The study was encouraged and guided by Prof. Prakasa Rao. Later it became the basis for a Ph.D. work at Delhi University. Sundaram's contributions in the Indo-British Seminar was greatly appreciated and it led to his being awarded a Senior Nuffield Fellowhip for studies in the Centre of South Asian Studies in the University of Cambridge (U.K). Dr. B.H. Farmer of Cambridge University wrote: "he impressed me, as he impressed other British participants previously unaware of him and his work, as a man of great ability destined to make a great contribution to geography, to the study of development and to his country".[1]

It was during the tenure of this fellowship (1978-79) that he wrote his book titled *Geography of Underdevelopment — The Spatial Dynamics of Underdevelopment* (Concept, 1983). As Nuffield Fellow, he lectured in a number of universities, both in U.K. and Europe. These included the University College of Swansea (Wales), University of Birmingham, University of Bradford and University of London in U.K., University of Utrecht and the Institute of Social Studies in The Hague in Netherlands, University of Bordeaux in France, University of Copenhagen in Denmark, University of Augsburg, Technical University at Aachen and University of Heidelberg in West Germany. Following his stay in Cambridge, Sundaram was invited as a Visiting

Professor to U.S.A. by the Centre of South Asian Studies, University of Michigan, Ann Arbor, and the Department of Geography, Boston University.

In 1973, he was invited by the United Nations Centre for Regional Development at Nagoya, Japan, as consultant, where he joined a research team and conducted a multi-national comparative study on the "growth of medium-sized towns in relation to their rural regions", covering case studies in three countries, viz., Japan, The Philippines and India. In 1974, the Planning Commission, Government of India, decided to create a position at senior middle level for a geographer. Sundaram was appointed against the post of Joint Director, with special responsibilities for multi-level planning.

From then on he held various positions as Joint Director, Director/Deputy Adviser and then as Joint Adviser of the Multi-level Planning Division of the Planning Commission. He left a good legacy in the Commission and wrote extensively on regional, local and multi-level planning. There was no published work on spatial planning during the 1970s and 1980s which did not have the imprint of Sundaram's thinking. It was during this period, and to be more specific in 1978, that he was honoured by Mysore University with a D. Litt, Degree (its highest Degree) for his book on *Urban and Regional Planning in India*. (Vikas, 1977).

He has written over 50 articles. Apart from his well-known book mentioned above he has been an author, a joint author or editor of a number of other books. A bibliography of his publications is given at the end of this profile.

Sundaram's activities in the Planning Commission, New Delhi concerned research, planning and project appraisal, advisory services, promotion of training activities and directing and managing some centrally sponsored projects, e.g., Western Ghats development and development of the North-east Region. His major contribution lies in micro-level planning at the District and Block levels and the promotion of training activities in multi-level planning.

In 1977, the Planning Commission appointed a Working Group under the Chairmanship of Prof. M.L. Dantwala to initiate block level planning in the country with a view to achieve full employment in ten years. Sundaram assisted this group in its deliberations and played a crucial role in preparing guidelines for block level planning. In 1982, the Planning Commission appointed a Working Group on District Planning under the Chairmanship of Prof. C.H. Hanumantha Rao with

Sundaram as the Member-convener of this group. The task entrusted to him was of stupendous magnitude, as it concerned with a planning activity at the sub-state level, which was characterised by tardy, hesitating and halting progress in the States, despite several efforts by the Planning Commission spanning over a number of plan periods. In this context, a very careful review was called for and the whole gamut of issues concerning decentralised District Planning had to be analysed and a new set of guidelines to assist the States in this direction had to be evolved. Sundaram started this work systematically. He set up seven sub-groups to discuss the various aspects of decentralised District Planning and organised four Regional Workshops in different regions of the country and convened more than 25 meetings, in what was a year-long study on District Planning. More than 90 persons consisting of senior officials at the Central and State levels and academicians in universities and research institutions were associated with this huge endeavour. For the first time, the State of art of District Planning in the various States in the country was systematically documented. As the States were at different stages of progress towards decentralised planning, the Working Group advocated a "Stages Approach" to District Planning, which all the State Governments in the country endorsed. Sundaram played a crucial role in preparing the report of the Working Group in two volumes and getting the State Governments and the Centre to agree on the recommendations of the Working Group. He also initiated certain important follow-up measures. The Working Group report became a classic and seminal document guiding the States on District Planning during the Seventh Plan.

Closely following the report of the Working Group on District Planning, the Planning Commission set up another Committee to review the existing administrative arrangements for rural development and poverty alleviation programmes (CAARD) under the Chairmanship of Shri G.V.K. Rao, a former Member of the Planning Commission. Sundaram was also associated with this committee and assisted in framing appropriate recommendations about administrative arrangements for decentralised planning at District level and below. The work done by Sundaram in the context of these two official committees laid down the basic guidelines for effecting systematic changes and re-orientations by the State Governments for initiating the process of planning from below.

Sundaram firmly believed in capability building ("the capacitation approach") of the personnel at the sub-national levels for ensuring the effective decentralisation of powers and functions and for initiating planning from below. He, therefore, vigorously advocated to the State Governments to select a few professional institutions in each State for imparting training in planning techniques to the planning personnel at the District and block levels and also to the volunteers and local leaders. As member of the Central Advisory Committee on Training, Government of India, he was instrumental for initiating centrally-assisted training programmes in District Planning, multi-level planning and integrated area development in more than a dozen institutions in the country. He collaborated with the Institute of Development Studies, Mysore, for running a correspondence training programme in micro-level planning for development administrators, with the Administrative Staff College of India, Hyderabad, for running a course on Multi-level Planning and with the Institute of Economic Growth, Delhi, for running courses in Project Planning and Development Planning. He was instrumental for initiating a Centrally-sponsored programme by the Planning Commission for strengthening the planning machinery at District level, which provides for the employment of a multi-disciplinary team of planners at the District level to prepare and monitor District plans. The inclusion of the post of a geographer in this team is to be particularly noted.

In 1984, the late Prime Minister Smt. Indira Gandhi heard about the extraordinary performance in rural development activities in Kundrakudi, a village in Ramnad District in Tamil Nadu, and wanted the Planning Commission to investigate into it. The task fell on the shoulders of Sundaram. He visited Kundrakudi, inspected all development projects and held discussions with development functionaries, local people and the scientists of the Central Electro-chemical Research Institute and prepared his report, in what became a well-known case study of a success story in local level planning for rural development. Setting out his conclusions, Sundaram summarised the achievements of Kundrakudi as stemming from a peculiar combination, called by him as "Technocratic, Administrative and Democratic Mix" (TAD Mix), which is rarely replicable. The Planning Commission, realising the importance of this study, published the report[2] and widely circulated it among the State Governments. Thus Sundaram brought to light what has been termed as "the Kundrakudi model of development" and made Kundrakudi, a place of pilgrimage for all development analysts and planners. The Lal Bahadur Academy of Public Administration in Mussoorie has prescribed this case study as an essential reading to I.A.S. probationers.

Another area in which he contributed significantly during his tenure of office in the Planning Commission is in relation to the setting up of information systems for planning at the sub-national levels. He collaborated with the Department of Science and Technology (Government of India) and initiated pilot projects in selected districts for the use of micro-computers for collecting, storing, processing and transferring data and information. This is an innovation which is now fast picking up in the country.

At the international level, he collaborated with the International Institute for Aerial Survey and Earth Sciences in Enschede (Netherlands) in 1980 on a research project on 'Information Requirements for Development Planning in Developing Countries" and later with UNESCO in Paris. In collaboration with UNESCO and the Institute for Coastal and Off-shore Research (INCOR) in Visakhapatnam, he was instrumental for organising an international seminar on "Information systems for sub-national planning", which ended with the issuing of a policy declaration, which has been termed the "Visakha Declaration". Sundaram advised the UNESCO in preparing training modules for "Information systems for sub-national development Planning". UNESCO has prepared a 'Data for development training kit', which has been tested in some training programmes. The work is still in progress.

International recognition for Sundaram's work came during the '80s, although he had been invited since the '70s by various international organisations. The international organisations which used his expertise in the fields of training, research related to training, rural development, local level planning, multi-level planning and information systems for sub-national development planning included the U.N. Centre for Regional Development, Nagoya, Japan, (1973-74; 1981-82), the German Foundation for Developing Countries (1981), the International Centre for Integrated Mountain Development (ICIMOD) (1987), UNESCO 1986), the International Centre for Aerial Survey and Earth Sciences (1980), The ESCAP (1980) and FAO (1983-84, 1986-87 and 1987-) more. The ESCAP utilised his services in its activities on local-level planning for rural development and for evolving appropriate guidelines on the basis of indepth analysis of the process of local level planning in individual countries in the South and South-East Asian Region (See the publication by ESCAP, : *The Practice of Local-Level Planning*, 1980). ICIMOD utilised his services for preparing a manuals for trainers' training in District Energy Planning. The FAO, on the basis of his work on Multi-level Planning in India, invited him in 1983 as a resource person to assist in conducting an "Expert Consultation on Multi-level Planning and the two-way process in Agricultural and Rural Development Planning", held at Bangkok. The Consultation noted the serious gaps in documentation on the state of the art of Multi-level Planning in the various countries and recommended that FAO should prepare the study and make a critical assessment of the experience gained in Multi-level Planning in the countries of the Asian and Pacific Regions. This responsibility was entrusted to Sundaram by FAO in 1984. He toured in six countries in Asia and prepared a monograph titled "Toward Improved Multi-level Planning for Agricultural and Rural Development in Asia and the Pacific" (FAO Economic and Social Development Paper 52, 1985), which is one of the most widely circulated publications by FAO. Following this, Multi-level Planning became an approved subject for technical assistance in the FAO and Sundaram was invited to Rome to conduct further studies and to advise the FA) suitably on various projects related to decentralized planning.

Sundaram took voluntary retirement from Government of India and joined the FAO in 1987. During his stay in the FAO Headquarters in 1987-88, he initiated several studies related to Multi-level Planning which also included studies on "Small Farmer Development". He was sent on a one-man mission to the Philippines during 1987 to advise on decentralized planning in the agriculture sector. Later, he was appointed as Project-Co-Manager and Chief Technical Adviser for an Inservice Training Project on Agricultural Project Analysis and Rural Development" in Nepal. In this capacity, he is now directing several training programmes in Nepal, including training programmes for decentralised District Planning. Currently he is engaged in preparing a training manual for decentralized District Planning, which is expected to give a big push to the decentralized District Planning process in Nepal.

Among other professional activities, mention must be made of his active collaboration with the Asian Institute of Technology (AIT) at Bangkok in promoting a "Rural Regional Development Network" in the South and South-East Asian Region, a project funded by the Government of Netherlands through the Institute of Social Studies, The Hague. As a result of the activities of this network, collaborative research bearing on the theme of "Decentralisation" was established with some institutions in India, Bangladesh, Thailand, Sri Lanka, The Philippines and Indonesia. This led to a number of critical studies on decentralisation and the A.I.T. held two workshops for discussing these contributions. These studies are now being published by the A.I.T. as occasional papers. In March 1988, the National Institute of Research Advancement (Japan) and the Japan Institute of Systems Research conducted an International Symposium on "the Development of Regional Agriculture and Environmental Conservation in South-East Asian Countries" in the Agricultural University at Kyoto (Japan). Sundaram was invited to deliver the keynote address. In October 1989, Sundaram was felicitated by the National Association of Geographers, India (NAGI), which held its 11th Geography Congress at Delhi University, Delhi, for his contributions in regional and local level planning.

If we stop at the above summary description of Sundaram, we would know only one side of the story. The other side is Sundaram as a man. He is an embodiment of humility. He is a very good listener. We have rarely seen him getting angry. He has always been charitable even to his critics, who, incidentally, have never been many.

Sundaram has a great habit of getting up at 4 a.m. in the morning. It is the time when he does his writing and reading. He is so regular and punctual, that no matter how busy he is, he is always on time for everything he takes up.

All those who have been associated with Sundaram, cherish his friendship. He is generous to the core and likes to share with others whatever he has. He leads a simple life and the very meeting with him generates a feeling of friendship, sacrifice and devotion to duty.

Girija, his wife, has always been a source of inspiration and support to him. His parents, says Sundaram, made him honest, sincere and humble; his wife made him achievement-oriented and a good human being; his children made him responsible and loving; and his friends made him share whatever little he has gained.

We convey our felicitations to Dr. Sundaram on his 60th birth day and wish him very many happy returns of the day.

NOTES

1. In the Foreword to the book *Geography of Underdevelopment: The Spatial Dynamics of Underdevelopment* by K.V. Sundaram (Concept, 1983).
2. Planning Commission, Government of India: "Towards Improved Local Level Planning for Rural Development — Lessons from some experiences",1986.

LIST OF MAJOR PUBLICATIONS
(BOOKS AND MONOGRAPHS)

(i) *Regional Development Planning in India - A New Strategy*; (Co-author) Vikas, New Delhi, 1974

(ii) *Urban and Regional Planning in India*, Vikas, New Delhi, 1977

(iii) *Rural Area Development: Perspectives and Approaches* (ed.), Sterling, New Delhi, 1979

(iv) *Multi-level Planning and Integrated Rural Development in India*, Heritage, New Delhi, 1980 (Co-author)

(v) *The Geography of Under-development*. Concept, New Delhi, 1983

(vi) *Rural Development Alternatives: Synthesis Report*, published by U.N. Centre for Regional Development, Nagoya, 1980 (Co-author)

(vii) *Geography and Planning*, (ed.) Concept, New Delhi, 1985.

(viii) *Rural Development – Capitalist and Socialist Paths* - Vol. 4, Prepared for United Nations Centre for Regional Development, Nagoya (Japan), published by Concept Publishing Company, New Delhi. 1985 (Co-author).

(ix) *Towards Improved Multi-level Planning in Agriculture and Rural Development in Asia and the Pacific* – FA0, Economic and Social Development paper 52, 1985

(x) *Report of the Working Group on District Planning*, prepared for Planning Commission, Government of India, New Delhi, 1984

(xi) *Population Geography* (ed) - Vol. 6 in the Series : "Contributions to Indian Geography", Heritage Publishers, New Delhi, 1985

(xii) *Impact of Policies and Programmes on the Small Farmer Development* - Prepared for FAO, 1986

(xiii) *Multi-level Planning Process for Forestry Development in Asia and the Pacific* - Prepared for FAO, 1986

(xiv) *Regional Decentralisation for Agricultural Development Planning in the Near East* - Prepared for FAO, 1986

(xv) *Towards Improved Local Level Planning for Rural Development*, Planning Commission, New Delhi, 1986

(xvi) *Guidelines for the Design of a Training Programme in District Planning*, Planning Commission of India, April, 1986

(xvii) *Guidelines for Block-level Planning*, Planning Commission, Government of India, 1979

(xviii) *Data and Information Needs for Sub-national Planning*, Keynote paper to UNESCO Seminar on "Information System for Sub-national Development Planning", Visakhapatnam, India 16-20 Dec. 1985

(xix) *An Integrated Approach to Training for the Establishment and Use of Information Systems for Sub-National Development Planning* – Paper to the Expert Group Meeting on Training in Information Systems for Local and Regional Planning in Developing Countries, United Nations Centre for Regional Development, Nagoya (Japan), 16-19 June, 1986

(xx) *Planning Exercise-Oriented Training Approach – Case Study of an International Training Experience*. Paper prepared for ESPT, FAO, April, 1987

(xxi) *"Small Farmer Development in Asia and the Pacific: Some lessons for strategy formulation land planning"* (with N.S. Randhawa), F.A.O. Economic and Social Development Paper, Food and Agricultural Organisation of United Nations, Rome, 1989.

Chapter Contributions in Books

1. "Some Recent Trends in Regional Development Planning in India in "*Regional Planning and National Development*, R.P. Misra et al. (Eds), Vikas Publishing House Pvt. Ltd., New Delhi, 1978.
2. "Delhi : The National Capital" Chapter Five in *Million Cities of India* R.P. Misra (Ed), Vikas Publishing House (Pvt) Ltd. New Delhi, 1978.
3. " Some Recent Trends in Rural Area Development Planning in India" - Chapter 2 in *Rural Area Development – Perspectives and Approaches*, R.P. Misra and K.V. Sundaram (Eds), Sterling Publishers Pvt. Ltd., New Delhi, 1979.
4. "The Practice of Local Level Planning – General Presentation and Comments" - Chapter 1 in *The Practice of Local Level Planning*, Case studies in selected rural areas in India, Nepal and Malaysia, United Nations Economic and Social Commission for Asia and Pacific, Bangkok, 1980.

5. "Economic Growth of Urban Areas: The Case of Meerut City" in *Municipal and Urban India,* Abhijit Datta (Ed), Indian Institute of Public Administration, New Delhi, 1980.
6. "Search for Strategy: Regional Development and Planning for the backward areas in India" in *Regional Development Alternatives* UNCRD Regional Development Series, Vol 2. A.L. Mobogunge and R.P. Misra (Eds), Maruzen Asia, Singapore, 1981.
7. "Experience of Area Development Planning in India - Alternative Approaches", Chapter 8 in *Rural Development: National Policies and Experiences*, R.P. Misra (Ed), UNCRD, Regional Development Series, Volume 4, Maruzen Asia, Singapore, 1981.
8. "Multi-level Planning: The Indian Experience" Chapter 4 in *Urban and Regional Policy Analysis in Developing Countries*, Lata Chatterjee and Peter Nijkamp (Eds), Gower Publishing Company, 1983.
9. "Multi-level Planning: The Indian Experience" in Report of the Expert Consultation on *Multi-level Planning and the two-way Process in Agriculture and Rural Development Planning*, FAO Regional Office for Asia and the Pacific, May, 1983.
10. "Metropolitan expansion in India: Spatial Dynamics and Rural Transformation" (with V.L.S. Prakasa Rao) Chapter 14 in *Understanding Green Revolution Agrarian Change and Development Planning in South Asia*, Tim Bayliss; Smith and Sudhir Wanmali, Cambridge University Press, Cambridge, 1984.
11. "India – Development Experience" in *Rural Development: Capitalist and Socialist Paths* Vol. 4 (India and Bangladesh) Studies Conducted by the United Nations Centre for Regional Development, R.P. Misra (Ed), Concept Publishing Company, New Delhi, 1985.
12. "India" -- (with R.K. Wishwakarma), Chapter 4 in *International Handbook on Land-Use Planning*, Nicholas N. Patricios (Ed), Greenwood Press, New York, 1986.
13. "Case Study of Kundrakudi" -- Chapter 1, in *Towards Improved Local Level Planning for Rural Development -- Lessons from some Experiences* Planning Commission, Government of India, New Delhi, 1986.
14. "The Challange and Response to Decentralisation: The Indian Experience, an overview" Chapter 2 in *Decentralisation: Area*

Development in Practice in Asia, Harvey Demaine and Romana E. Malong (Eds), Asian Institute of Technology, Bangkok, 1987.

15. "Planning Exercise-Oriented Training: An International Training Experience" – Case Study No 9 in *Training for Decentralised Planning – Lessons from experience – Case Studies*, Food and Agriculture Organisation of the United - Nations, Rome, 1987.
16. "Rural Development and Environmental Conservation" – Keynote Speech in Proceedings of International Symposium, *The Development of Regional Agriculture and Environmental Conservation in South-East Asian Countries*, National Institute for Research Advancement, Tokyo, June, 1988.
17. "Multi-level Planning: Concept, Principles and some Aspects of its Application to Sectoral Planning" in *Regional Planning and Development – Essays on Space, Society and Development* – in honour of Professor R.P. Misra, Edited by K.V. Sundaram, A Ramesh and P.S. Tiwari, Heritage Publishers, New Delhi, 1989.
18. "Prof. R.P. Misra – A Review and Assessment of his Contributions" Chapter 3 in *Regional Planning and Development – Essays on Space, Society and Development* – in honour of Professor R.P. Misra, Edited by K.V. Sundaram, A. Ramesh and P.S. Tiwari, Heritage Publishers, New Delhi. 1989.
19. "Decentralised District Planning – An Agenda for a Training Manual for Nepal" in *Report of the Expert Group Meeting for Designing a Training Manual on Decentralised District Planning* APROSC/FAO, July 1989.
20. "Pre-requisites for decentralised planning in view of ensuring appropriate utilisation of trained manpower" Paper No. 3.4 in *Training for Decentralised Planning* – Proceedings of the Expert Consultation, Kathmandu, Nepal, Food and Agriculture Organisation of the United Nations, Rome, 1989.
21. Multi-level Planning (with R.P. Misra) – Chapter 4 in *Regional Development*, Moonis Raza (Ed) – Contributions to Indian Geography, R.P. Misra (Gen. Editor), Heritage Publishers, New Delhi, 1988.
22. "Territorial division of labour for optimum resource use in India" Chapter 5 in *Regional Development* Moonis Raza (Ed), Contributions to Indian Geography Vol X, R.P. Misra (Gen.

Editor), Heritage Publishers, New Delhi, 1988.

23. "Prakasa Rao: The Planner" Chapter 5 in *Geography and Planning*" – Essays in honour of V.L.S. Prakasa Rao, K.V. Sundaram (Ed), Concept Publishing Company, New Delhi, 1985.
24. "Inter-regional Disparities: Country Experiences, Policies and Strategies", Chapter 6 in *Geography and Planning* – Essays in honour of V.L.S. Prakasa Rao, K.V. Sundaram (Ed), Concept Publishing Company, New Delhi, 1985.
25. "District Planning – (i) Revitalising Panchayat Raj and (ii) Encouraging Localism," in *Economic Times*, New Delhi, June 9 - 10, 1988.
26. "Minimum Needs Programme – The Indian Experience", Chapter 19 in *Rural Transformation Readings*, Silver Jubilee Volume, National Institute of Rural Development, Hyderabad, 1984.
27. Changing Data and Information needs for Agricultural Planning: The Challenge for the Developing Countries in Information Systems for Government and Business: Trends, Issues, Challenges, UNCRD, Nagoya, 1988.
28. Meeting Basic Minimum Needs of People – (with Prof. R.P. Misra) – *Deccan Herald*, 1978.
29. Development of Hill Areas in India – Some lessons for strategy formulation and planning (with K.V. Palanidurai) – *Indian Journal of Regional Science*, Vol. XX, No. 1, 1988.
30. Rural–urban relationships in the process of Development – *Administrative change*, Vol. 6, No. 1-2, July 1978 – June 1979 – included as chapter XIX in Rural Geography Edited by H.N. Mishra, contributions to *Indian geography*, Vol. 9, general Editor, R.P. Misra, Heritage Publishers, New Delhi, 1987
31. Service Centre Planning for Agricultural Development – Chapter XIX in *Agricultural Geography* Edited by P.S. Tiwari, Contributions to Indian Geography, General Editor R.P. Misra, Heritage Publishers, 1986.
32. Underdevelopment in India – Spatial Perspectives and Government Polices, Chapter 7 in R.P. Misra (Ed.) Humanizing Development, Maruzen Asia, Singapore, 1981.

List of articles published in various journals

Not available.

INDEX